INFLATION IN DEVELOPING COUNTRIES

An econometric study of Chilean inflation

CONTRIBUTIONS
TO
ECONOMIC ANALYSIS

84

Honorary Editor

J. TINBERGEN

Editors

D. W. JORGENSON

J. WAELBROECK

NORTH-HOLLAND PUBLISHING COMPANY – AMSTERDAM • OXFORD
AMERICAN ELSEVIER PUBLISHING, COMPANY, INC. – NEW YORK

INFLATION IN DEVELOPING COUNTRIES

An econometric study of Chilean inflation

VITTORIO CORBO LIOI

Sir George Williams University
and
Internatonal Institute of Quantitative Economics

1974

NORTH-HOLLAND PUBLISHING COMPANY – AMSTERDAM • OXFORD
AMERICAN ELSEVIER PUBLISHING, COMPANY, INC. – NEW YORK

Library of Congress Catalog Card Number: 73 79104
North-Holland ISBN for this series: 0 7204 3100 X
North-Holland ISBN for this volume: 0 7204 3186 7
American Elsevier ISBN for this volume: 0 444 10525 5

Publishers:

NORTH-HOLLAND PUBLISHING COMPANY–AMSTERDAM
NORTH-HOLLAND PUBLISHING COMPANY, LTD.–OXFORD

Sole distributors for the U.S.A. and Canada:

AMERICAN ELSEVIER PUBLISHING COMPANY, INC
52 VANDERBILT AVENUE
NEW YORK, N.Y. 10017

PRINTED IN THE NETHERLANDS

To the many who made it all possible,
especially to my parents and Verónica

INTRODUCTION TO THE SERIES

This series consists of a number of hitherto unpublished studies, which are introduced by the editors in the belief that they represent fresh contributions to economic science.

The term *economic analysis* as used in the title of the series has been adopted because it covers both the activities of the theoretical economist and the research worker.

Although the analytical methods used by the various contributors are not the same, they are nevertheless conditioned by the common origin of their studies, namely theoretical problems encountered in practical research. Since for this reason, business cycle research and national accounting, research work on behalf of economic policy, and problems of planning are the main sources of the subjects dealt with, they necessarily determine the manner of approach adopted by the authors. Their methods tend to be 'practical' in the sense of not being too far remote from application to actual economic conditions. In addition they are quantitative rather than qualitative.

It is the hope of the editors that the publication of these studies will help to stimulate the exchange of scientific information and to reinforce international cooperation in the field of economics.

The Editors

PREFACE

This book is a revised version of my PhD thesis presented at the Economics Department of MIT in February 1971.

I wish to express my gratitude to the members of my thesis committee: Professors Richard Eckaus, Franklin Fisher and Robert Solow, whose detailed comments on various drafts of this work deeply influenced the final product; and in particular the influence of Professor Fisher is clear in most of the work. Earlier discussions with Professors Zvi Griliches, Arnold Harberger and Edwin Kuh were very helpful also.

Various portions of this work have benefited from having been presented and commented upon at seminars in the University of Chicago, Universidad Católica and Universidad de Chile. Professor Harberger, who read the first three chapters of the manuscript, helped me to clarify the sections of this book dealing with some of his important work on Chilean inflation. In Chile I wish to thank my former colleagues: Sergio Baeza, Jorge Cauas, Ricardo Ffrench-Davis, Eduardo García, Tomas Reichmann and Ernesto Tironi, all of whom read portions of the manuscript and made valuable suggestions.

I am especially indebted to my friends and fellow students at MIT, Walter Corson and ManMohan Agarwal, who not only made suggestions on the content of this work, but also corrected my English and improved the style in the first version of this manuscript. The language and style in this revised version was corrected first by Roy Wyscarver and later by Mohan Munasinghe, to both of whom I am thankful.

The revisions of the first three chapters of the original manuscript were done while I was working at the Universidad Católica in Santiago, Chile, in the period February 1971–February 1972. The remaining chapters, except the last two, were revised while I was at Clark University in spring 1972, and while I was a post-doctoral fellow at MIT in summer 1972. The final two chapters were revised at the International Institute of Quantitative Economics (IIQE) in Montreal, Canada.

The estimations for this work were done using the Econometric Software Package at the Institute Processing Center of MIT. The simulations of chs. 3 and 11 were done using the Troll system* at MIT and at IIQE in Montreal, respectively, with the assistance of Mr Paul Hubert.

I am grateful to the Rockefeller Foundation who, by financing my studies at MIT and by providing me with a post-doctoral fellowship at MIT in summer 1972, enabled me to do part of the revision of the manuscript. I owe special thanks to my wife Verónica who sacrificed numerous weekends (to help have this book finished), and provided at home the atmosphere essential for the completion of this work.

Finally, I would like to thank the referees who provided valuable comments, as well as all the secretaries who participated in the typing of the various drafts of the manuscript, particularly Miss Maureen Baril of Clark University and the IIQE staff.

Montreal, Canada   Vittorio Corbo Lioi

---

* The Troll system was developed at MIT and further extended at the Computer Research Center of the National Bureau of Economic Research in Cambridge, Massachusetts under the direction of Mr M. Eisner and Professor E. Kuh.

CONTENTS

PART III: AN ANNUAL STUDY OF INFLATION

Contents

INTRODUCTION

My interest in the study of inflation in a developing country dates back to the period 1965–1967, when I was working at the National Planning Office in Chile. At that time I was dissatisfied with the existing explanations and empirical works on inflation in developing countries. After spending some time on the subject I realized that, with the exception of the work of Professor Jorge Ahumada, most of the explanations of Chilean inflation in particular were incomplete. In general, there appeared to be confusion between change in relative prices and increase in the price level. On the empirical side the most valuable work existing at that time, and even today, was the work by Professor Arnold Harberger. Professor Harberger also has the honor of having made the first serious empirical study of Chilean inflation.

After examining all this work I came to the conclusion that the only interesting way to study the behavior of the price level from the analytical and especially from the policy-maker's point of view was to work with a complete macroeconomic model.

From an analytical point of view this is the correct way to approach the problem because it allows one to consider the most important interrelations among the main macro-variables, in contrast to the use of single equations in which all these feedbacks are disregarded. The second advantage of this approach is from the policy point of view. Especially in the last 15 years, the political authorities are interested not only in the stability of price levels but also in their relationship to other variables. Thus, if the side effect of stability is a substantial increase in unemployment and a lower level of output, then the political authorities would like to know more precisely the consequences of their policies. One can agree completely with Professor Milton Friedman that stability has a cost in terms of output and unemployment only in the short run, but the policy makers are still very much concerned with the short run (which could be a period of several years) consequences of their policies.

This book is a first attempt towards building a macroeconomic model to study the interaction among the main macroeconomic variables. It is divided into three parts plus three appendixes. The first part deals with monetarism, structuralism and past studies of Chilean inflation. This part consists of two chapters: in ch. 1 we present in modern terminology the now famous controversy between monetarists and structuralists. Although there is no clear presentation in the literature of either of these two extreme viewpoints, we will try to examine in this chapter the main characteristics of these two positions. Ch. 2 contains a critical evaluation of the empirical studies of Chilean inflation.

The second part of this book deals with a quarterly model for industrial prices, industrial wages and inflation. This part comprises the whole of ch. 3 in which we specify and estimate a quarterly submodel which explains industrial prices, industrial wages, wholesale prices and the cost of living. We find from this chapter that, for a one percentage point increase in the rate of change of imported raw material prices, the direct effect is a 0.41 percentage point increase in the rate of change of industrial prices. Furthermore, the rate of change in wages has a direct effect of 0.684 for each percentage point of increase in industrial wages. This last coefficient is substantially higher than the 0.15 value that Professor Harberger obtained in his study. A possible explanation of this substantial difference is given in ch. 2, as a problem in specification error theory. We also use this model to run some simulations in which we consider the role of monetary and fiscal policy in moving toward a given level of unemployment and of capacity utilization in the industrial sector. We end this chapter by studying a steady state situation in which all the variables, except the four that we are explaining with this submodel, are assumed to be at some equilibrium level. From this last exercise we conclude that, even with constant international prices and agricultural prices, stability in the cost of living requires an unemployment rate of

12.6% in the industrial sector, a situation much more unfavorable than in other more developed countries.

Two important real variables used in the submodel of ch. 3 are the unemployment rate and the level of capacity in the industrial sector. To explain the behavior of these last two variables it is necessary to build a complete macroeconomic model.

The third part of the book is devoted to the specification, estimation and simulation of an annual econometric model of the Chilean economy. This part of the book includes chs. 4–12. In ch. 4 some characteristics of the Chilean economy from 1950 to 1970 are analyzed. In this chapter we show that the average rate of change in prices for the last 20 years has been 31.5% for the retail price index, 32.3% for the wholesale price index and 33.7% for the deflator of expenditures in gross domestic product. In this chapter we also show that for most of the period under study there is no clear-cut relation between inflation and growth. Therefore the evidence available does not support the contention that inflation is necessary to promote growth, with the limitation that this conclusion has not been arrived by a *ceteris paribus* experiment. In ch. 5, a simplified version of the macroeconomic model specified and estimated in chs. 6–10 is presented. In ch. 6 the technology of the economy is investigated as well as its relationship with output capacity and the employment of factors. In this chapter we make a grouping of the sectors of production into two groups: the sector producing commodities, and the sector producing services. For the sector producing commodities we assume first that the technology can be characterized by a constant elasticity of substitution production function. After estimating this function we can conclude that the elasticity of substitution is not significantly different from unity, and therefore we proceed to estimate a Cobb–Douglas production function. For the sector producing services we assume that there are no capacity limitations. We finish the chapter with the estimation of factor requirements functions.

In ch. 7 the expenditure side of the gross domestic product of output is developed. The chapter starts with the definition of real expenditure in gross domestic product and then continues with the specification and estimation of the equations for its different components. In ch. 8, equations are developed and estimated for the price of commodities, price of services, cost of living, wages in the commodity sector, and wages in the service sector. This chapter is based on the developments of ch. 3, with price equations of the mark-up variety and wage equations of the Phillips vintage. In ch. 9 the question of the government deficit in fiscal account is studied. The study of this deficit requires the consideration of the proceeds from the different taxes. In ch. 10 the demand and supply of money are developed. In this chapter some critical comments are made on the usual procedure of measuring the cost of holding money through a weighted average of past inflation rates. In ch. 11 the equations estimated in chs. 6–10, together with some miscellaneous equations, are put together to build a complete model of the Chilean economy. In chs. 6–11 the specification and estimation of the individual equations are studied. In these chapters only tests on the individual equations are performed.

In ch. 12 we start studying the performance of the full model. In this chapter three experiments are performed for the period which coincided with the Frei administration. In the first one we study a case in which it is assumed that in the period 1965–1970, for a constant unemployment rate, the real wage rate in the commodity sector is constant (instead of growing at the historical rate of approximately 15%). The consequences of this change are lower prices, an important increase in employment in the commodity sector and lower output. In the second experiment we study the consequences of a change in the policy of the Central Bank with respect to foreign reserves. In the experiment it is assumed that the Central Bank does not accumulate foreign exchange during the period 1965–1970, but instead maintains a level of foreign reserves equal to the average of the period 1962–1964, and uses the surplus for buying additional competitive imports, which are sold subsequently in the domestic market to relieve some of the pressure on the domestic supply. The consequence of this set of policies is a reduced level of output, especially in the years with the higher surplus of foreign reserves. Prices are also lower. Much more interesting is the third experiment presented in this chapter, in which it is assumed that the foreign reserves are used to finance an expansion in investment in plant and equipment. This requires a relaxation in the quantitative restrictions on imports. The consequences of this set of policies are more output, less unemployment and lower prices. Therefore the model shows very clearly the economic costs of the policy of increasing the level of foreign reserves. This does not imply that the increase in reserves was bad, since the benefits of such an accumulation, in terms of a more rational organization of the international trade and more economic independence, can be higher than its costs.

Finally, in appendix A we present the data used in the estimations of ch. 3. In appendix B we present the data used in the estimations of the third part of the book. In appendix C we discuss some problems with the use of the Kmenta approximation to estimate a CES production function.

In most of the equations, to start with we assume autocorrelation in the disturbances and the Fair (1970) method is used to estimate them. We follow this procedure because we believe that the specifications used for the different equations (because of the generality of our theories and the lack of data) include only the most important explanatory variables, and therefore there is room for autocorrelations to appear in the disturbances, through variables left out.

PART I

MONETARISM, STRUCTURALISM
AND PAST STUDIES OF CHILEAN INFLATION

CHAPTER 1

THE MONETARIST AND STRUCTURAL VIEWS
OF CHILEAN INFLATION: A SURVEY

With the increase in the rate of inflation in the first half of the 1950s and the stabilization policy that followed, a debate started in Chile and elsewhere concerning the causes of this inflation. Among the various explanations presented, two extremes can be distinguished: the monetarist view and the structuralist view. Although there is no clear presentation in the literature of either of these two extremes, we try to present here what we think are their main characteristics.

The main difference between the two views is in their statement of how the economy really works. In the pure monetarist view, the real structure of the economy can generate stability and growth. Inflation and stagnation have been produced, not by an inadequate structure, but by erroneous policies (such as price controls, foreign trade policies, fiscal policies). It is not the structure that is faulty, but the values taken by the policy variables which have generated those results. In the extreme structuralist view, on the other hand, the structure itself is not able to generate stability and growth, independently of the values of the policy variables. Therefore, to stop inflation and to increase growth, the structure should be changed.

In this chapter, we will present a summary of both views in relation to the Chilean case.

1.1. The monetarist view

The monetarist view of inflation, in Chile, was associated from the beginning with the International Monetary Fund (IMF). Owing to the fixed exchange rate system, inflation led to balance of payments problems and the IMF stepped in to try to solve them. Its recommendations centered on measures to stop inflation, and these measures presuppose a view of the economy which is now called the monetarist view.

If the balance of payments problem had been tackled using methods accepted by the IMF, then it would not have stepped in and the monetarist viewpoint would not have been associated with it. Furthermore, without the IMF support, these specific policy proposals would not have been implemented.

The IMF, which was created to solve the problem of temporary scarcity of liquidity for international transactions, was faced with a problem for which it was not prepared: how to bridge the chronic foreign trade gap of the underdeveloped countries in a fixed exchange rate system. The periodical devaluations necessary to bridge the gap with exchange rate policy could hardly be the kind of devaluations allowed under the 'structural disequilibria' category of the IMF. All IMF policy was centered around the fixed exchange rate system.

To ensure implementation of its measures, the IMF set conditions on the credits that it gave to the underdeveloped countries with persistent balance of payments problems. Furthermore, the other lenders (including the USA) made their offers of new credits and foreign aid conditional on the borrowing countries' fulfillment of the IMF stabilization program.

In most of the IMF studies, inflation is a problem of excess demand which is analyzed through Fisher's version of the quantity theory of money. Among the IMF writings we find statements like the following (Bernstein and Patel, 1952, p. 368):

'... This is the basic framework for the inflation process, when aggregate demand for all purposes — consumption, investment, and government — exceeds the supply of goods at constant prices.'

Later on, Bernstein again wrote (1958, p. 323):

'Although the basic causes of inflation vary widely in different countries and at different times, the process of inflation always shows strikingly similar characteristics. Eventually, it is caused by the excessive expectations of government, business, or labor in the use of the national product and is associated with the excessive creation of credit.'

He finished the same paper (1958, p. 339) with the statement that:

'The only way to escape from the disorder caused by inflation is to create an environment in which the distribution and use of real income are responsive to economic forces and the monetary system cannot be used to generate an excessive demand or to support a claim for an uneconomic level of wages. That is the task of the monetary authorities.'

The IMF recommendations, based as they were in the quantity theory of money, were centered around different ways of controlling the money supply.

So we find among the IMF studies statements like the following (Ahrensdorf, 1959, p. 286):

'Suppose that in any given country the growth of productive capacity, as a result of a given investment pattern is expected to permit annual increases in real output of, say $50 million. Also, assume that income velocity is 5 and is constant. Abstracting from the various qualifications stated earlier, monetary stability would call for an annual increase in effective demand of $50 million, or a monetary expansion of $10 million.'

In these studies, we find a model either explicit or implicit in which inflation is caused by excess demand. Furthermore, the aggregate demand is determined by Fisher's version of the quantity theory of money. In the recommendations to achieve monetary stability, it is implicit that prices and wages are flexible.

Economic measures of the IMF kind suggested for Chile consisted mainly of the following:

(1) restrictive monetary policy;

(2) wages and salary adjustments limited to less than the previous year's inflation rate;

(3) reduction of the multiplicity of foreign exchange rates and import controls;

(4) increase in public utility rates to eliminate deficits in state-owned enterprises; and

(5) restrictions on government expenditures, mainly govern-

ment investment in the construction industry.

As we said at the beginning, the main logic behind this set of policies is that the structure is able to generate stability and growth if we make some policy changes mainly in the monetary and fiscal area.

Although some decrease in inflationary pressures resulted from these policies, this was only transitory and was associated with a deterioration of real wages, with unemployment and with general economic recession.

1.2. The structural view

Structuralism was associated from the beginning with the dual objectives of growth and stabilization. From a study of the interaction between these two objectives, we can obtain a picture of the working of the economic system.

In the structuralist view, the structure of the system is such that it generates certain disequilibria: mainly inflation, unemployment, public deficit, balance of payments disequilibria, stagnation, etc.

Osvaldo Sunkel (1958, p. 570), the leader of structuralist thought in Latin America, wrote the following about the monetarist type of stabilization policies applied in Chile in 1956–1957 by the Klein-Saks mission[1]:

'As the stabilization program did not eliminate the various inflationary pressures, inflation continued. The only difference was that under the new conditions, deprived of the free action of the propagation mechanism, inflation brought along a substantial regressive shift in income distribution and a limitation of real public expenditures, on top of a general rise in prices. It might be argued that these effects are not too high a price to pay for stability. But whoever thinks along those lines will be falling into an error of logic because those are not the real alternatives. In an underdeveloped country, the objective is, almost by definition to achieve economic development, and the methods that are being used to stabilize the Chilean economy are jeopardizing the country's possibilities of long-term economic progress.

[1] The Klein-Saks mission was a private consulting firm hired by the Chilean Government in the second half of 1955.

In the structuralist view, we should distinguish between the causes of the inflationary pressures and the mechanisms by which inflation develops. From among the causes of the inflationary pressures, they make a distinction between the structural limitations of the system and the cumulative inflationary pressures. The structural limitations are reflected in the inability of some sectors to adjust to changes in the level and composition of aggregate demand. The basic structural features in Chile are usually taken to be:

(1) the stagnation of food supply in the face of expanding demand,

(2) inelasticity and instability of the purchasing power of exports,

(3) bottlenecks in the supply of social overhead capital and skilled labor, and

(4) structural deficiencies in the tax system, mainly inflexibility of revenues and the regressivity of the tax structure.

In the structuralist view, inflation cannot be stopped if these structural limitations are not eliminated. The cumulative inflationary pressures are distortions generated by the inflationary process itself which are an increasing function of the rate of inflation. The main cumulative factors are:

(1) distortions of the price system, mainly caused by the price control policies associated with inflation; and

(2) misallocation of resources, mainly investment funds.

These primary causes of inflation, structural and cumulative, need a propagation mechanism for inflation actually to develop. The propagation mechanism works at two levels. Firstly, there is the continuous struggle among the different economic groups to improve their shares in total income. This manifests itself in the struggle between wage-earners and profit-earners. Secondly, there is the struggle between the private and public sectors to increase their share of real resources. This works through the level of the government expenditures and revenues and the way the government deficit is financed.

To explain the structuralist view, we will develop three models that have been presented by this school at various historical moments to explain Chilean inflation. The first one we find to be the most explicit, whereas the other two are implicit in the writing of the structuralists.

The first model applies to the period after the great depression (1930–1945) and can be built with the elements presented in the excellent paper by Ahumada (1958).

The second model applies to the period 1945–1960 and is implicit in the writings of such prominent structuralists as Sunkel (1958) and Pinto (1960).

The third model applies to sub-periods going from 1930 up to the present date, and it incorporates explicitly the dual objectives of economic growth and stabilization. This model has been developed mainly by Seers (1962) and Pinto (1964).

To understand the first model, we have to go back in history to the pre-crisis period. During this period, Chile was very receptive to international trade and therefore the behavior of exports provided the dynamic element in their growth process. Aggregate demand, linked to the existing level and the distribution of income, was highly diversified. The demand for industrial products was the major component of demand while agriculture and mining constituted the major components of the production sector. Sectoral equilibrium between supply and demand was provided through imports. At this time, tax revenue was generated, primarily, through the foreign trade sector, and redistributed in part to those areas in the economy where economic activity was less pronounced.

In the first model, we start with the crisis in the foreign trade sector brought about by the great world depression. The value of exports decreased and the economy had to adjust to this new situation. In this case there were, in principle, three policies or combinations of them open to the policy maker to try to reach equilibrium in the foreign trade sector. The first, similar to a gold standard policy, was to depress the level of income and in this way reduce the level of imports. The second was to change the exchange rate and, finally, the third possibility was to produce domestically the commodities that were previously imported. This last policy combined discriminatory controls on imports (quotas, tariffs, etc.) and compensatory fiscal and monetary policy in order to maintain the level of aggregate demand.

In the structuralist view, the first course was not feasible for, without domestic industry, the people unemployed in the mining sector would have to be employed in agriculture but wages in this sector were already near the subsistence level and further cuts necessary to generate additional employment would not have been feasible.

Furthermore, the first course was not politically feasible for a country like Chile which had a high proportion of the population in the urban sector and a high level of per capita income. Since most of the urban labor force owned no agricultural land, they had nothing to fall back upon if their employment in the industrial sector was terminated. This would have had undesirable political repercussions.

A similar argument has usually been used by the trade theorist to refer to the failure of the gold standard. In the literature, we find arguments such as the following (Grubel, 1970, p. 21):

'When most of the world's population lived off the land in relative self sufficiency, and cyclical instabilities characteristic of capital economies had relatively minor effects, the gold standard worked well. But as the countries began to industrialize and population shifted into urban centers, cyclical fluctuations in employment had increasingly more significant effects on the well-being of the public. Pressures mounted on governments to engage in deliberate counter-cyclical policies.'

The second approach was not open either, for during the big depression most countries were closing their doors to international trade, thereby forcing the price elasticity of Chilean exports very low. Furthermore, most Chilean imports did not have domestic substitutes and so their elasticity continued to remain low. In this framework, devaluation could not be counted on to close the balance of payment deficit.

In this way, we arrive at the conclusion that the only real possibility (*during the world crises*) was the third. This consisted of absorbing the excess demand by substituting domestic production of goods for part of those goods previously imported. This approach was supplemented with discriminatory controls on imports (quotas, tariffs, etc.) and compensatory fiscal and monetary policy to maintain the level of money aggregate demand. This set of policies has been called the model of domestically oriented growth, because the dynamic element, instead of being the export sector, is private and public investment in the import substitution industry.

In the Ahumada model, the mix of compensatory policy and domestic protection produced two simultaneous effects: (1) an increase in domestic prices, and (2) a change in relative prices in favor of imported commodities (mainly industrial products) and domestically produced commodities subject to tariffs.

The change in relative prices was necessary in order to develop the domestic industry, but the increase in the price level was a consequence of the economic structure of the country. The economic structure was such that, as the level of exports dropped off, men and machines employed by the mining sector suddenly became unemployed. But, as the level of money aggregate demand was re-established (via compensatory policy), only men were available as a factor to the industrial sector; thereby a difference was generated between money aggregate demand and aggregate supply which forced prices up.

Until now, we have explained only the increase in prices associated with the beginning of the import substitution experience. To go on from here and explain the ensuing period of inflation, we must analyze the remaining set of missing pieces.

Before 1920, most of the industrial wage-goods were imported; therefore the protectionist measures had an important role in the determinations of the real income of wage-earners. Among the various measures taken to compensate for the negative effect of price increases on the real income of wage-earners was a system of multiple exchange rates. This system resulted in an overvaluation of domestic money for export transactions and in the end led to maintaining a low level of exports. Following this, wages increased and domestic prices followed suit to bring about a worsening of the balance of payments and the need for more protection. The cycle, once begun, continued on to produce a seemingly endless spiral.

The second model of the structuralist school can be built with the ideas developed by Pinto (1960) and Sunkel (1958).

To understand this model, it is necessary to present a general picture of the Chilean economy at the end of the Second World

War. Although a major development of domestic industry grew out of the previous period (1930–1945), Chile was very much dependent on its international trade. During this period, export earnings were needed to purchase imported raw materials and capital goods in addition to the consumption goods that were not domestically produced (primarily durables). Consequently, the investment process and the normal flow of raw materials was conditioned to export earnings. Taxes on exports continued to be an important source of government revenue. Furthermore, owing in part to the change in relative price of the previous period and the land tenure system, agriculture was very backward[2].

In this model, inflation starts with a cyclical crisis in the trade sector. The control measures pursued in closing the balance of payments deficit (devaluation, tariffs, etc.) increased the cost of imported raw materials needed by domestic industry and simultaneously, but independent of the market organization, the price of imported products increased. The prices in domestic currency of goods that were internationally traded were also increased[3].

In the structuralist view, if these increases in costs had not been financed by the monetary authority (through a higher level of money demand), additional unemployment would have been generated.

An additional source of pressure on the monetary authority came from the fall in taxes. Since an important part of government revenue came from taxes on exports and specific taxes on imports, the decrease in foreign trade values diminished the revenue of the government. Simultaneously, public expenditures could not be allowed to decrease for two reasons: first, most of public expenditures on current accounts were for wages and salaries and social security payments which are very inflexible downward; second, the government was urged to take compensatory fiscal policy to keep the level of unemployment no higher than the maximum socially acceptable level. The only way to finance this deficit in an

---

[2] See especially Ahumada (1958).

[3] If the exported goods are also consumed domestically (wheat and meat in Argentina), then a devaluation will increase domestic prices too, as long as the international prices do not fall by the full amount of the devaluation.

economy without a well developed market for government bonds was through an increase in the quantity of money. Even if compensatory fiscal and monetary policy maintained the level of real aggregate demand, its composition would have changed against exportable goods. Since the existing productive capacity was not geared to this demand composition, additional pressure on prices would have been generated.

In addition to the government deficit on current account, there were pressures to increase the government's capital budget.(because of investment in capital-intensive sectors like steel, electricity, provision of social overhead capital, etc.). This generated pressures to finance it through the monetary authority[4].

In a second stage, the propagation mechanism began to work through pressures of the wage-earners to keep their share of real income. Costs went up again, industrial prices went up and the spiral started to work.

The third model of the structuralist school is more a theoretical model and does not apply to any period in particular. It can be built with the ideas developed by Seers (1962) and Pinto (1964). In this model, the dynamic element is the government-promoted expansion in domestic industry to stimulate growth. The model is formulated for periods in which the economy is stagnant. The models that result can be interpreted as being of the same kind as the Bruno—Chenery—Strout model (Chenery and Bruno, 1962).

Here we start with an expansion in economic activity through government-financed investment in the industrial sector. Such an expansion should cut back the unemployment generated by a secular growth of the supply of labor in the face of a stagnant demand for labor.

The structuralist in this case would advocate that the increase in aggregate demand associated with the expansion in the industrial sector generates pressures in the agricultural sector in terms of

---

[4] At the beginning, the policy followed was to finance these investments through public sector bonds. Unfortunately, to increase the incentives for the private sector, these bonds were allowed to be used as primary reserves by the banking system, thus increasing the money base.

demand for food and raw materials. Owing to the low price elasticity of supply in this sector (a structural problem), a substantial increase in relative prices in favor of agriculture is necessary to clear the market. In the structuralist view, this is aggravated by the fact that in the foreign trade sector, where the situation is very tight to start with, we need to make room for imported raw materials and capital goods necessary to the expansion of domestic industry. Therefore, imports of food cannot be increased.

If unemployed resources could have been moved to the industrial sector to increase output and if industrial prices were flexible downward, we could have a change in relative prices without inflation. However, because of the low mobility of resources and the inflexibility of industrial prices, we need a monetary expansion to finance the price increase necessary for the change in relative prices. Parallel to this, the development of the industrial sector generated additional demand for imported raw materials and capital goods and created demand pressures on social overhead capital, which has been built mainly for the export sector.

We can summarize this model by saying that structural inflationary pressures are basically the result of lack of adaptation of domestic supply to a changing pattern and level of demand. This problem is aggravated by the inelasticity and instability of exports which do not allow changing import levels to achieve sectoral equilibrium. Neither do industrial prices move to equate demand and supply, particularly if they have to move downward.

Alternatively, in the nomenclature of tradeoff theory, the structural position can be summarized by saying that the structure of the economy is such that it generates a tradeoff between unemployment and changes in prices which is very unfavorable for policy measures. As an illustration, to cut inflation from 40% to 25% may require an increase in the rate of unemployment from 7% to 12%. In their view, given this tradeoff, the only real alternative open to cut unemployment and promote growth is to change the structure which would be equivalent to shifting the tradeoff curve towards the origin (see fig. 1.1). In the no-long-term-tradeoff theory of Friedman (1968) and Phelps (1968), when the natural rate of unemployment is too high the only real alternative for reducing unemployment is to change the structure which

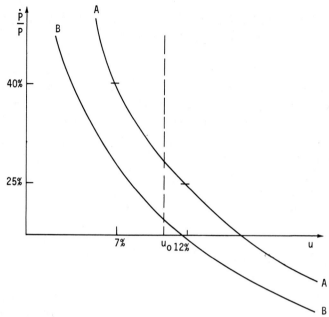

Fig. 1.1. *AA*: tradeoff with the present structure. *BB*: tradeoff after structural changes. $\dot{P}/P$: rate of change in prices. u: rate of unemployment. u_0: maximum socially acceptable rate of unemployment.

would be equivalent to a shift in the vertical tradeoff curve towards the origin, thus reducing the natural rate of unemployment.

The two-gap model formulation can be summarized as follows:

If we want to grow at a socially acceptable rate — say 5% per year — the economic system will generate, at the given exchange rate (this point is not always made clear), a foreign trade gap. This comes from the inelasticity of the supply of exports (a structural problem) together with rapidly expanding imports. The increase in imports is caused by additional requirements of raw materials and capital goods in the industrial sector and of foodstuffs for consumption. The latter one is aggravated by the inelasticity of agricultural supply.

Another disequilibrium will occur from the savings—investment gap. To be able to grow at a given rate, the economy requires some level of investment which is higher than the desired savings at that level of income. Public savings are limited by the inflexibility of the tax system and private savings are discouraged by the distortionary effects of inflation that hinder the emergence of a capital market.

In the structuralist view, inflation emerges in the process of making the two gaps equal *ex post*. This should be manifested through the two struggles for the limited resources: the one between wage-earners and profit-earners, and the other between the private sector and the public sector. In this case, the structuralists would say (like everybody else with training in economics) that the economy is not able to grow at the given rate because it does not have (*given its structure*) the real resources. If the government tries, through fiscal and monetary policy, to make the economy grow at this rate, we will only have inflation (see Corbo, 1968).

In the structuralist view, the only way of achieving the 'socially acceptable' rate of growth is, again, by changing the economic and social structure.

The problem with the structuralist thesis is that in the period 1965–1970 most of the traditional structural limitations were eliminated in Chile (notably the inelasticity and instability of the purchasing power of exports, the structural deficiencies in the tax system, and the old land-tenure system) but inflation continued. It is important to note that the main reason for the failure of the stabilization program of this period was attributed by the Frei government to the behavior of wages.

This brings up the point of the relation between cost inflation and the monetarist and structuralist views of inflation. In the monetarist view, there clearly is no room for cost inflation because prices and wages always move to whatever level is necessary to clear the markets and aggregate demand is determined by the supply of money via the quantity theory. To include cost inflation in the structural school is to stretch too much the structural view. Cost inflation is not related at all to the structural causes usually given, such as inelasticity of food supply, inelasticity and instability of the purchasing power of exports, deficiencies in the tax structure, etc. Although cost inflation is clearly related to the economic structure (through the price formation mechanism) it was not among the structural causes of inflation. Therefore, cost inflation can be considered as a separate view of inflation.

1.3. Conclusions

The problem with these alternative views of Chilean inflation is that there is no discussion of the explicit mechanisms by which the main variables interact. To work out any serious stabilization program, it is necessary to have some idea of the consequences of the different policies. The study of this mechanism is the main objective of this book.

We accept from the start the hypothesis that, for an inflation of the magnitude of the Chilean one, the main long-run factor will be found to be the increase in the quantity of money. But it is important to study why this increase has taken place. This sets up two important questions. First: what is the mechanism through which money affects prices? The answer to this question is fundamental for the formulation of a short-run anti-inflationary program. Second: what is the mechanism through which the quantity of money increases? The study of the answers to these questions will occupy us in the coming chapters.

CHAPTER 2

EMPIRICAL STUDIES OF CHILEAN INFLATION: THE STATE OF THE ART

Looking carefully at the literature concerning Chilean inflation (García, 1964; Deaver, 1961; Harberger, 1963; Lüders, 1968; Behrman, 1970; Cauas, 1970), nowhere can we find an explicit model of how the main variables involved interact with each other in the inflationary process. All the works start out by saying that their main objective is to specify the mechanism that generates inflation.

Harberger (1963, p. 220), in the first serious empirical work on Chilean inflation, says:

> '*In this paper I try to explore in some detail the mechanism by which the Chilean inflation was generated.* Hypotheses about this mechanism abound, and opinions are strong and sometimes vehemently expressed. This study was motivated by the belief that only by hard empirical work and close examination of the evidence, can we resolve such conflicts of view as those regarding the Chilean inflation... . It [the paper] *seeks to discover the dynamic process by which monetary expansion has its effects upon the current rate of price rise, and to clarify somewhat the role that wage changes played in the Chilean inflationary process.*' (The italics are mine.)

After this he goes on to say:

> 'It is perfectly obvious that the effects of increases in money supply upon the price level do not occur instantaneously. The path by which such effects take place through time is of interest not only from a scientific point of view, but also from the standpoint of the policy maker.'

And then (p. 222):

'One way of capturing the lag pattern by which money-supply changes affect the price level is by introducing money-supply changes with different lags as explanatory variables for the rate of inflation. Thus, if P_t represents the percentage change in the price level during year t, and M_t represents the percentage change in the money supply during the same year, and M_{t-1} the percentage change in money supply during the previous year, and so on, we may write:

$$P_t = a_0 + a_1 M_t + a_2 M_{t-1} + \ldots .'$$

If this equation is a reduced form of a bigger model, as later claimed by Harberger (1966b), then we miss the study of the mechanism by which money affects prices. Furthermore, besides the behavior of prices, most of the time the policy makers want to know also the behavior of other macro variables like unemployment, gross domestic product, etc. To study the movements in all these variables, we need to formulate a full macro model. This last will be the road that we will follow in our work.

Another difference between Harberger's work and ours is the role of wages in the price equation. In a different paper (1966a, p. 43), commenting on the role of wages, he refers to his paper on Chilean inflation and to other unpublished papers, concluding that:

'The coefficient measuring the direct effect of a 1 per cent wage rise on the price level was .04 when consumer price changes were being explained, and .15 when wholesale price changes were being explained. The former of these coefficients was not statistically significant, a result duplicated in Blanco's work on Chile for a later period. The latter coefficient was highly significant... but it indicates that the direct effect of wage rises was small, a 10 per cent rise in the wage rate producing only a 1.5 per cent price rise.'

We want to stress that these results depend crucially on the specification of the price equation. We will consider an alternative specification of the price equation which corresponds more to a structural equation rather than to a reduced form equation as in Harberger's study. We shall assume that wages affect prices through some kind of a mark-up equation which is affected by the level of excess demand in the market[1]. Specifically, let us assume

---

[1] This is a sound hypothesis for a country characterized by the statement

that the rate of change in prices is described by eq. (3.10) in ch. 3:

$$\frac{\dot{P}^{\mathrm{I}}(t)}{P^{\mathrm{I}}(t)} = \alpha_0 + \alpha_1 \frac{U\dot{L}C(t)}{ULC(t)} + \alpha_2 \frac{\dot{P}^{\mathrm{M}}(t)}{P^{\mathrm{M}}(t)} + \alpha_3 f\left(\frac{D(t)-Q(t)}{Q(t)}\right) + \mu(t),$$

where

$\dfrac{\dot{P}^{\mathrm{I}}(t)}{P^{\mathrm{I}}(t)}$ = rate of change of industrial prices,

$\dfrac{U\dot{L}C(t)}{ULC(t)}$ = rate of change of the unit cost of labor,

$\dfrac{\dot{P}^{\mathrm{M}}(t)}{P^{\mathrm{M}}(t)}$ = rate of change of import prices,

$\dfrac{D(t)-Q(t)}{Q(t)}$ = excess demand as a proportion of output, and

$\mu(t)$ = a random error.

This equation implies that to study the impact of wages, forgetting about the simultaneity of the model for the moment, we should keep the other variables in the equation, like excess demand, constant, including them as regressors. If wages increase, everything else remaining the same — in the Harberger case these would be real income, money and the rate of exchange (see footnote 2) — we will expect absolute prices to be marked upward. At the same time, we will expect that for a higher nominal income (through the increase in wages) demand will shift towards the right. If the shift in demand and the increase in the price are such that at the new price excess production is created, then we will expect downward pressure in prices.

Figure 2.1 illustrates the effect of a shift in price function RR upward to $R'R'$ due to an increase in money wages. Thus, the new price at the old quantity is P_1. However, this is only part of the effect on prices, for the increase in wages shifts the demand func-

that 'Industry in Chile is typically monopolistic or oligopolistic' (Harberger, 1963, p. 245). See also ch. 3.

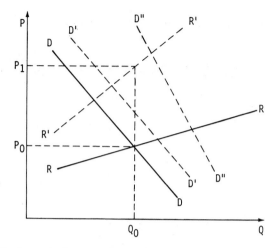

Fig. 2.1. The impact of excess demand or excess production on prices.

tion DD towards the right. If the new level of demand is at $D'D'$, then at a price of P_1 we will have excess production and downward pressure on prices. Alternatively, if the new level of demand is at $D''D''$, then at a price of P_1 we will have excess demand and upward pressure on prices.

In the Harberger case, the impact of a possible excess demand or excess production on prices is mixed with the one from the other regressors included in his equation. Replacing capacity utilization in the regression model by the change in the money supply and the change in real income, when the true model is a mark-up one, will make all the estimates biased. To obtain some idea of the bias we can apply the Theil specification error theorem (Theil, 1961) [2].

[2] Specifically let us write the true model as

$$\frac{\dot{P}(t)}{P(t)} = \beta_0 + \beta_1 \frac{\dot{w}(t)}{w(t)} + \beta_2 \frac{\dot{P}^m(t)}{P^m(t)} + \beta_3 f\left(\frac{D(t)-Q(t)}{Q(t)}\right) + v(t) , \tag{1}$$

with $f' > 0$,
where

$$\frac{\dot{P}(t)}{P(t)} = \text{rate of change in prices,}$$

$\dfrac{\dot{w}(t)}{w(t)}$ = rate of change in wage rate,

$\dfrac{\dot{p}^m(t)}{p^m(t)}$ = rate of change in the price of imported raw materials,

$\dfrac{D(t) - Q(t)}{Q(t)}$ = excess demand, and

$v(t)$ = random error.

But instead of this we estimate (Harberger equation):

$$\frac{\dot{P}(t)}{P(t)} = \alpha_0 + \alpha_1 \frac{\dot{w}(t)}{w(t)} + \alpha_2 \frac{\dot{p}^m(t)}{p^m(t)} + \alpha_3 \frac{\dot{M}(t)}{M(t)} + \alpha_4 \frac{\dot{Y}(t)}{Y(t)} + u(t) , \qquad (2)$$

where

$\dfrac{\dot{M}(t)}{M(t)}$ = rate of change in the money supply,

$\dfrac{\dot{Y}(t)}{Y(t)}$ = rate of change in real income, and

$u(t)$ = random error.

We will assume that the regressors in (2) are independent of the error term in (1). Let us call α the least-squares estimates of the coefficients in (2). Then, using the Theil specification error theorem, we have

$$E[\alpha_i] = \beta_1 + P_{i3}\beta_3 \qquad i = 0,1,2$$

$$E[\alpha_i] = P_{i3}\beta_3 \qquad i = 3,4.$$

The P_{i3}'s are the coefficients in the auxiliary regression

$$f\left(\frac{D(t) - Q(t)}{Q(t)}\right) = P_{03} + P_{13}\frac{\dot{w}(t)}{w(t)} + P_{23}\frac{\dot{p}^m(t)}{p^m(t)} + P_{33}\frac{\dot{M}(t)}{M(t)} + P_{43}\frac{\dot{Y}(t)}{Y(t)} .$$

In the case in which at the new price an excess production is created (this case corresponds to a price equation $R'R'$ and a demand $D'D'$ in fig 2.1), P_{13} and P_{23} will be negative. Besides, we expect β_3 to be positive and therefore α_1 and α_2 to be biased downward. As for the sign of P_{33}, we expect that with constant wages, constant price of imported raw materials and constant real income, an increase in the money supply will generate excess demand in the commodity market. In a traditional IS–LM Keynesian model, this will be caused by an increase in the money supply which shifts the LM curve to the right and brings about a new equilibrium with a higher effective demand and a

The magnitude of the biases will depend on the absolute value of the various coefficients involved.

Thus, we reach the conclusion that if the mark-up price equation is the true one and if the assumptions of ordinary least squares are true, then the coefficients estimated by Harberger for the wage and the foreign exchange variable could be downward biased. Another explanation of his low coefficient for the wage variable, and maybe the most important one, is the particular definition used for the wage variable. He used the minimum wage which describes only the behavior of white-collar workers and not of the industrial workers. When we employ a simultaneous estimation procedure and alternative definitions for the wage variable, we obtain a coefficient for the rate of change in the wage rate[3] that exceeds 0.50.

Harberger did not consider the effect of the prices of imported raw materials in his first study (1963), but they were considered important in some of his subsequent work (1969).

In another work concerned with Chilean inflation, Behrman concentrates his attention again on the money market. He starts with a section on 'The demand for per capita real monetary balances and aggregate price determination' where he studies the restrictions that can be imposed on the different coefficients of a demand-for-money equation. Assuming that the money supply is exogenous, he focuses on the price adjustment relationship.

Justifying the expression for the rate of change in prices, Behrman says (1970, pp. 7–8):

> 'Let us hypothesize that the determination of the rate of change of prices may be approximated by a linear function of the relevant variables:

lower interest rate. (We exclude the liquidity trap case.) In a Modigliani–Patinkin model, we have to add to the Keynesian model a real-balance effect. In our model, we will expect a positive P_{33} due to the clearing mechanism of the money market. When persons have more real money to hold than they wish, the demand for durables will increase and therefore, *ceteris paribus*, excess demand will develop.

[3] In our quarterly model, we employed an index of wage payments in the industrial sector (see ch. 3), and in our annual model we employed the average wage rate from the National Accounts (see ch. 5). None of these data were available when Harberger's work was done.

$$r(P)_t = \sum_{i=0}^{m} a_i r\left(\frac{M}{N}\right)_{t-1} + \sum_{i=0}^{n} b_i r\left(\frac{Y}{NP}\right)_{t-i} + \sum_{i=0}^{p} c_i r(ER_{t-i})$$

$$+ \sum_{i=0}^{q} d_i r\left(\frac{W(1 + TXR^{SS})}{GDP/L}\right) + \text{constant} + u_t \qquad (1)$$

where

$r(X)$	= annual rate of change of X,
P	= annual average deflator for gross domestic product,
M/N	= nominal average annual per capita money supply,
$Y/(NP)$	= real average annual per capita income,
ER	= average annual exchange rate,
$\dfrac{W(1 + TXR^{SS})}{GDP/L}$	= average annual wage rate, adjusted for employer's social security contribution, relative to average value added per domestic laborer,
a_i, b_i, c_i, d_i	= parameters to be estimated, and
u	= disturbance term.'

He then studies 'what can we say about the pattern of lagged responses', under the assumption that this equation comes from the equilibrium between a demand and an exogenous supply of money.

Upon examination of Behrman's equation, we are somewhat skeptical of the role of a foreign exchange rate and an average wage rate corrected by labor productivity in a demand for money. Unfortunately, there is no justification of why they are included. After discussing the expected pattern of the $\Sigma\ a_i$ and the $\Sigma\ b_i$ in the context of a demand-for-money equation, he states that (1970, p. 12):

'The comments of this paragraph, *appropriately modified to allow for the expectation that* $\Sigma_{i=0}^{p} c_i > 0$ *and* $\Sigma_{i=0}^{q} d_i > 0$, apply to the pattern of lagged adjustment to the other two right-hand variables in relation (1).' (The italics are mine.)

On failing to find a justification for the inclusion of the last two variables in the theoretical formulation, when we go to the empirical results we will be disappointed again.

With respect to the impact of the rate of change in the foreign exchange rate on prices, he says (1970, p. 19):

'The estimated response is rapid and substantial. The rapidity presumably reflects the almost *immediate transmission of news about exchange rate alternatives to the relevant sectors of the economy.* The size of the response reflects the substantial role of exports and imports (and close substitution for both) in the Chilean economy.' (The italics are mine.)

What is the relation of all this with a demand for money? With respect to the role of wages he concludes:

'The evidence of a major direct causal role of wage changes in the determination of the aggregate rate of change of prices, therefore is not strong.'

He finishes this section by comparing his results with those of Harberger and concludes that the main difference in their results is the pattern of lagged response to changes in the rate of change of nominal monetary balances. He attributes this difference to the procedure used by Harberger to select the number of lagged values.

The section on sectoral prices does not help in providing a justification for the specification used. Justifying the equation that he uses, Behrman says (1970, p. 23) the following with respect to the variables included in his equation:

'Both general and sector-specific pressures operating on the demand and on the supply side are represented as well *as is possible given the available data and the author's imagination.*' (The italics are mine.)

So we see that, in Berhman's work, there is no clear discussion of the mechanism that is generating the inflation.

Another important work on Chilean inflation is Lüder's excellent monetary history of Chile. He starts by taking Harberger's price equation as the true one with distributed lags in money and real income as regressors and concentrates on explaining the divergences between the predicted value and the observed values. He concludes (1968, p. 12):

'As expected from the results of the econometric work done in this field, there are some periods in which the divergence between actual and predicted changes is significant.

'These divergences can be explained mainly by two factors: (a) *"cost" factors* such as relative changes in wages and costs of imported products (1932–38, 1941–42, 1942–45, 1950) and (b) price expectations (especially 1953–1955).' (The italics are mine.)

The question that immediately comes to mind is: what is the mechanism through which these *economic* variables affect prices? But again, nowhere is there a discussion of the mechanism by which these variables affect prices.

The common feature of all these studies is that they start from the money market equilibrium condition and the assumption that the demand-for-money equation is very stable.

In the otherwise excellent survey of inflation theories by Johnson (1967), the matter is not clarified either. After describing the Keynesian theory of inflation, he says (pp. 122–123):

'The basic postulate of the quantity theory models of inflation is that there is a stable demand for money in real terms, into which the rate of inflation enters as a cost of holding real balances, which cost influences the quantity of real balances held. *Given this function, the rate of increase of the nominal stock of money determines the rate of inflation,* the public eventually coming to expect that rate of inflation and adjusting its stock of real balances to it.' (The italics are mine.)

However, we must qualify his conclusion. His conclusion does not apply for an economy with mild inflation and a well developed financial market in which the alternative to holding idle balances is not to hold commodities with their high storage costs but short-term financial assets which clearly dominate them as a portfolio choice. On the other hand, his conclusion does apply for a country with a high inflation rate and without a well developed financial market (in most cases both go together) where holding commodities, foreign equities or foreign exchange are better alternatives to holding idle cash balances.

In this last case, the problem is to prove that there exists a price level that simultaneously will clear the money and commodity markets. This problem is not analysed in any of the quantity theory versions.

García's (1964) work is the first in which an explicit model of how the main variables interact is developed. He begins with a cost model which is generalized to include the role of government and monetary institutions. The basic model with which he begins is as follows.

General price level equation

$$p_t = \alpha p_{at} + \beta p_{It} + \gamma p_{mt} \tag{2.1}$$

$$(\alpha + \beta + \gamma = 1),$$

Agricultural price equation

$$p_{at} = p_t + A_t, \tag{2.2}$$

Industrial price equation

$$p_{It} = a W_{t-1} + b p_{mt-1} + c, \tag{2.3}$$

Industrial wage equation

$$W_t = k + j p_{t-1}, \tag{2.4}$$

Import price equation

$$p_{mt} = q_t + f_t, \tag{2.5}$$

Foreign exchange price equation

$$f_t = p_t + F_t, \tag{2.6}$$

where

p_{at} = rate of change of agricultural prices,
p_t = rate of change of the general price level,
A_t = rate of change of real agricultural prices (deflated by the general price level) in response to real phenomena,
p_{It} = rate of change of industrial prices,

W_t = rate of change of industrial wages,
p_{mt} = rate of change of import costs,
q_t = rate of change of import prices in foreign currency,
f_t = rate of change of the exchange rate, and
F_t = rate of change of the real exchange rate in response to real factors such as the terms of trade and the growth of foreign and domestic income.

Combining eqs. (2.1)–(2.6), a non-homogeneous second-order difference equation with variable terms is obtained. Following García, let us write the equation as

$$p_t - bp_{t-1} - ajp_{t-2} = S_t, \tag{2.7}$$

where

$$S_t = ak + c + (\alpha/\beta)A_t + (\gamma/\beta)(q_t + F_t) + b(q_{t-1} + F_{t-1}). \tag{2.8}$$

Taking S_t as a given parameter independent of t, García studies the solution of (2.7). The stationary value of p_t will be given by

$$p_t^* = \frac{1}{1 - b - aj} S_t, \tag{2.9}$$

where $S_t = S$ for all t.

The purpose of García's work is to evaluate the different parameters involved in this model and to measure the weights of the different elements, here included, in the explanation of the rate of inflation.

In expression (2.9), García studies the implications of the structuralist and the cost push view of inflation. For García, both views have different hypotheses with respect to the role of the different parameters included in S.

In García's words (1964, p. 31):

> 'It should be clear now why structuralist thinking emphasizes the role of changes in the real magnitudes contained in S, especially increases in the relative prices of the lagging sectors of the economy, mainly agriculture and foreign trade, as primary causes of inflation. Any increase in A_t, q_t or F_t would indeed pose an inflationary stimulus to be propagated throughout the economy

by the multiplier factor of equation [2.9] till a new steady rate of inflation was achieved, provided that the system were stable.

'On the other hand a believer of wage-inflation would consider that the only relevant parameter in S is k, the autonomous increase in nominal wages, while an advocate of profit-inflation would argue that the driving force behind the increase in S is c, the autonomous change in the percentage mark-up.'

We agree in principle with this presentation of the basic cost-inflation model, but we do not agree with the way the model was extended to include the role of excess demand in prices.

In the final model, García includes the money supply in the industrial products price equation. Justifying this choice, he says (1964, pp. 54–56):

'A mixed inflation model blending cost and demand elements can be built up along Keynesian lines. Here however another approach will be taken by assuming that the rate of increase in industrial prices and wages is not a function of the "inflationary gap" but of the rate of increase in the money supply and related monetary categories, in addition to the cost elements already considered.

'Following Harberger's study of the Chilean inflation this approach can be framed by assuming that the rate of increase in prices is a function of the rate of increase in the money supply, current and/or lagged, the expected change in the cost of holding cash, to account for changes in the ratio of cash balances to income or in velocity, and of the rate of change in real income.'

Once again, the role of money is not studied in the context of a completely specified macro-model. He starts with a cost-determined price equation and curiously mixes it up with a demand-for-money equation.

It is interesting to note that the same approach was used by Behrman in the study already discussed in this chapter. Furthermore, it is of interest to note that García, at the end of his work, treats the money supply as an endogenous variable.

The main difference between García's work and the present study is twofold. First, we can concentrate on a complete model in which the price equation includes cost and excess-demand terms. The role of monetary variables in the model (especially in ch. 5) is derived only from an explicitly formulated model.

Second, since our model is a simultaneous one, we will use a simultaneous-equation estimation procedure whereas García used a single-equation estimation procedure. It should be obvious that this work complements García's work.

At the end of 1964, a new government came to power with a strong desire to stop inflation. In order to make policy decisions, a new model was formulated by Cauas (1970). The Cauas model, following García's work, incorporates cost factors in the determination of short-run prices. His basic model is an extension of the Leontief model. In addition, Cauas makes a couple of assumptions about the growth in intermediate inputs and primary factors.

Let us describe how he obtains the price equation in his model. The cost—revenue identity gives

$$P_j Q_j = \sum_{i=1}^{n} P_i Q_{ij} + \sum_{h=1}^{k} W_h F_{hj} , \qquad (2.10)$$

where Q_j is the production of j, P_i is the price of intermediate input i, W_h is the price of primary factor h, Q_{ij} is the intermediate input of i in the production of j, F_{hj} is the use of the primary factor h in the production of j, $i,j = 1, \ldots n$, and $h = 1, \ldots k$.

Taking time differentials in eq. (2.10), we get

$$p_j + q_j = \sum_{i} a_{ij}(p_i + q_{ij}) + \sum_{h} b_{hj}(w_h + f_{hj}) , \qquad (2.11)$$

where a_{ij} is the share of intermediate input i in the value of production of j; b_{hj} is the share of primary factor h in the production of j; $h = 1 \ldots k$; and $j = 1 \ldots n$. Small letters indicate the rate of change of variables in capital letters.

Let us assume that

$$q_{ij} = q_j, \qquad f_{hj} = q_j - \beta_h, \qquad \begin{matrix} i = 1, \ldots n \\ h = 1, \ldots k \\ j = 1, \ldots n . \end{matrix} \qquad (2.12)$$

This means that through time there are fixed coefficients in the use of intermediate inputs and that there is a productivity gain for each factor (β_h). This last assumption can reflect increasing returns to scale or technical progress.

Substituting (2.12) in (2.11), we get

$$p_j = \sum_i a_{ij}\, p_i + \sum_h b_{hj}\, w_h - \sum_h b_{hj}\, \beta_h \qquad j = 1, \ldots n. \qquad (2.13)$$

This last system of equations can be written in matrix form as

$$p = Ap + Bw - B\beta \qquad\qquad\qquad\qquad (2.14)$$

with the property that $A1 + B1 = 1$, where 1s are unit vectors of appropriate dimensionality. From (2.14) we get

$$p = (I - A)^{-1}\, B(w - \beta). \qquad\qquad\qquad (2.15)$$

It can be shown that

$$(I - A)^{-1}\, B\, 1 = 1. \qquad\qquad\qquad\qquad (2.15')$$

Let us assume now that the price index ($\bar{p}$) whose behavior we want to describe is a weighted sum of the price vector p, the weights being given by the vector ρ. Then

$$\bar{p} = \rho(I - A)^{-1}\, B(w - \beta), \qquad\qquad\qquad (2.16)$$

with

$$\rho 1 = 1. \qquad\qquad\qquad\qquad\qquad\qquad (2.16')$$

Let us now define $\rho (I - A)^{-1} B = \mu$. Then from (2.15′) and (2.16′) we have $\mu 1 = 1$. Hence

$$\bar{p} = \mu w - \mu\beta. \qquad\qquad\qquad\qquad\qquad (2.17)$$

The change in the price index is a weighted average of change in the price of the factors minus a weighted average of the changes in productivity.

From here, Cauas goes on to assume a different behavior for the price of primary inputs (the ws) in order to get the final change in $\bar{p}$. In this model, it is not necessary that sectoral compatibility of supply and demand exist. Therefore, it does not include sectoral demand pressures on prices. This is not a defect of the specification of the model, for it was built specifically for monetary programming and not to explain past inflation.

Besides the inclusion of demand pressures in the price equation, the main difference between Cauas's work and ours is the explanation of the wage rate. We explain wage behavior by a stable relation that is implicit in Chilean economic institutions. Cauas studied mainly the impact on prices of different alternatives for wage increases. Therefore our work is complementary to his.

PART II

A QUARTERLY MODEL FOR INDUSTRIAL PRICES, INDUSTRIAL WAGES AND INFLATION

CHAPTER 3

INDUSTRIAL PRICES, INDUSTRIAL WAGES
AND INFLATION IN CHILE: A QUARTERLY MODEL

This chapter is divided into five sections. In the first one, we will study the formation of prices in the industrial sector. In the second section, we will study the specification of the industrial wage equation (in both these sections, we use ordinary least squares as a searching procedure to select alternative specifications of the different equations of the subsystem that will be estimated using a simultaneous equation estimation procedure)[1]. In the third section, we estimate the simultaneous model. In the fourth, we discuss the results and analyze their implications for stabilization policy by means of simulation experiments. Finally, we study the steady-state behavior of the model. The data used for the empirical estimations are presented in appendix A.

3.1. Prices in the industrial sector

It is hard to specify a price equation for an economy like the Chilean one where we have had a long history of price controls. In the period considered in this study, 1963–1968, we have had experiences of very tight price controls. The hypothesis that we wish to test is that even in a framework of price controls these prices keep a stable relationship to cost and demand elements.

---

[1] We made only limited use of this strategy because, in the context of a simultaneous model, ordinary least square estimates are not only biased but also inconsistent.

For commodities with free prices we arrive at this hypothesis from different theoretical models that are developed below. They include, among others, the case of a method of pricing consisting of a mark-up over average variable cost, and the case of a mono-polist in the commodity market that faces a demand for his pro-duct with constant price elasticity.

For commodities under price controls, this hypothesis implies that in the price negotiations between public officials and pro-ducers the objective factors are the behavior of cost elements and demand pressures. This last element arises through the interest of the public official in the elimination of shortages even at the cost of some price increases.

Another problem in specifying the price equation is that, in an economy with price control, most of the prices are adjusted in the same season, usually at the beginning of the year, and therefore any specification of a price equation should consider this. Fortun-ately, this is not the case in the industrial sector where the adjust-ment in prices is distributed throughout the year as is shown in table 3.1.

TABLE 3.1
Price increases in the industrial sector*.

Year and quarter			Year and quarter		
1964	1		1968	1	28.3
	2	56.2		2	29.3
	3	54.2		3	32.3
	4	50.9		4	36.8
1965	1	30.6	1969	1	34.5
	2	26.2		2	34.9
	3	26.1		3	37.1
	4	26.1		4	35.7
1966	1	34.6	1970	1	39.8
	2	28.6		2	38.8
	3	27.9		3	36.2
	4	25.8		4	34.5
1967	1	28.2			
	2	28.1			
	3	26.4			
	4	23.3			

* Rate of change with respect to the same quarter of the previous year. (Source: various issues of the *Monthly Bulletin*, Central Bank of Chile.)

3.1.1. The model

The industrial sector in Chile has a predominantly non-competitive structure, which we would expect in any small economy.

Some evidence in this respect shows that (Lagos, 1966, p. 104):

> 'The level of industrial concentration is rather high; the 52 largest firms of the country (they represent less than 1% of all firms) generate 38% of the value added in the industrial sector.'

Garretón and Cisternas (1970, p. 8) conclude that for 1966, 'about 17% of all enterprises control 78.2% of total assets in the corporate sector'.

In our work we will begin by assuming a pricing method that consists of a mark-up over variable cost. This mark-up will be modified by the demand conditions in the market for industrial products[2].

For commodities subject to price controls, this mark-up is the result of price negotiations.

3.1.1.1. Full cost pricing
In this case, it is assumed that

$$
\begin{aligned}
P^I(t) \quad &= \lambda\, TVC(t), \\
P^I(t) \quad &= \text{industrial prices}, \\
TVC(t) \quad &= ULC(t) + UIMC(t) + UDMC(t), \\
ULC(t) \quad &= \text{unit labor cost}, \\
UIMC(t) \quad &= \text{unit imported material cost}, \\
UDMC(t) \quad &= \text{unit domestic material cost, and} \\
\lambda - 1 = \mu \quad &= \text{mark-up coefficient}.
\end{aligned}
$$

This is a behavioral equation and as such is entirely compatible with the identity between price and average cost of production

$$P^I(t) = ULC(t) + UIMC(t) + UDMC(t) + R(t), \tag{3.1}$$

where $R(t)$ is the residual.

[2] The most important works on the specification of a price equation of the mark-up over variable cost variety are Eckstein and Fromm (1968), Lipsey and Parkin (1970), and Bodkin (1966).

Eq. (3.1) implies that, given the unit costs variable, the residual (which includes the unit cost of capital) is a consequence of the pricing method. Furthermore, this equation is incompatible, in general, with the assumption of short-run profit maximization. However, it can be compatible with long-run profit maximization (see below).

If we differentiate (3.1) with respect to time and then divide through by $P^I(t)$, we obtain

$$\frac{\dot{P}^I(t)}{P^I(t)} = \frac{\dot{\lambda}}{\lambda} + \lambda\frac{ULC(t)}{P^I(t)}\frac{U\dot{L}C(t)}{ULC(t)} + \lambda\frac{UIMC(t)}{P^I(t)}\frac{UI\dot{M}C(t)}{UIMC(t)}$$

$$+ \lambda\frac{UDMC(t)}{P^I(t)}\frac{UD\dot{M}C(t)}{UDMC(t)}, \tag{3.2}$$

where the dots indicate time differentials.

If we assume that the shares of labor cost, domestic material cost and imported materials cost in the value of production are constant (this is equivalent to the fixed value coefficients assumed by the Cauas model to which we referred in ch. 2) we obtain

$$\frac{\dot{P}^I(t)}{P^I(t)} = \alpha_1\frac{U\dot{L}C(t)}{ULC(t)} + \alpha_2\frac{UI\dot{M}C(t)}{UIMC(t)} + \alpha_3\frac{UD\dot{M}C(t)}{UDMC(t)} + \frac{\dot{\lambda}}{\lambda}, \tag{3.3}$$

where $\alpha_1 = \lambda ULC(t)/P^I(t)$, $\alpha_2 = \lambda UIMC(t)/P^I(t)$, and $\alpha_3 = \lambda UDMC(t)/P^I(t)$. If this is so, the ratio of the coefficients in (3.3) will have a clear interpretation in terms of relative cost.

To derive the final price equation, we need a hypothesis for the behavior of the mark-up factor (λ) through time. We will assume that what firms think a reasonable mark-up is determined by demand pressures in the market. Explicitly, we will assume that

$$\frac{\dot{\lambda}}{\lambda} = f\left(\frac{D(t) - Q(t)}{Q(t)}\right),$$

where $D(t)$ is the demand for industrial products and $Q(t)$ is the production of industrial products. The specification of the function f will be studied in detail below. Introducing this in eq. (3.3) yields a final price equation of

$$\frac{\dot{P}^l(t)}{P^l(t)} = \alpha_1 \frac{U\dot{L}C(t)}{ULC(t)} + \alpha_2 \frac{UI\dot{M}C(t)}{UIMC(t)} + \alpha_3 \frac{UD\dot{M}C(t)}{UDMC(t)} + f\left(\frac{D(t) - Q(t)}{Q(t)}\right).$$

(3.4)

3.1.1.2. Profit maximization case

Now we will derive an equation similar to (3.4) for a producer who maximizes profits in the short run. Let us consider the case of a monopolist in the commodity market who faces fixed prices in the factor market (the results would be the same up to a constant if the producer is at the same time a monopsonist in the market for factors with constant elasticity of demand for factors). Let us assume further that he faces a demand for his product with constant elasticity and that its technology can be represented by a Cobb–Douglas production function. Then it can be shown from a fundamental theorem of duality that the price of the product is a Cobb–Douglas function of the price of inputs with the same exponents as the production function.

This means that

$$P = BW_1^{\alpha_1} W_2^{\alpha_2} \ldots W_n^{\alpha_n},$$

(3.5)

where W_j is the price of input j, α_j is the constant elasticity of production with respect to factor j, and B is a constant related to the constant of the production function, the elasticities of production and the elasticity of demand for the product.

From (3.5) we can obtain

$$\frac{\dot{P}^l(t)}{P^l(t)} = \sum_i^n \alpha_i \frac{\dot{W}_i(t)}{W_i(t)}.$$

(3.6)

Let us now assume that in the short run we have three inputs: labor, imported raw materials and domestic materials.

Therefore, (3.6) can be written as

$$\frac{\dot{P}^l(t)}{P^l(t)} = \alpha_1 \frac{\dot{W}_L(t)}{W_L(t)} + \alpha_2 \frac{\dot{W}_{DM}(t)}{W_{DM}(t)} + \alpha_3 \frac{\dot{W}_{IM}(t)}{W_{IM}(t)},$$

(3.7)

where α_1 is the elasticity of production with respect to labor, α_2 is the elasticity of production with respect to domestic materials, α_3 is the elasticity of production with respect to imported materials, W_L is the price of labor services, W_{DM} is the price of domestic materials, and W_{IM} is the price of imported materials.

Let us now transform eq. (3.5) from an equation in the price of inputs to an equation in unit costs. Using the assumption that the production function is homogeneous of first degree, we have

$$P^I = \beta' \left(\frac{W_1 V_1}{Q} \right)^{\alpha_1} \left(\frac{W_2 V_2}{Q} \right)^{\alpha_2} \cdots \left(\frac{W_m V_m}{Q} \right)^{\alpha_m},$$

where Q is output, V_i is the physical amount of input i and β' is a contant. From this we obtain

$$\frac{\dot{P}^I(t)}{P^I(t)} = \sum_i \alpha_i \frac{U\dot{V}_i C(t)}{UV_i C(t)},$$

where $UV_i C(t)$ is the unit cost of input i in period t.

Let us again assume that we have in the short run the same three inputs: labor, imported raw materials and domestic raw materials. In this case we have

$$\frac{\dot{P}^I(t)}{P^I(t)} = \alpha_1 \frac{U\dot{L}C(t)}{ULC(t)} + \alpha_2 \frac{U\dot{D}MC(t)}{UDMC(t)} + \alpha_3 \frac{U\dot{I}MC(t)}{UIMC(t)}. \qquad (3.8)$$

Because of the assumption of constant returns, we will expect the coefficients in (3.8) to add up to one minus the elasticity of production with respect to capital.

Now we will add to the dynamic behavior of prices (due to cost elements expressed in eq. (3.8)) the demand pressures in the market for industrial products [3]. The final expression for the price changes will be given by

---

[3] These demand pressures will come in through their impact on the elasticity of demand for the product.

$$\frac{\dot{P}^I(t)}{P^I(t)} = \alpha_1 \frac{U\dot{L}C(t)}{ULC(t)} + \alpha_2 \frac{U\dot{D}MC(t)}{UDMC(t)} + \alpha_3 \frac{U\dot{I}MC(t)}{UIMC(t)} + f\left(\frac{D(t)-Q(t)}{Q(t)}\right)$$

$$+ \eta(t).$$

This equation is equivalent to eq. (3.4). Therefore we have shown that an equation of the form of (3.4) can be derived for a profit-maximizing monopolist. In the analysis that follows, we will use the mark-up justification for this equation.

In order to have an explicit price equation, we need to specify the function f. We will distinguish three cases.

Case 1. In this case we will assume that pressures on prices coming from the commodity market are a linear function of excess demand in the commodity market. Specifically, we will assume that

$$f\left(\frac{D(t)-Q(t)}{Q(t)}\right) = h_0 + h_1 \left(\frac{D(t)-Q(t)}{Q(t)}\right) = (h_0 - h_1) + h_1 \frac{D(t)}{Q(t)},$$
$$(3.9)$$

where h_0 takes care of some upward pressures in prices even if $D(t) = Q(t)$. This will be generated in the case of a nonsymmetric response of price changes to excess demand pressures by disequilibria at the industry level. This is primarily caused by changes in the composition of the industrial sector demand.

Unfortunately, we do not have any direct measure of demand pressures in the market for industrial products (such as unfilled orders, inventory change, etc.). Therefore, this necessitates that we try to find a proxy for excess demand.

We will specifically assume that, in this *non-competitive* system, the pricing equation already discussed assumes a target level use of capacity. If the price determined in eq. (3.4) is too high, there will be excess capacity and prices will therefore be marked down.

Therefore, we could approximate, for a world of price makers, the demand pressures in the market by an index of capacity utilization[4].

---

[4] This point arose from discussions with Professor F.M. Fisher.

Introducing this in (3.4) we have

$$\frac{\dot{P}^I(t)}{P^I(t)} = \delta_0 + \delta_1 \frac{\dot{ULC}(t)}{ULC(t)} + \delta_2 \frac{\dot{UDMC}(t)}{UDMC(t)} + \delta_3 \frac{\dot{UIMC}(t)}{UIMC(t)} + \delta_4 CU(t)$$

$$+ \eta(t),\tag{3.10}$$

where $CU(t) = D(t)/Q(t)$ is an index of capacity utilization, used as a measure of the demand pressures in the market for industrial products.

Case 2. In this case, we will assume that the pressures coming from the demand side are some non-linear function of the excess demand in the market[5]. Specifically, we will assume that

$$f\left(\frac{D(t)-Q(t)}{Q(t)}\right) = k_0 + k_1 NLCU(t),$$

where non-linear capacity utilization

$$NLCU(t) = \left[\text{sign}\left(\frac{D(t)}{Q(t)} - M\left(\frac{D(t)}{Q(t)}\right)\right)\right]\left(\frac{D(t)}{Q(t)} - M\left(\frac{D(t)}{Q(t)}\right)\right)^2,$$

and $M(D(t)/Q(t))$ is the sampling mean of $D(t)/Q(t)$. Introducing this in (3.4) yields

$$\frac{\dot{P}^I(t)}{P^I(t)} = \epsilon_0 + \epsilon_1 \frac{ULC(t)}{ULC(t)} + \epsilon_2 \frac{UDMC(t)}{UDMC(t)} + \epsilon_3 \frac{UIMC(t)}{UIMC(t)} + \epsilon_4 NLCU(t)$$

$$+ \eta(t).\tag{3.11}$$

The problem with cases 1 and 2 is that, after the capacity utilization index has achieved its maximum value, eqs. (3.10) and (3.11) will imply that no additional demand pressures on prices exist. Furthermore, they imply that the response of price changes to excess demand pressures is symmetric for situations both above and below average capacity utilization. To make this point clear,

---

[5] A similar treatment has been used by Solow (1969).

let us consider the following example. Assume that, in the first quarter of a year capacity utilization reaches its upper limit (let us say 90%) but that fiscal and monetary policy continue to be expansive in the following quarters. Eqs. (3.10) and (3.11) will imply that demand pressures remain the same as in the first quarter.

To take care of this shortcoming, we will consider another choice for the function f.

Case 3. Here, we will assume that

$$f\left(\frac{D(t)-Q(t)}{Q(t)}\right) = m_0 + m_1 \left(\frac{1}{r-CU(t)}\right) ,$$

with $CU(t) < r$ where r is defined to be the upper limit on capacity utilized in the industrial sector. In this specification, when capacity utilization approaches its ceiling r, the pressures on prices become higher and higher, approaching infinity in the limit.

Substituting this in (3.4), we have

$$\frac{\dot{P}^I(t)}{P^I(t)} = \zeta_0 + \zeta_1 \frac{\dot{ULC}(t)}{ULC(t)} + \zeta_2 \frac{\dot{UDMC}(t)}{UDMC(t)} + \zeta_3 \frac{\dot{UIMC}(t)}{UIMC(t)} + \zeta_4 \frac{1}{r-CU(t)}$$

$$+ \eta^*(t) . \tag{3.12}$$

This is illustrated graphically in fig. 3.1.

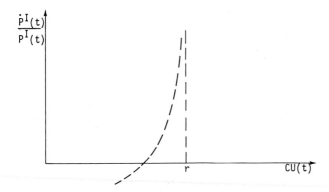

Fig. 3.1. Price response to demand pressures under the formulation of eq. (3.12) under given values of the unit cost variables.

Before estimating eq. (3.12), we will assume that the rate of change in unit domestic raw material costs is the same as the rate of change in industrial prices. This is a sound hypothesis in a highly inflationary economy where most of the increase in unit cost is due to an increase in prices. With this additional assumption, we can write

$$\frac{\dot{P}^I(t)}{P^I(t)} = \chi_0 + \chi_1 \frac{U\dot{L}C(t)}{ULC(t)} + \chi_2 \frac{U\dot{I}MC(t)}{UIMC(t)} + \chi_3 \frac{1}{\eta - CU(t)} + \eta^{**}(t),$$

(3.13)

where

$$\chi_0 = \frac{\zeta_0}{1-\zeta_2}, \quad \chi_1 = \frac{\zeta_1}{1-\zeta_2}, \quad \chi_2 = \frac{\zeta_2}{1-\zeta_2}, \quad \chi_3 = \frac{\zeta_3}{1-\zeta_2},$$

and

$$\eta^{**}(t) = \frac{\eta^*(t)}{1-\zeta_2}.$$

In our empirical work we cannot estimate eq. (3.13) because we do not have data on unit imported raw material cost. Because of this, we have to split the change in unit imported raw material cost into two components: the change in imported raw material prices and the change in imported raw material requirements per unit of production.

In this way, we can rewrite (3.13) as

$$\frac{\dot{P}^I(t)}{P^I(t)} = \chi_0 + \chi_1 \frac{U\dot{L}C(t)}{ULC(t)} + \chi_2 \frac{\dot{P}^M(t)}{P^M(t)} + \chi_2 \frac{U\dot{I}M(t)}{UIM(t)} + \chi_3 f\left(\frac{D(t)-Q(t)}{Q(t)}\right)$$
$$+ \pi^{**}(t),$$

(3.13')

where $UIM(t)$ is the unit imported raw materials in period t and $P^M(t)$ is the price of imports in period t. We now proceed to estimate

$$\frac{\dot{P}^I(t)}{P^I(t)} = \chi_0 + \chi_1 \frac{U\dot{L}C(t)}{ULC(t)} + \chi_2 \frac{\dot{P}^M(t)}{P^M(t)} + \chi_3 f\left(\frac{D(t)-Q(t)}{Q(t)}\right) + \psi(t).$$

(3.13'')

If model (3.13) is correct, when we estimate (3.13″) we are making a specification error which we should consider in the interpretation of the final results. It is interesting to note that, if the rate of change in $UIM(t)$ is steady, its effects will be included in the constant in (3.13″). Furthermore, in the Leontief constant coefficient case, this rate will be zero.

3.1.2. Definition of variables

3.1.2.1. Quarterly price index of industrial commodities
We use the manufacturing industry component of the wholesale price index with a base year of 1947. The dependent variable in our regressions is the overlapping four quarters annual rate of change in this index.

3.1.2.2. Unit labor cost
This is defined as the product of an index of wages and salaries in the industrial sector and an index of labor requirements per unit of production. The index of wages and salaries in the industrial sector begins in April 1963. The index of labor requirements per unit of production was defined as a ratio between an index of industrial employment and an index of industrial production. There are two different production indexes: one computed by the National Institute of Statistics and the other by the Association of Industrial Entrepreneurs (the first one has a broader coverage). In the estimations, both indexes were used and the results were slightly better for the National Institute of Statistics index. Only the results obtained with the latter index are reported here.

In the empirical analysis that we will discuss, we consider different numbers of quarters in the definition of the index of labor requirements. The rate of change of the unit labor cost is defined as the overlapping four quarters annual rate of change in the unit labor cost.

3.1.2.3. Quarterly price index of imported raw materials
We use the imported raw materials component of the wholesale price index with a base year of 1947. The rate of change is defined as the overlapping four quarters rate of change of this price index.

3.1.2.4. Capacity utilization

This is defined as the ratio between a quarterly index of industrial production and a quarterly index of maximum industrial production. This last index was built using linear interpolation from the peaks in the monthly index of industrial production. We made a correction for the level of this variable using the capacity utilization figures estimated by the Institute of Economic Research of the University of Chile (1963, p. 18); the figures estimated by the Institute of Economic Research were obtained in the second half of 1961 from a survey of 42 industrial firms.

3.1.3. Results

We can see in table 3.2 the results of estimating the model just described[6]. From this table, it is clear that, independently of the specification of the equation, the coefficient of the rate of change in imported raw material prices is fairly steady. Several distributed lags for this variable were also tried but they did not improve the results.

In the estimations, we can try different distributed lags for the other explanatory variables but better results are always obtained without them. This can be attributed to the high speed of adjustments to price changes for an economy with a long history of inflation.

In terms of t-statistics and $\bar{R}^2$, the eqs. (C), (D) and (B) are the best, in that order. For most of the cases, the sum of the coefficients for the unit labor cost and the imported raw materials variables was not significantly different from unity, as we expected *a priori*.

It is important to note that, owing to the simultaneity of the model, the coefficients and the associated t-statistics do not have much value if we do not study the specific bias introduced in the

---

[6] In this section, we consider only the specification corresponding to case 1 for the capacity utilization variable. Because most of the estimations were done before these alternative cases were thought of, it was not thought worthwhile to re-run these regressions, since we are mainly interested in the model of section 3.3 which is estimated by a procedure that takes into consideration the simultaneity of the model. At that time, we consider these alternative formulations.

estimation of the coefficients and in their standard errors. This same argument applies to the Durbin—Watson statistic which is now only a descriptive statistic.

In the estimation of the equations of table 3.2, we implicitly introduced the assumption that the coefficient of the rate of change in wages and the coefficient of the rate of change in unit labor requirements were the same. Now we want to split the unit labor cost into its two components and use regression to estimate their impact on the price variable.

In table 3.3, the same equations are presented, the only difference being that the unit labor cost has been split into the rate of change in the index of wages and salaries and into the rate of change in unit labor requirements.

As we see from table 3.3, the rate of change of unit labor requirements has a very poor showing. In some cases, it has the wrong sign and it never has a t-statistic over 1.753 for all periods considered. Here there is almost no difference between (F), (G), (H), (I) and (J).

What puzzles us is the poor showing of the labor requirements variable. An explanation for this can be attributed to the fact that the dominant element in unit labor cost is the rate of change in industrial wages, which is around 30% for most of the period; and therefore it is this variable that should be used as a proxy for labor cost in pricing policy. In the light of this last comment, we can leave out the rate of change of unit labor requirements [7] and obtain the results that appear in eq. (K).

We see that, in terms of t-statistics and $\bar{R}^2$, eq. (K) is slightly better than the other equations in table 3.3. Furthermore, the sum of the coefficients of the price variables is close to unity. This is what we should expect in accordance with the discussion at the beginning of this section. This means that the data do not disprove the hypothesis that the wage variable is the main element considered as a proxy for unit labor cost in the pricing mechanism. In the last section of this chapter, we will test for non-linearities in this price equation within the context of a simultaneous model.

---

[7] This equation corresponds to eq. (3.7) in the text, with the assumption that $\dot{W}_{DM}(t)/W_{DM}(t) = \dot{P}^I(t)/P^I(t)$.

Inflation in developing countries

TABLE 3.2*

Equation	Constant	Rate(a) of change, unit labor cost (2)	Rate of change, unit labor cost (4)	Rate of change, unit labor cost (6)	Capacity(b) utilization (4)	Rate of change, imported raw material prices	R^2(d)	DW(e)
(A)	-2.586 (-4.513)(c)	0.430 (4.775)			3.344 (4.463)	0.362 (6.184)	0.882	1.38
(B)	-2.643 (-5.612)		0.508 (6.224)		3.369 (5.471)	0.390 (7.807)	0.917	1.81
(C)	-2.817 (-6.806)			0.596 (7.166)	3.531 (6.519)	0.447 (9.389)	0.933	2.04

Equation	Constant	Rate of change, unit labor cost (8)	Rate of change, unit labor cost (12)	Capacity utilization (4)	Rate of change, imported raw material prices	R^2	DW
(D)	-3.115 (-7.210)	0.574 (6.556)		3.927 (7.003)	0.434 (8.623)	0.923	1.72
(E)	-3.237 (-6.497)		0.644 (5.298)	4.058 (6.269)	0.420 (7.243)	0.897	1.30

* The sample size for all these regressions was 19.
(a) The number in parentheses indicates the numbers of quarters used in the definition of the index of unit labor requirements.
(b) The number in parentheses indicates the number of quarters utilized in the definition of the variable.
(c) The numbers in parentheses are the t-statistics of the respective coefficients.
(d) R^2 is the coefficient of multiple determination.
(e) DW is the Durbin and Watson statistic.

TABLE 3.3*

Equation	Constant	Rate of change, wages and salaries	Rate of change, unit labor requir. (2)	Rate of change, unit labor requir. (4)	Rate of change, unit labor requir. (6)	Capacity utilization (4)	Rate of change, prices of imported raw material	$\bar{R}^2$	DW
(F)	-2.427 (-4.648)	0.651 (5.480)	0.020 (0.079)			3.035 (4.364)	0.394 (7.136)	0.889	1.47
(G)	-2.458 (-4.726)	0.648 (5.881)		-0.145 (-0.206)		3.077 (4.475)	0.391 (7.354)	0.891	1.40
(H)	-2.355 (-4.646)	0.666 (6.061)			0.573 (0.836)	2.931 (4.357)	0.403 (7.614)	0.895	1.66

Equation	Constant	Rate of change, wages and salaries	Rate of change, unit labor requir. (8)	Rate of change, unit labor requir. (12)	Capacity utilization (4)	Rate of change, prices of imported raw material	$\bar{R}^2$	DW
(I)	-2.445 (-4.920)	0.664 (6.087)	1.068 (0.871)		3.039 (4.627)	0.420 (6.990)	0.896	1.75
(J)	-2.594 (-4.787)	0.673 (6.083)		1.552 (0.756)	3.227 (4.596)	0.416 (6.913)	0.895	1.50
(K)	-2.436 (-4.944)	0.647 (6.077)			3.048 (4.678)	0.393 (7.704)	0.897	1.45

* See notes at the end of table 3.2.

It is important to note that the use of eq. (K) to predict changes in industrial prices ignores the feedbacks that are possible. The most obvious feedback begins with industrial prices and is transmitted to the cost of living and from there to industrial wages. We will study this in more detail after studying wages in the industrial sector.

3.2. Wages in the industrial sector

For the last twenty years, Chile has had periodic laws of wage increases. The main objective of these laws has been to 'protect' wage-earners against the loss in real income produced by inflation[8]. The laws are dictated for the public sector and include some rules for the private sector. These rules have been in the form of minimum wage increases or general recommendations for wage increases. The importance of this legislation for our work is that it can introduce non-market elements in the wage behavior of the industrial sector.

The other important point is timing. Wage laws are usually enacted for a calendar year. If in the industrial sector the increase in wages is concentrated in the first quarter of the year there is no point in building a quarterly model. Fortunately, this is not the case for the industrial sector. The different firms have wage negotiation all year long, as can be seen in table 3.4.

3.2.1. The model

Again, given the structure of labor organizations in Chile, we can expect some mix of competitive and non-competitive market behavior in the determination of industrial wages. On the competitive side, we will assume that

$$\frac{\dot{w}(t)}{w(t)} = \beta_1 + \beta_2 \left(\frac{d(t) - s(t)}{s(t)} \right) + \frac{\dot{CL}(t)}{CL(t)} + \theta(t) , \qquad (3.14)$$

---

[8] Ramos (1970) shows that the behavior of real wages has not been significantly influenced by the wage legislation.

TABLE 3.4
Wages in the industrial sector*.

Year and quarter			Year and quarter		
			1968	1	30.4
1964	2	48.6		2	31.7
	3	57.1		3	28.1
	4	45.9		4	31.5
1965	1	34.9	1969	1	38.8
	2	43.5		2	38.9
	3	47.8		3	40.8
	4	47.3		4	35.1
1966	1	52.0	1970	1	34.7
	2	43.7		2	40.4
	3	37.4		3	44.0
	4	39.4		4	43.2
1967	1	38.2			
	2	28.2			
	3	30.7			
	4	32.4			

* Rate of change with respect to the same quarter of the previous year. (Source: various issues of the *Monthly Bulletin,* Central Bank of Chile.)

where $\dot{w}(t)/w(t)$ is the rate of change in the nominal wage rate, $d(t)$ is the quantity demanded of labor, $s(t)$ is the quantity supplied of labor (labor force), $\dot{CL}(t)/CL(t)$ is the rate of change in the cost of living, and $\theta(t)$ is the random error.

If we add to this the pressures on wages due to non-competitive elements in the organization of the labor market, we will have

$$\frac{\dot{w}(t)}{w(t)} = \beta_1 + \beta_2 \left(\frac{d(t)-s(t)}{s(t)} \right) + \beta_3 \frac{\dot{CL}(t)}{CL(t)} + \omega(t) . \qquad (3.15)$$

The amount by which β_3 differs from unity is an indication of non-competitive elements in the labor market as well as a measure of the speed of adjustment of wages to price changes.

Given the fact that we do not have observations for $d(t)$, we have to introduce some transformations to (3.15) before proceeding to estimate it.

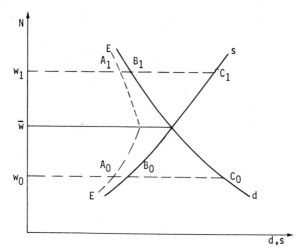

Fig. 3.2. Employment and the demand and supply of labor. d is the demand for labor, s is the supply of labor, EE is employment, and $\bar{w}$ is equilibrium wage.

Let us describe the labor market as illustrated in fig. 3.2[9]. The distance between s and EE for $w \leqslant \bar{w}$, and between d and EE for $w \geqslant \bar{w}$, is a measure of frictional unemployment. This frictional unemployment is due mainly to a lack of information among suppliers and demanders. For a wage rate w_0 below the equilibrium rate $\bar{w}$, we will have $B_0 C_0$ = excess demand for labor, $A_0 C_0$ = unfilled vacancies, and $A_0 B_0$ = measured unemployment.

For a wage rate w_1, above the equilibrium rate $\bar{w}$, we will have $B_1 C_1$ = excess demand for labor (negative), $A_1 B_1$ = unfilled vacancies, and $A_1 C_1$ = measured unemployment.

From our characterization of the labor market, it is clear that for conditions where $w < \bar{w}$, measured unemployment is a very bad proxy for excess demand in the labor market. For $w > \bar{w}$, the higher w is, the better is unemployment as a proxy for excess demand (negative in this case).

In general, we will have

$$d - s = V - U, \tag{3.16}$$

[9] After the first draft of this chapter was written, a paper by Hansen (1970) where he presents a similar theoretical analysis came to our attention.

where V is the total unfilled vacancies, and U is the total unemployment.

It is easy to see that $V = d - E$ and $U = s - E$, where E = total employment. Therefore, equilibrium in the labor market ($d = s$) implies that the number of people looking for jobs (U) is equal to the number of unfilled vacancies (V).

The problem is that we do not have observations on V; therefore, we need to relate it to some variable for which we have observations. We will study three different cases.

Case 1. In this case, we are interested in estimating the relation for points where $w \geqslant \bar{w}$. This is the case in which unemployment is due mainly to the inflexibility of wages. Here we can approximate the excess demand in the labor market by the level of unemployment. Specifically, we will have $d(t) - s(t) \approx -U(t)$, and, introducing this in (3.15), we get

$$\frac{\dot{w}(t)}{w(t)} = \beta_1 - \beta_1 \frac{U(t)}{s(t)} + \beta_3 \frac{\dot{CL}(t)}{CL(t)} + \omega(t) . \qquad (3.17)$$

Case 2. Here we will consider the simple Phillips curve kind of argument approximating $[d(t) - s(t)]/s(t)$ by $a + b/[U(t)/s(t)]$. Introducing this in (3.15), we get

$$\frac{\dot{w}(t)}{w(t)} = \gamma_1 + \gamma_2 \frac{1}{U(t)/s(t)} + \gamma_3 \frac{\dot{CL}(t)}{CL(t)} + \chi(t) . \qquad (3.18)$$

Case 3. The last case we will study corresponds to a steady-state solution which is derived from the basic Lipsey (1960) model. Following Lipsey, for a given wage rate, we will assume a steady state in which the number of people leaving jobs is equal to the number of unemployed that find jobs.

We need to introduce some additional terms, viz. R = number of employed that leave employment per unit of time and F = number of unemployed finding jobs per unit of time. We will assume [10]

[10] It is important to note that Lipsey assumes that R is not a function of V. We do not know what his reason was for including it in F and excluding it

that $R = f_1(E, V)$, and $F = f_2(U, V)$. In the steady state, $R = F$ implying that $f_1(E, V) = f_2(U, V)$. We can solve this for $V = g(E, U)$ and introduce this in (3.16) to get a relation among observed variables.

In this case, we assume that f_1 and f_2 are linear in their arguments and are homogeneous. Therefore, $R(t) = a_1 E(t) + a_2 V(t)$, and $F(t) = b_1 U(t) + b_2 V(t)$.

In the steady state,

$$V(t) = \frac{b_1}{a_2 - b_2} U(t) - \frac{a_1}{a_2 - b_2} E(t) \, .$$

Introducing this in (3.15), we obtain

$$\frac{\dot{w}(t)}{w(t)} = \delta_1 \frac{E(t)}{s(t)} + \delta_2 \frac{U(t)}{s(t)} + \delta_3 \frac{\dot{CL}(t)}{CL(t)} + \mu(t) \, . \tag{3.19}$$

Here we have excluded the constant, as otherwise we would have had perfect collinearity among the regressors.

Before presenting the estimation of these three equations, we will define the variables used in the regressions.

3.2.2. Definition of variables

$$\frac{\dot{w}(t)}{w(t)} = \frac{w(t) - w(t-4)}{w(t-4)} =$$ overlapping four quarters annual rate of change in the index of wages and salaries in the industrial sector,

$$\frac{U(t)}{s(t)} =$$ last four quarters weighted average rate of unemployment in the industrial sector, where the weights are the employment levels,

$$\frac{\dot{CL}(t)}{CL(t)} =$$ overlapping four quarters annual rate of change in the index of retail prices, and

$$\frac{E(t)}{s(t)} =$$ last four quarters weighted average rate of employment in the industrial sector.

in R. If we introduce V into his specification of the functions f_1 and f_2, then, in the steady-state solution, V will cancel and we will not be able to solve for V.

TABLE 3.5

Equation	Constant	Unemployment rate	Reciprocal of unemployment rate	Employment rate	$\dfrac{Ci\,(t)}{CL\,(t)}$	$\dfrac{Ci(t-1)}{CL(t-1)}$	R^2	DW
(L)	0.888 (4.253)	−9.556 (−2.359)					0.247	0.59
(M)	0.853 (7.651)	−12.885 (−5.762)			0.718 (6.544)		0.795	2.11
(N)	0.796 (6.555)	−11.327 (−4.765)				0.612 (5.847)	0.760	1.89
(O)	−0.078 (−0.382)		0.024 (2.314)				0.240	0.56
(P)	−0.463 (−3.812)		0.033 (5.941)		0.731 (6.780)		0.804	2.17
(Q)	−0.368 (−2.955)		0.029 (5.016)			0.627 (6.153)	0.774	1.94
(R)	—	−8.674 (−2.256)		0.881 (4.253)			0.248	0.59
(S)	—	−12.032 (−5.651)		0.853 (7.651)	0.718 (6.544)		0.801	2.11

3.2.3. Results

Here we will present the estimates that were obtained using ordinary least squares for the equations just presented. The results are shown in table 3.5.

In examining the results, we see that (R) and (S) are very similar to eqs. (L) and (M) with the constants of the latter pair playing the role of the employment rate variable in the former. This should be obvious, for the employment/unemployment ratio is very close to unity. Having observed this, we discard (R) and (S).

Another important point to mention is that the coefficients of the change in the cost of living are very stable and substantially less than unity for eqs. (M), (N), (P) and (Q). Furthermore, it is worth noticing that the unemployment rate or its reciprocal explains no more than 25% of the variance in the rate of change of wages and that introducing the rate of change of the cost of living improves the results quite substantially. It is important to note that, even when we incorporated a distributed lag in the cost of living, our results did not improve and the coefficient of the cost of living variable was still less than unity. We will comment on this further in section 3.4 where the results of our complete model are analyzed. Finally, we can see from table 3.5 that there is little difference between eqs. (L)–(N) and (O)–(Q).

In order to study the interaction between the price and wage equation in the determination of the cost of living, we go to the following section where we present a simultaneous model.

3.3. Industrial prices, industrial wages and cost of living

In this section we will consider, in the context of a simultaneous model, the equations that we studied in the first two sections. We will discuss the problems arising from the indiscriminate use of two-stage least squares in the estimation of this type of subsystem, and later we will estimate it using instrumental variables.

3.3.1. The price subsystem

Let us consider first the simultaneous submodel

$$\frac{\dot{w}^I(t)}{w^I(t)} = a_1 + a_2 \frac{1}{U(t)/s(s)} + a_3 \frac{\dot{CL}(t)}{CL(t)} + \epsilon^{w^I}(t), \qquad (3.20)$$

$$\frac{\dot{P}^I(t)}{P^I(t)} = b_1 + b_2 \frac{\dot{w}^I(t)}{w^I(t)} + b_3 CU(t) + b_4 \frac{\dot{P}^m(t)}{P^m(t)} + \epsilon^{P^I}(t), \qquad (3.21)$$

$$\frac{\dot{P}(t)}{P(t)} = c_1 \frac{\dot{P}^f(t)}{P^f(t)} + c_2 \frac{\dot{P}^I(t)}{P^I(t)} + c_3 \frac{\dot{P}^m(t)}{P^m(t)} + \epsilon^P(t), \qquad (3.22)$$

$$\frac{\dot{CL}(t)}{CL(t)} = d_1 + d_2 \frac{\dot{P}(t)}{P(t)} + d_3 \frac{\dot{P}(t-1)}{P(t-1)} + d_4 \frac{\dot{P}(t-2)}{P(t-2)} + d_5 \frac{\dot{P}(t-3)}{P(t-3)}, \qquad (3.23)$$

where the variables are

$\frac{\dot{P}(t)}{P(t)}$ = four quarters annual rate of change of wholesale prices,

$\frac{\dot{P}^I(t)}{P^I(t)}$ = four quarters annual rate of change of industrial prices,

$CU(t)$ = four quarters weighted average of capacity utilization,

$\frac{\dot{P}^m(t)}{P^m(t)}$ = four quarters annual rate of change of imported raw material prices,

$\frac{\dot{P}^f(t)}{P^f(t)}$ = four quarters annual rate of change of farm prices, and

$\frac{\dot{w}^I(t)}{w^I(t)}$ = four quarters annual rate of change of industrial wages.

The derivation of eqs. (3.20) and (3.21) has already been discussed. What we will do now is study eqs. (3.22) and (3.23). Although the wholesale price index is a linear combination of its different components with fixed weights, eq. (3.22) assumes that its rate of growth can be approximated by a linear combination of three of its components. In other words, we know that

$$P(t) = \alpha_f P^f(t) + \alpha_I P^I(t) + \alpha_m P^m(t) + \alpha_o P^o(t),$$

where $P^o(t)$ is a weighted average of the other prices of the index[11]. Then

$$\frac{\dot{P}(t)}{P(t)} = \frac{\alpha_f P^f(t)}{P(t)} \frac{\dot{P}^f(t)}{P^f(t)} + \frac{\alpha_I P^I(t)}{P(t)} \frac{\dot{P}^I(t)}{P^I(t)} + \frac{\alpha_m P^m(t)}{P(t)} \frac{\dot{P}^m(t)}{P^m(t)}$$

$$+ \frac{\alpha_o P^o(t)}{P(t)} \frac{\dot{P}^o(t)}{P^o(t)} \, .$$

We are assuming that there is not much change in relative prices and therefore we can write

$$\frac{\dot{P}(t)}{P(t)} = c_1 \frac{\dot{P}^f(t)}{P^f(t)} + c_2 \frac{\dot{P}^I(t)}{P^I(t)} + c_3 \frac{\dot{P}^m(t)}{P^m(t)} \, .$$

We will expect that the weights will add up to unity when we estimate this equation.

Eq. (3.23) is included to close the model and it implies that there is some kind of mark-up from wholesale prices to retail prices. If the constant mark-up is proportional to the wholesale price, then we will expect to get $\Sigma \, d_i = 1$. Furthermore, the constant will take care of part of this effect (the part correlated with $\dot{P}(t)/P(t)$ will be in d_2).

In the specification of eq. (3.23), we assume that the rate of change in the cost of living (retail prices) is a distributed lag of the rate of change in wholesale prices. The rate of change of wholesale prices is as an element of cost in retail prices. We should also add to this equation labor cost, but unfortunately there are no quarterly data for wages in the retail sector.

To estimate a model using two-stage least squares, as Perry (1966) did, is equivalent to assuming that the variables in each equation, excluding the four left-hand ones, are truly exogenous in

----

[11] We are leaving out the price of other imports and the price of mining products but we assume that these minor components which have a weight of 10% in the index will not bias the estimation too much.

the sense of being uncorrelated in the probability limit with the disturbances of that equation. This will not be true if any of the endogenous variables has some feedback on the unemployment rate or on capacity utilization variables as surely will be the case. Therefore, it is a mistake to assume that $CU(t)$ and $U(t)/s(t)$ are truly exogenous variables; hence, they cannot be used as instruments in the two-stages least squares estimation procedure. In the estimation procedure that we use, we assume that there are other equations in a larger system that describe the behavior of $CU(t)$ and $U(t)/s(t)$. We can employ other exogenous variables, such as the rate of change of the nominal supply of money as instruments in the estimation of this subsystem.

3.3.2. Results

We will start by presenting the results of the estimation of eq. (3.22). This is advantageous, for the form of the estimated equation is the same in each of the different price subsystems that we present. This is not a structural equation and therefore we estimated it using ordinary least squares.

From our estimation, we have

$$\frac{\dot{P}(t)}{P(t)} = \underset{(8.774)}{0.408} \, \frac{\dot{P}^l(t)}{P^l(t)} + \underset{(8.856)}{0.340} \, \frac{\dot{P}^f(t)}{P^f(t)} + \underset{(14.987)}{0.240} \, \frac{\dot{P}^m(t)}{P^m(t)}, \quad \underset{\text{olsq}}{(3.22)}$$

where $T = 24$ (number of observations). The sum of the coefficients is 0.99; therefore, for a $\sigma\%$ rate of growth in industrial prices, agricultural prices and imported raw material prices, the wholesale price index increases by a rate of 0.99σ. This is very close to our *a priori* expectation of σ.

We estimate the other equations of the price subsystem using instrumental variables. In this subsystem, the price of farm products can be considered exogenous because most of the farm products (including wheat and all kinds of meat) have government-fixed prices. The price of imported raw materials – which is determined by its international price, the foreign exchange rate and the tariff structure – can be considered exogenous because its international price is determined by conditions outside the Chilean economy (we assume that a small country like Chile does not have monopsony power), the price of foreign exchange is determined by the Central Bank authority, and the tariff structure is policy-determined (without too much consideration of its price impact).

On the other hand, if the Central Bank fixes the price of foreign exchange in accordance with the movement in some of the prices in our system, as has been the policy since 1965, this will affect the exogenous character of the price of imported raw materials. When we analyze this hypothesis, we do not find a high correlation between imported materials prices and the cost of living for the period under study. Nevertheless we can expect some correlation from the reduced form of our model.

In the complete system to which (3.20) − (3.23) belong, there will be a money sector and in the money sector there will be a variable called the *nominal* supply of money. We can take the rate of change of the nominal supply of money as an instrument to be used in the subsystem in which we are interested. We are not saying that the money supply will not affect prices. The money supply will, in general, affect prices in the Chilean economy in two ways.

(1) The disequilibrium in the money market spills over to the commodity market. This is captured through including, *à la* Patinkin, the difference between supply and demand for money in the demand function of the commodity market.

(2) There is a credit rationing mechanism that makes the opportunity cost of borrowing more related to the amount of credit from the banking system to the private sector than to the rate of interest. The credit rationing effect is captured by including real banking credit to the private sector in demand for durables and investment goods.

In our model, these two effects will reinforce each other and will affect industrial prices via the capacity utilization and the unemployment variables. What we are saying is only that the money supply in itself does not depend on other endogenous variables of our larger system to which (3.20) − (3.23) belong[12].

---

[12] In general, the money supply is an endogenous variable in the sense that it depends on the behavior of financial intermediaries (through their

The results that we obtain for our entire submodel using instrumental variables are as follows:

$$\frac{\dot{w}^I(t)}{w^I(t)} = \underset{(-3.762)}{-0.523} + \underset{(5.698)}{0.037} \frac{1}{U(t)/s(t)} + \underset{(6.234)}{0.704} \frac{\dot{CL}(t)}{CL(t)}. \qquad (3.20) \text{ i.v.}$$

Instruments:

$$\frac{\dot{M}(t-1)}{M(t-1)}, \frac{\dot{M}(t-2)}{M(t-2)}, \frac{\dot{P}^m(t)}{P^m(t)}, \frac{\dot{P}^f(t)}{P^f(t)}, C,$$

$T = 19 \qquad\qquad DW = 2.17$

where $\dot{M}(t)/M(t)$ is the overlapping four quarters annual rate of growth in the nominal money supply and C is a constant. The significant constant term and its negative value in this equation is not surprising in light of our earlier discussion of the form of the relation between excess demand and the unemployment rate.

For the industrial price equation in section 3.1, we obtained

$$\frac{\dot{P}^I(t)}{P^I(t)} = \underset{(-1.331)}{-0.77} + \underset{(5.520)}{0.738} \frac{\dot{w}^I(t)}{w^I(t)} + \underset{(4.276)}{0.016} NLCU(t-1)$$

$$+ \underset{(7.603)}{0.407} \frac{\dot{P}^m(t)}{P^m(t)}. \qquad\qquad (3.21) \text{ i.v.}$$

Instruments:

$$\frac{\dot{P}^m(t)}{P^m(t)}, \frac{\dot{P}^m(t-1)}{P^m(t-1)}, \frac{\dot{P}^f(t)}{P^f(t)}, \frac{\dot{M}(t-1)}{M(t-1)}, \frac{\dot{M}(t-2)}{M(t-2)}, \frac{N\dot{M}(t-1)}{NM(t-1)}, C,$$

$T = 19 \qquad\qquad DW = 1.60$

where the new variable introduced is $N\dot{M}(t)/NM(t)$ = square of the

choice of the level of free reserves) and of the public (through their choice of the ratio of currency demand to deposit). For a first approximation, we can take this last ratio to be a constant and, for an economy with a long history of inflation, we can take free reserves to be near zero. Therefore, we can take the money supply as exogenous. For an alternative formulation see chs. 5 and 10.

deviation from the mean of $\dot{M}(t)/M(t)$, keeping the sign of the original deviation.

When we considered the alternative specification for the non-linearity in this equation we obtained

$$\frac{\dot{P^I}(t)}{P^I(t)} = \underset{(-3.565)}{-0.166} + \underset{(5.484)}{0.688} \frac{\dot{w^I}(t)}{w^I(t)} + \underset{(4.909)}{0.0050} \frac{1}{0.84-CU(t-1)}$$

$$+ \underset{(8.387)}{0.406} \frac{\dot{P^m}(t)}{P^m(t)}. \qquad\qquad (3.21)\ \text{i.v.}'$$

Instruments:

$$\frac{\dot{P^m}(t)}{P^m(t)}, \frac{\dot{P^m}(t-1)}{P^m(t-1)}, \frac{\dot{P^f}(t)}{P^f(t)}, \frac{\dot{M}(t-1)}{M(t-1)}, \frac{\dot{M}(t-2)}{M(t-2)}, \frac{N\dot{M}(t-1)}{NM(t-1)}, C.$$

$T = 19 \qquad\qquad DW = 1.68$

The significant constant term and its high absolute value in this equation is consistent with our *a priori* expectations for we will expect no demand pressures on prices when $CU(t)$ is close its average value (around 0.80). In fact, for $CU(t)$ equal to the average capacity utilization rate, we have

$$-0.166 + 0.005 \frac{1}{(0.84-0.80)} = -0.041 .$$

Therefore, for a situation without cost changes

$$\frac{\dot{w^I}(t)}{w^I(t)} = \frac{\dot{P^m}(t)}{P^m(t)} = 0 ,$$

and without demand pressures $CU(t-1) = 0.80$, this equation yields what we expected *a priori*: $\dot{P^I}(t)/P^I(t) \approx 0$.

When capacity is at its average value, we would expect that, for an equal rate of change in wages and raw material prices, industrial prices would increase at the same rate. Therefore, we should test whether the sum of the coefficients of the wage variable and the imported price variable is unity. The covariance between the two coefficients was found to be 0.02214. Upon conducting the test, our results allow us to accept the null hypothesis that the coefficients add up to unity.

Considering these empirical results along with the theoretical discussion in section 3.1, we will use specification (3.21) i.v.' for the industrial price equation in what follows.

For the cost of living equation, we assume that the weights of the distributed lag of wholesale prices follow a second-degree polynomial. Furthermore, it was assumed, *a priori*, that in the explanation of the cost of living we should allow for the rate of change in the wholesale index with a maximum lag of three periods. When this equation is estimated using Hall's (1967) program, we obtain

$$
\frac{\dot{CL}(t)}{CL(t)} = \underset{(2.553)}{0.0391} + \underset{(4.411)}{0.3461} \frac{\dot{P}(t)}{P(t)} + \underset{(17.251)}{0.2416} \frac{\dot{P}(t-1)}{P(t-1)} +
$$

$$
+ \underset{(4.437)}{0.1491} \frac{\dot{P}(t-2)}{P(t-2)} + \underset{(2.007)}{0.0685} \frac{\dot{P}(t-3)}{P(t-3)} . \qquad (3.23)\,\text{i.\,v.}
$$

Instruments:

$$
\frac{\dot{M}(t-1)}{M(t-1)}, \; \frac{\dot{M}(t-2)}{M(t-2)}, \; \frac{\dot{P}^m(t)}{P^m(t)}, \; \frac{\dot{P}^m(t-1)}{P^m(t-1)}, \; \frac{\dot{P}^f(t)}{P^f(t)}, \; C.
$$

$T = 21$ mean lag = 0.926
                                     (4.273)

Eq. (3.23 i.v.) implies that, for a steady rate of growth of $\gamma\%$ in wholesale prices, retail prices will increase only at a rate of $0.805\,\gamma + 0.039$. This result could be explained by the fact that we are leaving out wages in the service sector which may be growing at a higher rate than wholesale prices.

As we saw in ch. 1, a basic element in any formulation of the structural model of inflation is the downward inflexibility of industrial prices. To test for this inflexibility, we estimate eq. (3.21) i.v. for the periods in which the capacity utilization equation index was lower than in the previous quarter. The results are

$$\frac{\dot{P^I}(t)}{P^I(t)} = \underset{(-3.475)}{-0.162} + \underset{(5.711)}{0.684} \frac{\dot{w^I}(t)}{w^I(t)} + \underset{(4.829)}{0.0048} \frac{1}{0.84-CU(t-1)}$$

$$+ \underset{(7.788)}{0.407} \frac{\dot{P^m}(t)}{P^m(t)} . \qquad\qquad (3.21) \text{ i.v.''}$$

Instruments:

$$\frac{\dot{P^m}(t)}{P^m(t)}, \frac{\dot{P^m}(t-1)}{P^m(t-1)}, \frac{\dot{P^f}(t)}{P^f(t)}, \frac{\dot{M}(t-1)}{M(t-1)}, \frac{\dot{M}(t-2)}{M(t-2)}, \frac{\dot{NM}(t-1)}{NM(t-1)}, C.$$

$T = 13$ $\qquad\qquad$ $DW = 2.80$

We cannot estimate eq. (3.21) i.v.'' for the rest of the sampling period since we do not have enough degrees of freedom to run the first stage of the instrumental variables procedure. Therefore, we can conduct a Chow test for the case of negative degrees of freedom in order to determine if there are differences between eq. (3.21) i.v.'' and the one for the rest of the period. The computed F is such that we accept the null hypothesis of no differences in the complete vector of regression coefficients in both periods[13]. Making the same test for the coefficient of the non-linear capacity variable alone, we are able to accept the null hypothesis again.

If industrial prices were inflexible downward we would have obtained a smaller coefficient for the non-linear capacity variable during the period of demand slackness in the market for industrial products (a period of demand slackness occurs when the capacity utilization index is lower than in the previous quarter). To see this, let us consider eq. (3.21) with the alternative definition of the capacity utilization employed in eq. (3.21) i.v.'. In this case, after differentiating, we have

$$\frac{\partial \frac{\dot{P}(t)}{P(t)}}{\partial CU(t-1)} = \frac{b_3}{[0.84-CU(t-1)]^2} .$$

[13] For a description of Chow tests see Fisher (1970). This test as carried out here is limited in that we do not know their small sample properties.

Therefore, for the inflexibility hypothesis to be true, we would expect that during the period of demand slackness b_3 would be smaller than in the rest of the period. Hence, we form the null hypothesis that b_3 was the same in both periods and our test indicates that this is indeed so[14].

3.4. Analysis of the results

The more important features of our results are given below.

(1) We obtain better results (with the exception of the demand element in the price equation and the cost of living equation) when we use unlagged right-hand variables in the original model. This makes sense for an economy that has had inflation for the last 100 years. Even more important is the fact that this inflation has been more or less steady in the last half of the sampling period (around a 30% four quarter annual rate of change in the cost of living index).

(2) The coefficient of the cost of living variable in the wage equation shows that, even in an economy with high inflation where people are very sensitive to price changes, the structure of the labor market is such that money wages do not adjust instantaneously to maintain a constant rate of change in real wages for a given excess demand. This supports the Harberger (1970, p. 1013) contention that:

> 'My belief that wages should probably be readjusted more often than once a year rather than less often is regarded as heretical by some. But, in point of fact, real wages have historically tended to fall in periods of growing inflation, forcing workers to bear a disproportionate share of the burden.'

This contention is also supported by Ramos (1970).

(3) The rate of change in the prices of imported raw materials is an important factor in the explanation of the rate of change of industrial prices. For a 1% point increase in the rate of growth of

---

[14] This test is equivalent to putting a multiplicative dummy in the regression for the capacity utilization variable where the dummy variable takes the value one when capacity utilized decreases from one quarter to the next and zero otherwise.

prices of imported materials, *the direct effect is a 0.41% point increase in the rate of growth of industrial prices.* This in turn will affect the rate of change of the cost of living through eqs. (3.22) olsq and (3.23). This result is in agreement with the structuralist theory of inflation regarding the propagation of inflation, through increases in the price of imported raw materials[15].

(4) The coefficient of the non-linear response to demand pressures in the industrial sector (measured by $1/[0.84-CU(t-1])$ is significantly different from zero [16]. Therefore, this lends some support to the hypothesis that prices are determined by demand and costs.

(5) There is no evidence of downward inflexibility in the rate of change of industrial prices. Therefore, no empirical evidence exists to support the main foundation of the structuralist model of inflation. However, in order to reach a final conclusion on this point, we would need additional empirical evidence.

(6) The coefficient of the excess demand variable in the wage equation is higher than the coefficients obtained for more competitive economies. This implies that the tradeoff between unemployment and inflation is less favorable for an economy like the Chilean one than for competitive economies. This supports the structuralist thesis of slow adjustments of the economic structure.

Now let us study the following system of equations:

$$\frac{\dot{w}^I(t)}{w^I(t)} = a_1 + a_2 \frac{1}{U(t)/s(t)} + a_3 \frac{\dot{CL}(t)}{CL(t)} \ ,$$

$$\frac{\dot{P}^I(t)}{P^I(t)} = b_1 + b_2 \frac{\dot{w}^I(t)}{w^I(t)} + b_3 \frac{1}{0.84-CU(t-1)} + b_4 \frac{\dot{P}^m(t)}{P^m(t)} , \qquad (3.24)$$

$$\frac{\dot{P}(t)}{P(t)} = c_1 \frac{\dot{P}^f(t)}{P^f(t)} + c_2 \frac{\dot{P}^I(t)}{P^I(t)} + c_3 \frac{\dot{P}^m(t)}{P^m(t)} ,$$

[15] For a summary of the structuralist and monetarist theory of inflation, see ch. 1.

[16] This result is based on the asymptotic standard errors of the coefficients.

$$\frac{\dot{CL}(t)}{CL(t)} = d_1 + d_2\frac{\dot{P}(t)}{P(t)} + d_3\frac{\dot{P}(t-1)}{P(t-1)} + d_4\frac{\dot{P}(t-2)}{P(t-2)} + d_5\frac{\dot{P}(t-3)}{P(t-3)}.$$

It is important to note that (3.24) is not a closed model. In this system, $U(t)/s(t)$ and $1/[0.84-CU(t-1)]$ are endogenous variables generated by structural equations that have not been specified. In the structural equation for $U(t)/s(t)$, the wage rate will be one of the right-hand variables and, in the structural equation for $CU(t)$, industrial prices will be one of the right-hand variables. Therefore, to consider (3.24) as a closed model is equivalent to ignoring these feedbacks. The only way to eliminate this problem is to consider a complete model and, as stated in the beginning, that is not possible because of the lack of quarterly national accounts. When we attempt to build quarterly national account data from quarterly indexes, the results are discouraging. Consequently, we can formulate a complete model using annual data (this is presented in the next chapters).

Keeping the above point in mind, we will investigate the solution of (3.24) for $\dot{w}(t)/w(t)$, $\dot{P}(t)/P(t)$, $\dot{P}^I(t)/P^I(t)$ and $\dot{CL}(t)/CL(t)$, ignoring the feedbacks.

This case is interesting in itself, for it answers questions such as: Suppose that the monetary and fiscal authority controls unemployment and the level of demand (see below). Then with these two variables at certain target levels, what will happen to industrial wages, industrial prices, wholesale prices and cost of living?

Before proceeding to study different policy alternatives, let us study how well the model works during the sampling periods. This test is interesting because until now we have only tested how the different equations perform by themselves but not in the context of a simultaneous model.

When we simulated our model for the part of the sampling period that is in common with the estimation of our four equations, we obtain the results in tables 3.6–3.13.

These tables reveal that in general terms the model does quite well. The mean square errors are very low, the highest being 0.049 for the wage equation.

The simulation results for the last quarter of 1966 through the third quarter of 1967 suggest that something is missing. Our model

TABLE 3.6

Actual and simulated values of rate of change in wages (DS).

Variable: DS – Endogenous					
Year	Qt	Simulated	Actual	Error	Percent
1964	2	0.5093278	0.4868350	0.0224928	4.02
1964	3	0.4975605	0.5712260	−0.0736655	−12.90
1964	4	0.4639998	0.4601430	0.0038568	0.84
1965	1	0.4063440	0.3491010	0.0572430	16.40
1965	2	0.3941727	0.4356090	−0.0414363	−9.51
1965	3	0.4268641	0.4780120	−0.0511478	−10.70
1965	4	0.4475075	0.4725590	−0.0250515	−5.30
1966	1	0.5141248	0.5202500	−0.0061252	−1.18
1966	2	0.4439697	0.4373180	0.0066517	1.52
1966	3	0.4428312	0.3751780	0.0676532	18.03
1966	4	0.4459516	0.3944690	0.0514826	13.05
1967	1	0.3932936	0.3819060	0.0113876	2.98
1967	2	0.3937480	0.2822590	0.1114890	39.50
1967	3	0.3604976	0.3069060	0.0535916	17.46
1967	4	0.2710520	0.3229710	−0.0519189	−16.08
1968	1	0.2994830	0.3040500	−0.0045670	−1.50
1968	2	0.3089498	0.3171090	−0.0081591	−2.57
1968	3	0.3101956	0.2806440	0.0295516	10.53
1968	4	0.3824940	0.3151520	0.0673420	21.37

Error statistics, 19 observations: 1964 2 to 1968 4.
Mean error: 0.0116142.
RMS error: 0.0487295.

TABLE 3.7

Actual and simulated values of rate of change in industrial prices (DQINP).

Variable: DQINP – Endogenous					
Year	Qt	Simulated	Actual	Error	Percent
1964	2	0.5632418	0.5556980	0.0075438	1.36
1964	3	0.5429908	0.5293160	0.0136748	2.58
1964	4	0.5097376	0.5233790	0.0136414	−2.61
1965	1	0.3039706	0.2706820	0.0332886	12.30
1965	2	0.2584108	0.2648500	−0.0064392	−2.43
1965	3	0.2561664	0.2916670	−0.0355006	−12.17
1965	4	0.2556107	0.2851240	−0.0295133	−10.35
1966	1	0.3413119	0.3330540	0.0082579	2.48
1966	2	0.2804431	0.2877250	−0.0072819	−2.53
1966	3	0.2730301	0.2694270	0.0036031	1.34
1966	4	0.2695248	0.2480660	0.0214588	8.65
1967	1	0.2935988	0.2519370	0.0416618	16.54
1967	2	0.2937089	0.2234760	0.0702329	31.43
1967	3	0.2762394	0.2184350	0.0578044	26.46
1967	4	0.2290991	0.2261040	0.0029951	1.32
1968	1	0.2786817	0.2542070	0.0244747	9.63
1968	2	0.2881664	0.2992090	−0.0110426	−3.69
1968	3	0.3187229	0.3475570	−0.0288341	−8.30
1968	4	0.3644831	0.3491560	0.0153271	4.39

Error statistics, 19 observations: 1964 2 to 1968 4.
Mean error: 0.0088458.
RMS error: 0.0291201.

TABLE 3.8
Actual and simulated values of rate of change in wholesale prices (DWO).

Variable: DWO – Endogenous

Year	Qt	Simulated	Actual	Error	Percent
1964	2	0.5189139	0.5220320	−0.0031181	−0.60
1964	3	0.4932775	0.5110590	−0.0177815	−3.48
1964	4	0.4466203	0.4701220	−0.0235017	−5.00
1965	1	0.2546006	0.2481580	0.0064426	2.60
1965	2	0.2447956	0.2423200	0.0024756	1.02
1965	3	0.2298350	0.2447550	−0.0149200	−6.10
1965	4	0.2294881	0.2383100	−0.0088219	−3.70
1966	1	0.2837893	0.2778090	0.0059803	2.15
1966	2	0.2170627	0.2196200	−0.0025573	−1.16
1966	3	0.2349674	0.2173800	0.0175874	8.09
1966	4	0.2277440	0.2064590	0.0212850	10.31
1967	1	0.2293105	0.1931690	0.0361415	18.71
1967	2	0.2469757	0.2007490	0.0462267	23.03
1967	3	0.2221808	0.1857140	0.0364668	19.64
1967	4	0.2099159	0.1936210	0.0162949	8.42
1968	1	0.2763241	0.2688430	0.0074811	2.78
1968	2	0.2785448	0.2853960	−0.0068512	−2.40
1968	3	0.3402002	0.3334950	0.0067052	2.01
1968	4	0.3467675	0.3337380	0.0130295	3.90

Error statistics, 19 observations: 1964 2 to 1968 4.
Mean error: 0.0072929.
RMS error: 0.0197179.

TABLE 3.9
Actual and simulated values of rate of change in the cost of living (DCL).

Variable: DCL – Endogenous

Year	Qt	Simulated	Actual	Error	Percent
1964	2	0.4583508	0.4879700	−0.0296192	−6.07
1964	3	0.4450257	0.4669900	−0.0219643	−4.70
1964	4	0.4261186	0.4190800	0.0070386	1.68
1965	1	0.3442895	0.3103760	0.0339135	10.93
1965	2	0.2856018	0.3193860	−0.0337842	−10.58
1965	3	0.2462657	0.2728450	−0.0265793	−9.74
1965	4	0.2278933	0.2581390	−0.0302457	−11.72
1966	1	0.2436691	0.2764730	−0.0328039	−11.87
1966	2	0.2327172	0.2056910	0.0270262	13.14
1966	3	0.2307636	0.2410290	−0.0102654	−4.26
1966	4	0.2264033	0.1986740	0.0277293	13.96
1967	1	0.2233030	0.1680550	0.0552480	32.87
1967	2	0.2299031	0.1813590	0.0485441	26.77
1967	3	0.2253854	0.1765330	0.0488524	27.67
1967	4	0.2178515	0.1981370	0.0197145	9.95
1968	1	0.2353216	0.2521630	−0.0168414	−9.68
1968	2	0.2486847	0.2588240	−0.0101393	−3.92
1968	3	0.2795392	0.2730630	0.0064762	2.37
1968	4	0.3016873	0.2788080	0.0228793	8.21

Error statistics, 19 observations: 1964 2 to 1968 4.
Mean error: 0.0044831.
RMS error: 0.030034.

TABLE 3.10

Plotted values for rate of change in wages (DS).

Variable plotted – DS

Simula = Y   Actual = X

	0.271	0.309	0.346	0.384	0.421	0.459	0.496	0.534	0.571
1964							X Y		X
1965			X	Y	X Y	XY			
1966		X Y			Y	X X			
1967	Y X	X	X Y Y		X Y Y	YX			
1968	Y	YX Y Y X		Y					
1969		X X		Y					

TABLE 3.11

Plotted values for rate of change in industrial prices (*DQINP*).

Variable plotted – *DQINP*

Simula = Y   Actual = X

	0.218	0.262	0.305	0.348	0.391	0.434	0.477	0.520	0.563
1964									X Y
1965		X	Y					Y.X X Y	
1966				X–Y					
1967	X	X	Y	Y					
1968	X	X	Y	X X					
1969				Y					YX

TABLE 3.12
Plotted values for rate of change in wholesale prices (DWO)

Variable plotted - DWO
Simula = Y Actual = X

TABLE 3.13

Plotted values for rate of change in cost of living (DCL)

Variable plotted - DCL

Simula = Y Actual = X

systematically overshoots the actual values for the different endogenous variables. If we stop to investigate the explanation underlying our results, we find that this period was characterized by tight controls for the prices of products in the cost of living index[17]. There are two reasons why our model overshoots the actual figures. First, our high simulated rate of change in cost of living creates an overshooting in wages. Second, this overshooting in wages plus the increase in capacity utilized in the *industrial* sector (associated with the increase in quantity demanded coming from the low retail prices) implies an overshooting in industrial prices. From there on, the dynamics of our model continue to work.

It is important to indicate that this expansion in the industrial sector was obtained in spite of a decline in economic activity that came mainly from a decrease in government expenditure in public housing. Hence, we find that our model does not pick up the impact of price controls.

The easiest way of incorporating the price controls in our model is through a dummy variable that will take care of the downward pressures in retail prices for the four quarters already discussed.

We can do this for the (cost of living) equation and obtain

$$\frac{\dot{CL}(t)}{CL(t)} = \underset{(3.708)}{0.0598} - \underset{(-2.349)}{0.0325d(t)} + \underset{(4.615)}{0.3237}\frac{\dot{P}(t)}{P(t)}$$

$$+ \underset{(16.56)}{0.2277}\frac{\dot{P}(t-1)}{P(t-1)} + \underset{(4.615)}{0.1417}\frac{\dot{P}(t-2)}{P(t-2)} + \underset{(2.187)}{0.0658}\frac{\dot{P}(t-3)}{P(t-3)}.$$

$$(3.23) \text{ i.v.}'$$

Instruments:

$$\frac{\dot{P}^m(t)}{P^m(t)}, \frac{\dot{P}^m(t-1)}{P^m(t-1)}, \frac{\dot{P}^f(t)}{P^f(t)}, \frac{\dot{M}(t-1)}{M(t-1)}, \frac{\dot{M}(t-2)}{M(t-2)}, P(t), C,$$

$$T = 21 \quad \text{mean lag} = \underset{(4.823)}{0.934}$$

[17] For a study which shows that, with Law No. 16464 of 1966, price controls were intensified in the 1966–1967 period, see De La Cuadra (undated).

Using a one-tail test, we find all of the coefficients to be significant at a 2.5% level. Therefore, we see that the introduction of a dummy for the price controls of the period 1966 4 to 1967 3 captures the downward pressure of approximately 3.3% in the rate of change of the cost of living.

In order to determine how the incorporation of eq. (3.23) i.v.′ affects the working of the model we simulate, the model formed by eqs. (3.20) i.v., (3.21) i.v.′, (3.22) olsq and (3.23) i.v.′ for the sampling period. The results of our simulation are given in tables 3.14–3.21.

We find that all the RMS errors are now lower. Using the simulated values of this case as benchmark values, let us now use this system to study different policies.

TABLE 3.14

Actual and simulated values of rate of change in wages (DS) (includes a dummy variable in the cost of living equation).

Variable: DS – Endogenous					
Year	Qt	Simulated	Actual	Error	Percent
1964	2	0.5068643	0.4868350	0.0200293	4.11
1964	3	0.4954881	0.5712260	−0.0757379	−13.26
1964	4	0.4628269	0.4601430	0.0026830	0.58
1965	1	0.4090424	0.3491010	0.0599414	17.17
1965	2	0.3995998	0.4356090	−0.0360092	−8.27
1965	3	0.4340676	0.4780120	−0.0439444	−9.19
1965	4	0.4555450	0.4725590	−0.0170140	−3.60
1966	1	0.5214971	0.5202500	0.0012472	0.24
1966	2	0.4519317	0.4373180	0.0146137	3.34
1966	3	0.4509206	0.3751780	0.0757426	20.19
1966	4	0.4298078	0.3944690	0.0353389	8.96
1967	1	0.3760811	0.3819060	−0.0058249	−1.53
1967	2	0.3754551	0.2822590	0.0931961	33.02
1967	3	0.3420130	0.3069060	0.0351070	11.44
1967	4	0.2773139	0.3229710	−0.0456571	−14.14
1968	1	0.3060383	0.3040500	0.0019883	0.65
1968	2	0.3156358	0.3171090	−0.0014732	−0.46
1968	3	0.3158477	0.2806440	0.0352038	12.54
1968	4	0.3871923	0.3151520	0.0720403	22.86

Error statistics, 19 observations: 1964 2 to 1968 4.
Mean error: 0.0116564.
RMS error: 0.0452638.

TABLE 3.15

Actual and simulated values of rate of change in industrial prices (D*QINP*) (includes a dummy variable in the cost of living equation).

Variable: D*QINP* −	Endogenous			
Year	Qt	Simulated	Actual	Error	Percent
1964	2	0.5615469	0.5556980	0.0058489	1.05
1964	3	0.5415650	0.5293160	0.0122490	2.31
1964	4	0.5089307	0.5233790	−0.0144483	−2.76
1965	1	0.3058270	0.2706820	0.0351450	12.98
1965	2	0.2621446	0.2648500	−0.0027054	−1.02
1965	3	0.2611223	0.2916670	−0.0305447	−10.47
1965	4	0.2611405	0.2851240	−0.0239835	−8.41
1966	1	0.3463841	0.3330540	0.0133301	4.00
1966	2	0.2859210	0.2877250	−0.0018040	−0.63
1966	3	0.2785956	0.2694270	0.0091686	3.40
1966	4	0.2584179	0.2480660	0.0103519	4.17
1967	1	0.2817567	0.2519370	0.0298197	11.84
1967	2	0.2811235	0.2234760	0.0576475	25.80
1967	3	0.2635219	0.2184350	0.0450869	20.64
1967	4	0.2334073	0.2261040	0.0073033	3.23
1968	1	0.2831918	0.2542070	0.0289848	11.40
1968	2	0.2927663	0.2992090	−0.0064427	−2.15
1968	3	0.3226116	0.3475570	−0.0249454	−7.18
1968	4	0.3677155	0.3491560	0.0185595	5.32

Error statistics, 19 observations: 1964 2 to 1968 4.
Mean error: 0.0088748.
RMS error: 0.0247756.

Let us consider first a set of fiscal and monetary policies aimed at achieving a 5.0% rate of unemployment (against an average of 5.53 for the period 1960–1968) and at increasing the capacity utilization in the industrial sector to 0.81 (against an average of 0.796 for the period 1960–1968). Running this simulation while keeping the observed values of $\dot{P}^f(t)/P^f(t)$ and $\dot{P}^m(t)/P^m(t)$ yields the results that appear in tables 3.22–3.25.

From these tables we see that the targets with respect to unemployment and capacity utilization imply an increase in the rate of growth in cost of living of around 1.8 percentage points. Furthermore, for the year 1968 this increase is around 4.8 percentage points.

Now we will study the implications of a policy having the same targets for capacity utilization and unemployment but assuming

TABLE 3.16

Actual and simulated values of rate of change in wholesale prices (D*WO*) (includes a dummy variable in the cost of living equation).

Variable: D*WO* – Endogenous					
Year	Qt	Simulated	Actual	Error	Percent
1964	2	0.5182307	0.5220320	−0.0038013	−0.73
1964	3	0.4926920	0.5110590	−0.0183670	−3.59
1964	4	0.4462848	0.4701220	−0.0238372	−5.07
1965	1	0.2553158	0.2481580	0.0071579	2.88
1965	2	0.2463057	0.2423200	0.0039857	1.64
1965	3	0.2318555	0.2447550	−0.0128995	−5.27
1965	4	0.2317432	0.2383100	−0.0065667	−2.76
1966	1	0.2858768	0.2778090	0.0080678	2.90
1966	2	0.2192863	0.2196200	−0.0003337	−0.15
1966	3	0.2372352	0.2173800	0.0198552	9.13
1966	4	0.2232380	0.2064590	0.0167790	8.13
1967	1	0.2244857	0.1931690	0.0313167	16.21
1967	2	0.2418410	0.2007490	0.0410920	20.47
1967	3	0.2169896	0.1857140	0.0312756	16.84
1967	4	0.2116365	0.1936210	0.0180155	9.30
1968	1	0.2781719	0.2688430	0.0093289	3.47
1968	2	0.2804236	0.2853960	−0.0049724	−1.74
1968	3	0.3417917	0.3334950	0.0082967	2.49
1968	4	0.3480979	0.3337380	0.0143599	4.30

Error statistics, 19 observations: 1964 2 to 1968 4.
Mean error: 0.0073028.
RMS error: 0.0182041.

that tariffs and international prices are constant. Furthermore, we will asume that the devaluation rate is equal to the rate of change in the cost of living index and that the real agricultural prices improve at a 2% rate with respect to the cost of living. This set of policies is very similar to the one that was proposed at the beginning of 1965.

When we run the simulations with the above assumptions, we obtain the results given in tables 3.26–3.31. The simulation results indicate that this case yields a rate of inflation around 10.6 percentage points higher than the actual one. This casts some additional light on the importance of imported raw material prices on the rate of inflation. Furthermore, this also explains the role of imported raw material prices on the decline in the rate of inflation during the years 1965–1966. In addition, this shows that the set

TABLE 3.17

Actual and simulated values of rate of change in the cost of living (DCL) (includes a dummy variable in the cost of living equation).

Variable DCL - Endogenous					
Year	Qt	Simulated	Actual	Error	Percent
1964	2	0.4548514	0.4879700	−0.0331186	−6.79
1964	3	0.4420820	0.4669900	−0.0249080	−5.33
1964	4	0.4244526	0.4190800	0.0053726	1.28
1965	1	0.3481224	0.3103760	0.0377464	12.16
1965	2	0.2933107	0.3193860	−0.0260753	−8.16
1965	3	0.2564978	0.2728450	−0.0163472	−5.99
1965	4	0.2393102	0.2581390	−0.0188288	−7.29
1966	1	0.2541413	0.2764730	−0.0223317	−8.08
1966	2	0.2440269	0.2056910	0.0383359	18.64
1966	3	0.2422542	0.2410290	0.0012252	0.51
1966	4	0.2034718	0.1986740	0.0047978	2.41
1967	1	0.1988535	0.1680550	0.0307985	18.33
1967	2	0.2039189	0.1813590	0.0225599	12.44
1967	3	0.1991288	0.1765330	0.0225958	12.80
1967	4	0.2267462	0.1981370	0.0286092	14.44
1968	1	0.2446331	0.2521630	−0.0075299	−2.99
1968	2	0.2581818	0.2588240	−0.0006422	−0.25
1968	3	0.2875678	0.2730630	0.0145048	5.31
1968	4	0.3083609	0.2788080	0.0295529	10.60

Error statistics, 19 observations: 1964 2 to 1968 4.
Mean error: 0.004543.
RMS error: 0.0233879.

of policies proposed at the beginning of the Frei government was clearly inconsistent. The deceleration of inflation resulted because international prices declined.

Let us assume now that fiscal and monetary policy are oriented toward a 4.5% unemployment rate and a capacity utilization of 0.82. Running the simulation with historical figures for $\dot{P}^m(t)/P^m(t)$ and $\dot{P}^f(t)/P^f(t)$ yielded the results shown in tables 3.32–3.35.

From the tables, we find that an additional cut of 0.5 percentage points in the unemployment rate and an additional increase of one percentage point in capacity utilization in the industrial sector increases the inflation rate by an additional 4.8 percentage points (see tables 3.25 and 3.35). All of the results were estimated assuming historical values for $\dot{P}^m(t)/P^m(t)$ and $\dot{P}^f(t)/P^f(t)$.

TABLE 3.18

Plotted values for rate of change in wages (DS). (Includes a dummy variable in the cost of living equation.)

Variable plotted - DS

Simula = Y Actual = X

	0.277	0.314	0.351	0.388	0.424	0.461	0.498	0.534	0.571
1964							X . Y		X
							Y.		YX
1965			X	Y	X Y	I			
1966				X		Y. X			YX
				YX	Y	X Y			
1967	X	Y		X	Y				
	Y			Y					
1968	X	X	XY						
	X	Y	YX						
		X							
1969				Y					

TABLE 3.19

Plotted values for rate of change in industrial prices (DQINP). (Includes a dummy variable in the cost of living equation.)

Variable plotted - DQINP

Simula = Y Actual = X

	0.218	0.261	0.304	0.347	0.390	0.433	0.476	0.519	0.562
1964									XY
								. X Y	
							Y . X	
1965	X	Y						
	YX							
	Y	X						
	Y	X						
1966	. X Y							YX
		1						
1967	X Y . X	Y						
		Y						
	. Y							
1968	XY X	Y X .	Y	. X				
	. X			X				
1969				Y				

TABLE 3.20

Plotted values for rate of change in wholesale prices (*DWO*). (Includes a dummy variable in the cost of living equation.)

Variable plotted - *DWO*

Simula = Y Actual = X

	0.186	0.228	0.270	0.312	0.354	0.396	0.438	0.480	0.522

TABLE 3.21

Plotted values for rate of change in cost of living (DCL). (Includes a dummy variable in the cost of living equation.)

Variable plotted - DCL

Simula = Y   Actual = X

	0.168	0.208	0.248	0.288	0.328	0.368	0.408	0.448	0.488
1964	X							Y . Y	X
									X
1965			Y . Y X	. Y .	X	-Y-	XY		
			Y . Y X	X					
1966	X .	XY . Y	Y . XY .	- X -					
1967	X X . Y . Y . X	Y	- X-Y-	1					
1968				X . Y . X				Y	
1969									YX

TABLE 3.22
Simulation results for DS with $U(t)/s(t) = 0.05$ and $CU(t) = 0.81$.

Variable: DS − Endogenous				
Year	Qt	Simulated	Actual	Error
1964	2	0.5343138	0.5068643	0.0274495
1964	3	0.5250426	0.4954881	0.0295545
1964	4	0.5141847	0.4628269	0.0513578
1965	1	0.4619680	0.4090424	0.0529256
1965	2	0.4265022	0.3995998	0.0269024
1965	3	0.4019272	0.4340676	−0.0321403
1965	4	0.3906563	0.4555450	−0.0648887
1966	1	0.3992848	0.5214971	−0.1222123
1966	2	0.3951413	0.4519317	−0.0567904
1966	3	0.3958131	0.4509206	−0.0551075
1966	4	0.3690840	0.4298078	−0.0607238
1967	1	0.3683904	0.3760811	−0.0076908
1967	2	0.3743169	0.3754551	−0.0011382
1967	3	0.3749201	0.3420130	0.0329071
1967	4	0.4025277	0.2773139	0.1252138
1968	1	0.4203412	0.3060383	0.1143029
1968	2	0.4327526	0.3156358	0.1171168
1968	3	0.4563393	0.3158477	0.1404916
1968	4	0.4684225	0.3871923	0.0812303

Error statistics, 19 observations: 1964 2 to 1968 4.
Mean error: 0.0209874.
RMS error: 0.075344.

TABLE 3.23
Simulation results for D$QINP$ with $U(t)/s(t) = 0.05$ and $CU(t) = 0.81$.

Variable: D$QINP$ − Endogenous				
Year	Qt	Simulated	Actual	Error
1964	2	0.5302197	0.5615469	−0.0313272
1964	3	0.5293545	0.5415650	−0.0122105
1964	4	0.5137684	0.5089307	0.0048377
1965	1	0.3130154	0.3058270	0.0071883
1965	2	0.2899709	0;2621446	0.0278263
1965	3	0.2842893	0.2611223	0.0231670
1965	4	0.2869691	0.2611405	0.0258286
1966	1	0.3485815	0.3463841	0.0021974
1966	2	0.3367407	0.2859210	0.0503197
1966	3	0.3256197	0.2785956	0.0470240
1966	4	0.2977459	0.2584179	0.0393280
1967	1	0.3458669	0.2817567	0.0641102
1967	2	0.3573214	0.2811235	0.0761979
1967	3	0.3647565	0.2635219	0.1012346
1967	4	0.3946918	0.2334073	0.1612846
1968	1	0.4448517	0.2831918	0.1616599
1968	2	0.4535897	0.2927663	0.1608234
1968	3	0.5028333	0.3226116	0.1802217
1968	4	0.5068754	0.3677155	0.1391599

Error statistics, 19 observations: 1964 2 to 1968 4.
Mean error: 0.0647038.
RMS error: 0.0916371.

TABLE 3.24

Simulation results for DWO with $U(t)/s(t) = 0.05$ and $CU(t) = 0.81$.

Variable: DWO – Endogenous

Year	Qt	Simulated	Actual	Error
1964	2	0.5054982	0.5182307	−0.0127325
1964	3	0.4876802	0.4926920	−0.0050118
1964	4	0.4482320	0.4462848	0.0019471
1965	1	0.2582450	0.2553158	0.0029292
1965	2	0.2576266	0.2463057	0.0113200
1965	3	0.2413149	0.2318555	0.0094594
1965	4	0.2422771	0.2317432	0.0105339
1966	1	0.2868103	0.2858768	0.0009335
1966	2	0.2399448	0.2192863	0.0206584
1966	3	0.2564269	0.2372352	0.0191918
1966	4	0.2392959	0.2232380	0.0160579
1967	1	0.2506039	0.2244857	0.0261182
1967	2	0.2729109	0.2418410	0.0310699
1967	3	0.2582542	0.2169896	0.0412646
1967	4	0.2773467	0.2116365	0.0657102
1968	1	0.3441286	0.2781719	0.0659567
1968	2	0.3460408	0.2804236	0.0656172
1968	3	0.4152918	0.3417917	0.0735001
1968	4	0.4049393	0.3480979	0.0568414

Error statistics, 19 observations: 1964 2 to 1968 4.
Mean error: 0.0263877.
RMS error: 0.0373738.

TABLE 3.25

Simulation results for DCL with $U(t)/s(t) = 0.05$ and $CU(t) = 0.81$.

Variable: DCL – Endogenous

Year	Qt	Simulated	Actual	Error
1964	2	0.4507299	0.4548514	−0.0041215
1964	3	0.4375606	0.4420820	−0.0045214
1964	4	0.4221374	0.4244526	−0.0023151
1965	1	0.3479659	0.3481224	−0.0001565
1965	2	0.2975884	0.2933107	0.0042777
1965	3	0.2626807	0.2564978	0.0061829
1965	4	0.2466709	0.2393102	0.0073607
1966	1	0.2589273	0.2541413	0.0047860
1966	2	0.2530417	0.2440269	0.0090148
1966	3	0.2539958	0.2422542	0.0117416
1966	4	0.2160284	0.2034718	0.0125566
1967	1	0.2150431	0.1988535	0.0161897
1967	2	0.2234615	0.2039189	0.0195426
1967	3	0.2243183	0.1991288	0.0251895
1967	4	0.2635336	0.2267462	0.0367875
1968	1	0.2888370	0.2446331	0.0442039
1968	2	0.3064668	0.2581818	0.0482850
1968	3	0.3399707	0.2875678	0.0524028
1968	4	0.3571343	0.3083609	0.0487734

Error statistics, 19 observations: 1964 2 to 1968 4.
Mean error: 0.0176937.
RMS error: 0.0257472.

TABLE 3.26

Simulation results for DS with $U(t)/s(t) = 0.05$, $CU(t) = 0.81$ and D$QMRM$ and D$QAGR$ endogenous: D$QAGR$ = rate of change in imported raw material prices, D$QAGR$ = rate of change in agriculture prices.

Variable: DS − Endogenous

Year	Qt	Simulated	Actual	Error
1964	2	0.5313910	0.5068643	0.0245267
1964	3	0.5207773	0.4954881	0.0252892
1964	4	0.5168711	0.4628269	0.0540442
1965	1	0.5114286	0.4090424	0.1023862
1965	2	0.5079782	0.3995998	0.1083784
1965	3	0.5054685	0.4340676	0.0714010
1965	4	0.5035100	0.4555450	0.0479650
1966	1	0.5020868	0.5214971	−0.0194104
1966	2	0.5010267	0.4519317	0.0490950
1966	3	0.5002360	0.4509206	0.0493154
1966	4	0.4670917	0.4298078	0.0372838
1967	1	0.4562341	0.3760811	0.0801530
1967	2	0.4463068	0.3754551	0.0708517
1967	3	0.4380646	0.3420130	0.0960516
1967	4	0.4650771	0.2773139	0.1877632
1968	1	0.4712390	0.3060383	0.1652007
1968	2	0.4776650	0.3156358	0.1620292
1968	3	0.4833263	0.3158477	0.1674785
1968	4	0.4869463	0.3871923	0.0997541

Error statistics, 19 observations: 1964 2 to 1968 4.
Mean error: 0.0831346.
RMS error: 0.0994375.

TABLE 3.27

Simulation results for D$QINP$ with $U(t)/s(t) = 0.05$, $CU(t) = 0.81$ and D$QMRM$ and D$QAGR$ endogenous.

Variable: D$QINP$ − Endogenous

Year	Qt	Simulated	Actual	Error
1964	2	0.5474077	0.5615469	−0.0141391
1964	3	0.5339845	0.5415650	−0.0075805
1964	4	0.5290443	0.5089307	0.0201136
1965	1	0.5221611	0.3058270	0.2163341
1965	2	0.5177975	0.2621446	0.2556529
1965	3	0.5146235	0.2611223	0.2535011
1965	4	0.5121465	0.2611405	0.2510060
1966	1	0.5103465	0.3463841	0.1639625
1966	2	0.5090059	0.2859210	0.2230849
1966	3	0.5080058	0.2785956	0.2294102
1966	4	0.4660881	0.2584179	0.2076701
1967	1	0.4523564	0.2817567	0.1705998
1967	2	0.4398014	0.2811235	0.1586779
1967	3	0.4293774	0.2635219	0.1658554
1967	4	0.4635403	0.2334073	0.2301330
1968	1	0.4713332	0.2831918	0.1881414
1968	2	0.4794602	0.2927663	0.1866939
1968	3	0.4866201	0.3226116	0.1640085
1968	4	0.4911984	0.3677155	0.1234829

Error statistics, 19 observations: 1964 2 to 1968 4.
Mean error: 0.1677162.
RMS error: 0.1863281.

TABLE 3.28
Simulation results for DWO with $U(t)/s(t) = 0.05$, $CU(t) = 0.81$ and $DQMRM$ and $DQAGR$ endogenous.

Variable: DWO – Endogenous

Year	Qt	Simulated	Actual	Error
1964	2	0.4922542	0.5182307	−0.0259765
1964	3	0.4779783	0.4926920	−0.0147137
1964	4	0.4726392	0.4462848	0.0263544
1965	1	0.4653097	0.2553158	0.2099939
1965	2	0.4606333	0.2463057	0.2143276
1965	3	0.4572369	0.2318555	0.2253814
1965	4	0.4545883	0.2317432	0.2228450
1966	1	0.4526621	0.2858768	0.1667854
1966	2	0.4512279	0.2192863	0.2319416
1966	3	0.4501580	0.2372352	0.2129229
1966	4	0.4057558	0.2232380	0.1825178
1967	1	0.3908791	0.2244857	0.1663934
1967	2	0.3774720	0.2418410	0.1356310
1967	3	0.3663319	0.2169896	0.1493423
1967	4	0.4024297	0.2116365	0.1907932
1968	1	0.4109549	0.2781719	0.1327829
1968	2	0.4196248	0.2804236	0.1392013
1968	3	0.4272726	0.3417917	0.0854809
1968	4	0.4321786	0.3480979	0.0840807

Error statistics, 19 observations: 1964 2 to 1968 4.
Mean error: 0.1440045.
RMS error: 0.1635964.

TABLE 3.29
Simulation results for DCL with $U(t)/s(t) = 0.05$, $CU(t) = 0.81$ and $DQMRM$ and $DQAGR$ endogenous.

Variable: DCL – Endogenous

Year	Qt	Simulated	Actual	Error
1964	2	0.4465781	0.4548514	−0.0082733
1964	3	0.4315018	0.4420820	−0.0105802
1964	4	0.4259533	0.4244526	0.0015007
1965	1	0.4182224	0.3481224	0.0701000
1965	2	0.4133214	0.2933107	0.1200107
1965	3	0.4097565	0.2564978	0.1532586
1965	4	0.4069745	0.2393102	0.1676643
1966	1	0.4049528	0.2541413	0.1508116
1966	2	0.4034470	0.2440269	0.1594202
1966	3	0.4023239	0.2422542	0.1600696
1966	4	0.3552438	0.2034718	0.1517720
1967	1	0.3398212	0.1988535	0.1409677
1967	2	0.3257199	0.2039189	0.1218010
1967	3	0.3140122	0.1991288	0.1148834
1967	4	0.3523823	0.2267462	0.1256361
1968	1	0.3611349	0.2446331	0.1165018
1968	2	0.3702628	0.2581818	0.1120809
1968	3	0.3783044	0.2875678	0.0907366
1968	4	0.3834465	0.3083609	0.0750856

Error statistics, 19 observations: 1964 2 to 1968 4.
Mean error: 0.1059709.
RMS error: 0.1195629.

TABLE 3.30

Simulation results for $DQMRM$ with $U(t)/s(t) = 0.05$, $CU(t) = 0.81$ and $DQMRM$ and $DQAGR$ endogenous.

Variable: $DQMRM$ – Endogenous

Year	Qt	Simulated	Actual	Error
1964	2	0.4465781	0.3992900	0.0472881
1964	3	0.4315018	0.4128700	0.0186318
1964	4	0.4259533	0.3928800	0.0330733
1965	1	0.4182224	−0.0131000	0.4313224
1965	2	0.4133214	−0.0097600	0.4230814
1965	3	0.4097565	0.0178900	0.3918665
1965	4	0.4069745	0.0435900	0.3633845
1966	1	0.4049528	0.1807230	0.2242299
1966	2	0.4034470	0.1585800	0.2448671
1966	3	0.4023239	0.1300500	0.2722739
1966	4	0.3552438	0.1066900	0.2485539
1967	1	0.3398212	0.2263900	0.1134312
1967	2	0.3257199	0.2445600	0.0811599
1967	3	0.3140122	0.2618510	0.0521612
1967	4	0.3523823	0.2888000	0.0635823
1968	1	0.3611349	0.3821600	−0.0210251
1968	2	0.3702628	0.3826500	−0.0123872
1968	3	0.3783044	0.4639700	−0.0856656
1968	4	0.3834465	0.4534500	−0.0700035

Error statistics, 19 observations: 1964 2 to 1968 4.
Mean error: 0.1484119.
RMS error: 0.2223705.

TABLE 3.31

Simulation results for $DQAGR$ with $U(t)/s(t) = 0.05$, $CU(t) = 0.81$ and $DQMRM$ and $DQAGR$ endogenous.

Variable: $DQAGR$ – Endogenous

Year	Qt	Simulated	Actual	Error
1964	2	0.4755097	0.5686070	−0.0930973
1964	3	0.4601319	0.5077000	−0.0475681
1964	4	0.4544723	0.4244340	0.0300383
1965	1	0.4465869	0.3923330	0.0542539
1965	2	0.4415878	0.4165370	0.0250508
1965	3	0.4379516	0.3559590	0.0819926
1965	4	0.4351140	0.3374600	0.0976540
1966	1	0.4330519	0.2979610	0.1350909
1966	2	0.4315160	0.1896700	0.2418460
1966	3	0.4303703	0.2715860	0.1587844
1966	4	0.3823487	0.2710820	0.1112667
1967	1	0.3666176	0.1624530	0.2041646
1967	2	0.3522343	0.2013020	0.1500323
1967	3	0.3402924	0.1370750	0.2032174
1967	4	0.3794299	0.1383690	0.2410609
1968	1	0.3883576	0.2087560	0.1796016
1968	2	0.3976680	0.2033950	0.1942730
1968	3	0.4058705	0.2907270	0.1151435
1968	4	0.4111154	0.2626930	0.1484224

Error statistics, 19 observations: 1964 2 to 1968 4.
Mean error: 0.1174804.
RMS error: 0.1478177.

TABLE 3.32
Simulation results for DS with $U(t)/s(t) = 0.045$ and $CU(t) = 0.82$.

Variable: DS – Endogenous

Year	Qt	Simulated	Actual	Error
1964	2	0.6303045	0.5068643	0.1234402
1964	3	0.6314960	0.4954881	0.1360079
1964	4	0.6276578	0.4628269	0.1648309
1965	1	0.5791246	0.4090424	0.1700823
1965	2	0.5442041	0.3995998	0.1446043
1965	3	0.5198643	0.4340676	0.0857967
1965	4	0.5086728	0.4555450	0.0531278
1966	1	0.5173200	0.5214971	−0.0041772
1966	2	0.5131831	0.4519317	0.0612514
1966	3	0.5138568	0.4509206	0.0629362
1966	4	0.4871283	0.4298078	0.0573205
1967	1	0.4864348	0.3760811	0.1103537
1967	2	0.4923614	0.3754551	0.1169063
1967	3	0.4929646	0.3420130	0.1509516
1967	4	0.5205722	0.2773139	0.2432583
1968	1	0.5383858	0.3060383	0.2323475
1968	2	0.5507972	0.3156358	0.2351614
1968	3	0.5743839	0.3158477	0.2585361
1968	4	0.5864671	0.3871923	0.1992748

Error statistics, 19 observations: 1964 2 to 1968 4.
Mean error: 0.1369479.
RMS error: 0.1548491.

TABLE 3.33
Simulation results for D$QINP$ with $U(t)/s(t) = 0.045$ and $CU(t) = 0.82$.

Variable: D$QINP$ – Endogenous

Year	Qt	Simulated	Actual	Error
1964	2	0.6797612	0.5615469	0.1182144
1964	3	0.6860945	0.5415650	0.1445294
1964	4	0.6753378	0.5089307	0.1664072
1965	1	0.4771191	0.3058270	0.1712921
1965	2	0.4544499	0.2621446	0.1923052
1965	3	0.4489299	0.2611223	0.1878076
1965	4	0.4516644	0.2611405	0.1905239
1966	1	0.5132897	0.3463841	0.1669056
1966	2	0.5014534	0.2859210	0.2155324
1966	3	0.4903338	0.2785956	0.2117381
1966	4	0.4624604	0.2584179	0.2040425
1967	1	0.5105815	0.2817567	0.2288248
1967	2	0.5220360	0.2811235	0.2409125
1967	3	0.5294712	0.2635219	0.2659492
1967	4	0.5594065	0.2334073	0.3259992
1968	1	0.6095664	0.2831918	0.3263746
1968	2	0.6183043	0.2927663	0.3255380
1968	3	0.6675479	0.3226116	0.3449364
1968	4	0.6715900	0.3677155	0.3038746

Error statistics, 19 observations: 1964 2 to 1968 4.
Mean error: 0.2279846.
RMS error: 0.2375806.

TABLE 3.34
Simulation results for DWO with $U(t)/s(t) = 0.045$ and $CU(t) = 0.82$.

Variable: DWO – Endogenous				
Year	Qt	Simulated	Actual	Error
1964	2	0.5662774	0.5182307	0.0480467
1964	3	0.5516189	0.4926920	0.0589269
1964	4	0.5141448	0.4462848	0.0678599
1965	1	0.3251954	0.2553158	0.0698796
1965	2	0.3247334	0.2463057	0.0784277
1965	3	0.3084880	0.2318555	0.0766326
1965	4	0.3094728	0.2317432	0.0777295
1966	1	0.3540112	0.2858768	0.0681344
1966	2	0.3071475	0.2192863	0.0878612
1966	3	0.3236303	0.2372352	0.0863951
1966	4	0.3064994	0.2232380	0.0832614
1967	1	0.3178075	0.2244857	0.0933218
1967	2	0.3401145	0.2418410	0.0982734
1967	3	0.3254577	0.2169896	0.1084681
1967	4	0.3445503	0.2116365	0.1329138
1968	1	0.4113322	0.2781719	0.1331602
1968	2	0.4132444	0.2804236	0.1328208
1968	3	0.4824954	0.3417917	0.1407037
1968	4	0.4721429	0.3480979	0.1240450

Error statistics, 19 observations: 1964 2 to 1968 4.
Mean error: 0.0929927.
RMS error: 0.0969125.

TABLE 3.35
Simulation results for DCL with $U(t)/s(t) = 0.045$ and $CU(t) = 0.82$.

Variable: DCL – Endogenous				
Year	Qt	Simulated	Actual	Error
1964	2	0.4704041	0.4548514	0.0155527
1964	3	0.4720966	0.4420820	0.0300146
1964	4	0.4666447	0.4244526	0.0421921
1965	1	0.3977055	0.3481224	0.0495831
1965	2	0.3481024	0.2933107	0.0547917
1965	3	0.3135288	0.2564978	0.0570310
1965	4	0.2976318	0.2393102	0.0583216
1966	1	0.3099148	0.2541413	0.0557735
1966	2	0.3040385	0.2440269	0.0600116
1966	3	0.3049955	0.2422542	0.0627412
1966	4	0.2670289	0.2034718	0.0635570
1967	1	0.2660438	0.1988535	0.0671903
1967	2	0.2744623	0.2039189	0.0705434
1967	3	0.2753191	0.1991288	0.0761903
1967	4	0.3145344	0.2267462	0.0877883
1968	1	0.3398378	0.2446331	0.0952046
1968	2	0.3574676	0.2581818	0.0992858
1968	3	0.3909715	0.2875678	0.1034036
1968	4	0.4081351	0.3083609	0.0997742

Error statistics, 19 observations: 1964 2 to 1968 4.
Mean error: 0.0657342.
RMS error: 0.0696975.

TABLE 3.36
Simulation results for DS with $U(t)/s(t)$ = 0.045, $CU(t)$ = 0.82 and D$QMRM$ and D$QAGR$ endogenous.

Variable: DS – Endogenous

Year	Qt	Simulated	Actual	Error
1964	2	0.6310221	0.5068643	0.1241578
1964	3	0.6398706	0.4954881	0.1443825
1964	4	0.6537487	0.4628269	0.1909218
1965	1	0.6631456	0.4090424	0.2541032
1965	2	0.6696832	0.3995998	0.2700834
1965	3	0.6748361	0.4340676	0.2407686
1965	4	0.6785964	0.4555450	0.2230514
1966	1	0.6813849	0.5214971	0.1598878
1966	2	0.6834681	0.4519317	0.2315364
1966	3	0.6850126	0.4509206	0.2340920
1966	4	0.6536025	0.4298078	0.2237946
1967	1	0.6440344	0.3760811	0.2679533
1967	2	0.6350654	0.3754551	0.2596103
1967	3	0.6275353	0.3420130	0.2855223
1967	4	0.6550771	0.2773139	0.3777632
1968	1	0.6616323	0.3060383	0.3555940
1968	2	0.6683506	0.3156358	0.3527149
1968	3	0.6742292	0.3158477	0.3583815
1968	4	0.6780107	0.3871923	0.2908185

Error statistics, 19 observations: 1964 2 to 1968 4.
Mean error: 0.2550072.
RMS error: 0.2645051.

TABLE 3.37
Simulation results for D$QINP$ with $U(t)/s(t)$ = 0.045, $CU(t)$ = 0.82 and D$QMRM$ and D$QAGR$ endogenous.

Variable: D$QINP$ – Endogenous

Year	Qt	Simulated	Actual	Error
1964	2	0.7095411	0.5615469	0.1479942
1964	3	0.7207318	0.5415650	0.1791668
1964	4	0.7382836	0.5089307	0.2293529
1965	1	0.7501678	0.3058270	0.4443408
1965	2	0.7584360	0.2621446	0.4962914
1965	3	0.7649529	0.2611223	0.5038306
1965	4	0.7697086	0.2611405	0.5085681
1966	1	0.7732352	0.3463841	0.4268511
1966	2	0.7758698	0.2859210	0.4899488
1966	3	0.7778231	0.2785956	0.4092274
1966	4	0.7380986	0.2584179	0.4706807
1967	1	0.7259979	0.2817567	0.4442412
1967	2	0.7146547	0.2811235	0.4335312
1967	3	0.7051314	0.2635219	0.4416004
1967	4	0.7399636	0.2334073	0.5065563
1968	1	0.7482540	0.2831918	0.4650622
1968	2	0.7567507	0.2027663	0.4639844
1968	3	0.7641854	0.3226116	0.4415738
1968	4	0.7689679	0.3677155	0.4012524

Error statistics, 19 observations: 1964 2 to 1968 4.
Mean error: 0.4212139.
RMS error: 0.4346131.

TABLE 3.38

Simulation results for DWO with $U(t)/s(t) = 0.045$, $CU(t) = 0.82$ and $DQMRM$ and $DQAGR$ endogenous.

Variable DWO — Endogenous

Year	Qt	Simulated	Actual	Error
1964	2	0.5719516	0.5182307	0.0537209
1964	3	0.5847731	0.4926920	0.0920811
1964	4	0.6034537	0.4462848	0.1571689
1965	1	0.6161801	0.2553158	0.3608642
1965	2	0.6250318	0.2463057	0.3787261
1965	3	0.6319998	0.2318555	0.4001443
1965	4	0.6370885	0.2317432	0.4053453
1966	1	0.6408615	0.2858768	0.3549847
1966	2	0.6436800	0.2192863	0.4243937
1966	3	0.6457697	0.2372352	0.4085345
1966	4	0.6037140	0.2232380	0.3804760
1967	1	0.5905820	0.2244857	0.3660963
1967	2	0.5784714	0.2418410	0.3366304
1967	3	0.5682949	0.2169896	0.3513053
1967	4	0.6051088	0.2116365	0.3934724
1968	1	0.6141662	0.2781719	0.3359943
1968	2	0.6232317	0.2804236	0.3428081
1968	3	0.6311734	0.3417917	0.2893818
1968	4	0.6362979	0.3480979	0.2882000

Error statistics, 19 observations: 1964 2 to 1968 4.
Mean error: 0.3221225.
RMS error: 0.3383181.

TABLE 3.39

Simulation results for DCL with $U(t)/s(t) = 0.045$, $CU(t) = 0.82$ and $DQMRM$ and $DQAGR$ endogenous.

Variable: DCL — Endogenous

Year	Qt	Simulated	Actual	Error
1964	2	0.4714234	0.4548514	0.0165720
1964	3	0.4839923	0.4420820	0.0419103
1964	4	0.5037056	0.4244526	0.0792530
1965	1	0.5170534	0.3481224	0.1689310
1965	2	0.5263398	0.2933107	0.2330292
1965	3	0.5336593	0.2564978	0.2771615
1965	4	0.5390007	0.2393102	0.2996904
1966	1	0.5429616	0.2541413	0.2888203
1966	2	0.5459206	0.2440269	0.3018938
1966	3	0.5481145	0.2422542	0.3058602
1966	4	0.5034979	0.2034718	0.3000261
1967	1	0.4899069	0.1988535	0.2910534
1967	2	0.4771668	0.2039189	0.2732479
1967	3	0.4664706	0.1991288	0.2673418
1967	4	0.5055925	0.2267462	0.2788464
1968	1	0.5149039	0.2446331	0.2702708
1968	2	0.5244470	0.2581818	0.2662652
1968	3	0.5327972	0.2875678	0.2452294
1968	4	0.5381687	0.3083609	0.2298078

Error statistics, 19 observations: 1964 2 to 1968 4.
Mean error: 0.2334321.
RMS error: 0.2493575.

TABLE 3.40

Simulation results for $DQMRM$ with $U(t)/s(t) = 0.045$, $CU(t) = 0.82$ and $DQMRM$ and $DQAGR$ endogenous.

Variable: $DQMRM$ – Endogenous

Year	Qt	Simulated	Actual	Error
1964	2	0.4714234	0.3992900	0.0721334
1964	3	0.4839923	0.4128700	0.0711223
1964	4	0.5037056	0.3928800	0.1108256
1965	1	0.5170534	−0.0131000	0.5301534
1965	2	0.5263398	−0.0097600	0.5360999
1965	3	0.5336593	0.0178900	0.5157693
1965	4	0.5390007	0.0435900	0.4954107
1966	1	0.5429616	0.1807230	0.3622386
1966	2	0.5459206	0.1585800	0.3873406
1966	3	0.5481145	0.1300500	0.4180645
1966	4	0.5034979	0.1066900	0.3968079
1967	1	0.4899069	0.2263900	0.2635169
1967	2	0.4771668	0.2445600	0.2326068
1967	3	0.4664706	0.2618510	0.2046196
1967	4	0.5055925	0.2888000	0.2167925
1968	1	0.5149039	0.3821600	0.1327439
1968	2	0.5244470	0.3826500	0.1417970
1968	3	0.5327972	0.4639700	0.0688272
1968	4	0.5381687	0.4534500	0.0847187

Error statistics, 19 observations: 1964 2 to 1968 4 .
Mean error: 0.2758731.
RMS error: 0.3226535.

TABLE 3.41

Simulation results for $DQAGR$ with $U(t)/s(t) = 0.045$, $CU(t) = 0.82$ and $DAMRM$ and $DQAGR$ endogenous.

Variable: $DQAGR$ – Endogenous

Year	Qt	Simulated	Actual	Error
1964	2	0.5008519	0.5686070	−0.0677551
1964	3	0.5136722	0.5077000	0.0059722
1964	4	0.5337797	0.4244340	0.1093457
1965	1	0.5473945	0.3923330	0.1550615
1965	2	0.5568666	0.4165370	0.1403296
1965	3	0.5643325	0.3559590	0.2083735
1965	4	0.5697807	0.3374600	0.2323207
1966	1	0.5738208	0.2979610	0.2758598
1966	2	0.5768390	0.1896700	0.3871690
1966	3	0.5790767	0.2715860	0.3074907
1966	4	0.5335678	0.2710820	0.2624858
1967	1	0.5197050	0.1624530	0.3572520
1967	2	0.5067101	0.2013020	0.3054081
1967	3	0.4958000	0.1370750	0.3587250
1967	4	0.5357044	0.1383690	0.3973354
1968	1	0.5549359	0.2033950	0.3515409
1968	3	0.5634532	0.2907270	0.2727262
1968	4	0.5689321	0.2626930	0.3062391

Error statistics, 19 observations: 1964 2 to 1968 4.
Mean error: 0.2474908.
RMS error: 0.2771624.

When we study again the case with

$$\frac{\dot{CL}(t)}{CL(t)} = \frac{\dot{P}^m(t)}{P^m(t)} \quad \text{and} \quad \frac{\dot{P}^f(t)/P^f(t) - \dot{CL}(t)/CL(t)}{1 + \dot{CL}(t)/CL(t)} = 0.02 \;,$$

we obtain the results shown in tables 3.36–3.41.

Our last set of results implies that, in a situation with constant tariffs and constant international prices combined with a devaluation rate equal to the rate of inflation and a 2% improvement in agricultural prices, the increase in the rate of inflation is dramatic. The average increase is 23 percentage points for a four quarters rate of change. This result is substantially higher than the change of seven percentage points we obtained for the case in which the rates of change of imported raw material prices and agriculture prices were kept at their historical levels.

3.5. Steady-state behavior

Let us consider this last model in a steady-state situation characterized by

$$\frac{1}{U(t)/s(t)} = \alpha \;, \quad \frac{1}{0.84 - CU(t)} = \beta \;, \quad \frac{\dot{P}^m(t)}{P^m(t)} = \gamma \;, \quad \frac{\dot{P}^f(t)}{P^f(t)} = \delta$$

for all t.

In this case, the model reduces to the following system of difference equations[18]:

$$\frac{\dot{w}^I(t)}{w^I(t)} = -0.523 + 0.037\alpha + 0.704\frac{\dot{CL}(t)}{CL(t)} \;,$$

$$\frac{\dot{P}^I(t)}{P^I(t)} = -0.166 + 0.688\frac{\dot{w}^I(t)}{w^I(t)} + 0.005\beta + 0.406\gamma, \qquad (3.25)$$

---

[18] This is valid for the periods in which the dummy variable in the cost of living equation is equal to zero.

$$\frac{\dot{P}(t)}{P(t)} = 0.408 \frac{\dot{P}^I(t)}{P^I(t)} + 0.240\gamma + 0.340\delta \,,$$

$$\frac{\dot{CL}(t)}{CL(t)} = 0.0598 + 0.3237 \frac{\dot{P}(t)}{P(t)} + 0.2277 \frac{\dot{P}(t-1)}{P(t-1)}$$

$$+ 0.1417 \frac{\dot{P}(t-2)}{P(t-2)} + 0.0658 \frac{\dot{P}(t-3)}{P(t-3)} \,.$$

In this system, we want to study the behavior of the cost of living variable. Solving (3.25) for $\dot{CL}(t)/CL(t)$ we get

$$\frac{\dot{CL}(t)}{CL(t)} = -0.1101 + 0.0084\alpha + 0.0017\beta + 0.3289\gamma + 0.2757\delta$$

$$+ 0.0481 \frac{\dot{CL}(t-1)}{CL(t-1)} + 0.0299 \frac{\dot{CL}(t-2)}{CL(t-2)} + 0.0139 \frac{\dot{CL}(t-3)}{CL(t-3)}.$$

$$(3.26)$$

From the characteristic equation of the difference equation we find that the three roots are -0.2641; $0.15603 + 0.0965 \sqrt{(-3)}$; and $0.15603 - 0.0965 \sqrt{(-3)}$. Therefore, all of the roots are within the unit circle. The stationary equilibrium level for the rate of change in the cost of living is given by

$$Z = -0.1212 + 0.0093\alpha + 0.0019\beta + 0.3622\gamma + 0.3036\delta. \quad (3.27)$$

Let us look now at the behavior of Z as a function of the different parameters involved.

From (3.27) we have $\partial Z/\partial \gamma = 0.3622$. This means that for a 10 percentage point increase in the rate of growth of the price of imported raw materials (via devaluation, say), the rate of growth in the cost of living increases by 3.62 percentage points.

$\partial Z/\partial \delta = 0.3036$. Hence, a 10 percentage point increase in the rate of growth of the price of farm products yields an increase in the rate of growth in cost of living of 3.036 percentage points.

Another factor that we want to consider is the tradeoff between unemployment and cost of living for $\gamma = \delta = 0$ and a capacity utilization level equal to its average ($\beta = 1/(0.84-0.80) = 25$). Thus, we have from (3.27)

$$Z = -0.037 + 0.0093\alpha. \tag{3.28}$$

Solving (3.28) for α when $Z = 0$, we obtain what Friedman (1968) calls the 'natural rate of unemployment'. In this case, α would equal 12.6%. Therefore, we find that, with constant prices of imported raw materials and with constant prices of farm products, stability in the cost of living requires an unemployment rate in the industrial sector of 12.6%.

Turning now to the effects of different fiscal and monetary policies on Z, we will try to consider the case closest to reality in the Chilean economy. Assuming that the government follows a monetary and fiscal policy oriented towards: (a) keeping the unemployment rate in the industrial sector at 5% (against a 1960–1968 average of 5.53%); (b) keeping capacity utilization at the average for the period ($\beta = 25.0$); and (c) pursuing a long-run policy of improving the terms of trade for agriculture products by $100s\%$ per period $\delta - Z = s(1 + Z)$, then from (3,27) we will have

$$Z = \frac{0.1123}{1 - 0.3036(1 + s)} + \frac{0.3622\gamma}{1 - 0.3036(1 + s)} + \frac{0.3036s}{1 - 0.3036(1 + s)}.$$

Let us assume that the situation in the foreign trade sector is such that we do not need to devalue ($\gamma = 0$). Thus, it can be seen that even if we keep the agricultural terms of trade constant ($s = 0$), inflation will be 16.1%. If the four quarters devaluation rate is 25% and the improvement in the agricultural prices is 3%, then we obtain a four quarter rate of inflation of 30.5%. This rate is very close to the actual rate in Chile.

We conclude from this simple model that the problems facing the Chilean economy are more fundamental than the structuralist's thesis postulates. Even in the absence of structural problems (in the sense that the development of the agriculture and foreign trade sector allows growth with $\gamma = s = 0$), price stability requires an unemployment rate in the industrial sector of 12.6%.

Although this simple model is very powerful in the explanation of price behavior in Chile, the role of fiscal and monetary policy appears only implicitly. To study this explicitly, we must go to the following part, where the complete macroeconomic model is examined.

PART III

AN ANNUAL STUDY OF INFLATION

CHAPTER 4

SOME CHARACTERISTICS OF THE CHILEAN ECONOMY
FROM 1950 TO 1970

The study of the Chilean economy from 1950 to 1970 presents a very interesting opportunity to examine the interaction of the main macrovariables in the inflationary process[1]. During this period, there is enough variance in the variables to make it possible to test various hypotheses about their behavior.

It is impossible to write about the economic situation of Chile in the period 1950–1970 without devoting some time to the study of inflation and its relation to other variables: for example, inflation and growth; inflation and the distribution of income; and inflation and government revenues. In this chapter, we present the main developments in the Chilean economy during the last 20 years; but, in passing, we will have to concentrate part of our analysis on the consequences of inflation.

4.1. Inflation and its consequences

In a neoclassical model, where expectations are always fulfilled, the only long-run welfare effect of inflation is a loss in the overall efficiency of the economy resulting from individuals and firms economizing on money balances to hedge against inflation (Friedman, 1969, pp. 14–15; Samuelson, 1970; Johnson, 1967). Furthermore, if there are instantaneous adjustments to changes in the

---

[1] For an excellent description of the public policies pursued in this period, see Ffrench-Davis (1971).

rate of inflation, then this will be the only short-run effect as well. However, the characteristics of the neoclassical model are very different from those of the real world we live in, where prices are inflexible and institutions do not allow instantaneous adjustment in prices even if expectations are fulfilled. In such a world, inflation has not only short-run consequences but long-run consequences as well. Since the question of the long-run consequences of inflation is necessarily empirical (Solow, 1969), and since we as economists do not know very much about how expectations are formed, it has been very difficult to achieve agreement on the results of the empirical tests.

4.2. Inflation and growth

It is a common belief that, in a world in which prices are inflexible downward, a mild inflation (of about 1 or 2% per year) can be the vehicle to reallocate resources toward more productive sectors and in this way bring about an increase in short-term output. Advocates of this belief also say that inflation allows the economy to come closer to full employment. In the literature, one finds statements such as (Johnson, 1967, p. 140):

> 'Another argument with considerable validity is that a strong demand for labor increases mobility and, therefore, the efficiency of resource allocation and indirectly the rate of growth.'

Harberger (1964, pp. 321–322) favors a bias towards inflation because of its lower welfare cost in terms of unemployment of labor and capital. Comparing a deflation of 5% per annum with an inflation of the same magnitude he says:

> 'However, allowing deflationary forces to work themselves out would entail, in virtually any present-day economy, substantial unemployment of labor, and perhaps also of capital resources. This effect is present when the pressures are deflationary and absent when the pressures are inflationary. It seems to me self-evident that the social costs of allowing deflationary pressures at the rate of, say, 5 percent per annum are very much greater than the social costs of allowing inflationary pressures at the rate of 5

percent per annum to work themselves out in the economy. So long as there is this asymmetry between the social costs of a deflation of x percent per annum and the social costs of inflation of x percent per annum, it is clear that public policy should not operate on the assumption that one is as bad as the other. Some bias toward inflation should result from any rational calculation of the costs and benefits involved. The way in which this bias toward inflation might reasonably work itself out would be through a monetary and fiscal policy which was tight in periods of boom, and sufficiently loose in periods of slack to produce some rise in the general price level, as a consequence of the effort to eliminate or reduce the slackness in the economy. Just to put an order of magnitude on the kind of inflation that might result from this sort of policy, I can easily imagine that it could produce inflation at an average rate of 1, or 2, or 3 percent per annum. So as not to err in my judgment, let me set the limit as something like 10 percent per annum. It seems to me that it would be extremely difficult to defend a policy which produced inflation at more than 10 percent per annum on the ground that this rate of inflation was necessary to eliminate slackness in the economy.'

If the impact of inflation on the long-run rate of growth is to be a consideration in formulating policy, then the relation between inflation and growth must be specified; but it is exactly this relation which escapes us, for our knowledge of factors contributing to the growth process is very incomplete. In any case, the kind of inflation that Chile has had in the last 20 years can hardly be judged as necessary to promote growth and/or to allow for a high level of utilization of the existing resources. On the contrary, the high inflation rate and the associated price controls that followed have distorted relative prices and have hindered the existence of a capital market. Concurrently, the inflationary process transformed preferences to the point that durable assets and land (before the land reform of 1964) became the most desired form in which to hold private wealth.

In order to determine the relation between inflation and growth, we will investigate the statistical characteristics of price and output changes during the last 20 years. In the remainder of this section, we will try to measure the association between these variables rather than attempt to determine the causality. This is

TABLE 4.1
Inflation and growth (percentage changes).

Year	Retail prices (1)	Wholesale prices (2)	Expenditure on gross domestic product deflator (3)	Expenditure on gross domestic product (4)
1950	16.7	17.4	17.6	4.8
1951	22.3	30.8	21.8	4.3
1952	21.6	24.0	16.8	5.7
1953	26.2	22.9	34.9	5.2
1954	56.2	57.0	66.6	0.4
1955	76.3	76.4	76.6	−0.1
1956	65.8	63.9	59.4	0.5
1957	28.7	42.4	25.3	10.5
1958	25.9	25.4	24.9	3.8
1959	38.6	29.9	41.8	−0.5
1960	11.6	5.3	10.5	6.6
1961	7.7	0.8	6.6	6.2
1962	13.9	8.3	14.9	5.0
1963	44.3	53.7	41.5	4.7
1964	46.0	50.6	45.4	4.2
1965	28.8	24.3	34.2	5.0
1966	22.9	22.9	30.3	7.0
1967	18.1	19.3	28.3	2.3
1968	26.6	30.5	30.9	2.9
1969	30.3	36.5	41.1	3.3
1970	32.8	36.1	38.5	3.1
Mean	31.5	32.3	33.7	4.0
Standard deviation	17.68	19.41	17.94	2.63
Coefficient of variation	0.56	0.60	0.53	0.65

Sources: see appendix B.

the purpose of the next eight chapters where a full macromodel is developed.

From table 4.1 we find that the rate of change in retail prices ranges from a low of 7.7% in 1961 to a high of 76.3% in 1955. It is interesting to note that the inflation process accelerated from 1952 to 1955 but did not explode. The deceleration of the inflation process during 1955–1958 is associated with the implementation of the Klein-Saks mission's program of stabilization (see ch. 1; Klein-Saks, 1958; and Ffrench-Davis, 1971). Similarly, the deceleration of inflation during 1960–1962 is credited to the Alessandri stabilization program (Ffrench-Davis, 1971, pp. 27–39) and that of 1965–1967 to Frei's stabilization intent (Ffrench-Davis, 1971, pp. 40–55).

The average inflationary rate ranged between 31.5 and 33.7% (the result depending on which price index change one uses to measure inflation) while the standard deviation ranged from 17.68 to 19.41%. These results indicate that enough variability exists in the series to make attempts at determining the explanation of the different observed rates of inflation interesting if not fruitful.

Similarly, the behavior of the rate of growth in expenditure on gross domestic product (*EGDP*) is very erratic. The lowest rate is for 1955 (−0.1%) which coincides with the peak of inflation [2] and the highest for 1957 (10.5%) [3].

The average rate of growth for the period is 4.0% with a standard deviation of 2.63%. This implies that there is enough movement in the rate of growth in output to make further analysis worthwhile.

When we study the simple correlation between the rate of growth in output and the rate of change in prices we find that the correlation is negative for the period considered here. The correlation is −0.64 with the retail price index. It is −0.49 with the wholesale price index and −0.69 with the implicit deflator of expenditure in gross domestic product.

Although, again with the limitation that this is not a *ceteris paribus* experiment, the evidence presented until now does not support the contention that an inflation like the Chilean one is necessary to promote growth.

---

[2] For such a high rate of inflation, small errors of measurement in the price index have important consequences in the measurement of the rate of growth in output.

[3] We must be cautious in using this figure, for most of the statistics derived for this period show that 1957 was characterized by stagnation (Sunkel, 1960, pp. 24–26; Ffrench-Davis, 1971, pp. 245–246).

4.3. The structure of output and employment

4.3.1. Agriculture

As tables 4.2 and 4.3 show, in the last 20 years the share of agriculture in the expenditure of gross domestic product and in employment has been diminishing. It is difficult to judge whether this is a cause of inflation (as the structuralist school assumes) or a consequence of inflation (due to a deterioration in relative prices in the agriculture sector). An attempt was made to formulate an

TABLE 4.2

Output structure (share in the *EGDP*).

Year	Agri-culture	Mining	Indus-try	Rest of commo-dities*	Total commo-dities	Ser-vices [†]
1950	13.8	15.1	21.0	10.5	60.4	39.6
1951	12.5	16.7	19.9	9.7	58.8	41.2
1952	12.5	15.9	19.6	9.2	57.2	42.8
1953	12.1	12.5	21.3	10.4	56.4	43.6
1954	12.1	11.7	23.8	10.6	58.1	41.9
1955	12.6	12.3	24.3	9.6	58.7	41.3
1956	13.5	9.5	23.3	10.2	56.4	43.6
1957	12.1	9.2	22.3	10.0	53.5	46.5
1958	13.0	8.6	21.3	9.7	52.6	47.4
1959	13.4	9.6	22.2	10.1	55.3	44.7
1960	11.6	9.9	22.8	9.5	53.7	46.3
1961	11.3	9.8	23.3	10.1	54.4	45.6
1962	10.5	9.9	24.8	11.2	56.4	43.6
1963	10.5	10.1	24.7	11.5	56.8	43.2
1964	10.7	10.3	25.1	11.6	57.7	42.3
1965	10.0	9.9	25.4	11.8	57.0	43.0
1966	10.0	10.0	25.8	11.0	56.9	43.1
1967	10.5	9.9	25.9	10.9	57.2	42.8
1968	10.4	9.8	25.8	10.7	56.7	43.3
1969	9.2	10.7	25.7	11.0	56.6	43.4
1970	9.3	10.5	24.9	11.2	55.9	44.1

* 'Rest of commodities' includes: construction, electricity, gas and water, transportation and communication.

[†] 'Services' includes commerce, government services, personal services and owner-occupied houses.

Sources: see appendix B.

TABLE 4.3
Employment structure * (percentages).

Year	Agri-culture	Manu-factur-ing	Mining	Rest of commo-dities	Total commo-dities	Ser-vices
1960	30.7	17.8	4.0	11.3	63.8	36.2
1961	29.3	18.7	4.0	11.6	63.7	36.3
1962	28.6	18.7	3.8	12.7	63.8	36.2
1963	28.5	18.8	3.6	12.5	63.3	36.7
1964	27.1	18.8	3.6	13.5	63.0	37.0
1965	27.1	19.3	3.6	13.1	63.0	37.0
1966	26.6	19.5	3.5	12.9	62.4	37.6
1967	26.7	19.0	3.3	12.0	61.0	39.0
1968	25.6	18.9	3.3	11.9	59.7	40.3
1969	25.0	18.9	3.3	12.0	59.3	40.7
1970	24.6	18.8	3.3	12.2	58.9	41.1

* For the definitions of the columns, see table 4.2.
Sources: see appendix B.

econometric model of the agricultural sector in order to resolve this controversy, but it was not possible to isolate a stable relation for the supply of agricultural products. The inconclusiveness of these attempts can be attributed in part to the difficulties in measuring expected prices in an economic environment where agricultural prices have been politically, and furthermore rather irrationally, determined.

4.3.2. Mining

Output and employment in the mining sector achieved their peak during the Korean war and subsequently suffered an almost steady decrease. The decrease in employment's share during the last decade (in the face of a growing or constant output share) could be due in part to the change in the relative price of factors which made domestic labor more expensive. (This was a result of an increase in wages in this sector relative to the price of imports.) Employment finally stabilized around 3.3% of total employment and output around 10% of total output.

4.3.3. Industry

During the last 20 years, the industrial sector has had the highest rate of expansion in the production of commodities in terms of both its share in output and its share in employment. This was partially a result of the expansion in demand associated with the growth in national income and partially a result of the strong protection given to domestic industry by banning the importing of industrial products that could compete with those produced domestically.

4.3.4. Rest of commodities

This sector, which includes construction, electricity, gas and water, transportation and communications, has had an almost constant share in output and employment.

4.3.5. Services

The share of services in output has fluctuated between a low of 39.6% in 1950 and a high of 47.4% in 1958. The share of employment composed by the service sector has increased rather steadily for the last 11 years. The disparate behavior of output and employment could reflect an overexpansion (in terms of employment) in the service sector as well as a lack of employment opportunities in the commodity sector (especially during the years with low growth rates, namely, 1967–1970).

4.4. The foreign trade situation

For some time now, one of the most important elements in the structuralist view of inflation has been the inelasticity and instability of export earnings (see ch. 1). From the start, we should realize that it is hazardous to make inferences about a causal relationship between foreign trade and inflation, for the real world does not provide us with a *ceteris paribus* experiment but rather a

TABLE 4.4

Export/import data, 1950–1970 (millions of current US dollars and US cents per pound).

Year	Exports of goods and services (1)	Imports of goods and services (2)	Trade balance (3)	Copper price (4)	Share of copper * in the value of exports of goods (5)
1950	344.5	285.5	49.0	21.0	50.5
1951	426.2	397.1	29.1	25.0	45.1
1952	512.5	429.6	82.9	24.5	53.0
1953	406.9	397.6	9.3	23.8	47.3
1954	421.0	394.5	26.5	23.7	55.3
1955	537.6	445.3	92.3	34.1	64.5
1956	544.8	440.8	104.0	40.0	64.3
1957	450.3	507.8	−57.5	27.2	59.6
1958	416.8	467.8	51.0	24.4	52.2
1959	517.2	473.8	43.4	29.6	58.4
1960	551.7	603.8	−52.1	31.7	68.8
1961	547.8	705.7	−157.9	28.5	66.0
1962	586.9	616.5	−29.6	29.6	66.6
1963	586.9	664.7	−77.8	29.4	67.8
1964	687.0	706.2	−19.2	31.5	67.4
1965	788.1	697.7	90.4	37.4	70.6
1966	991.5	858.2	133.3	47.8	73.4
1967	1001.9	895.6	106.3	48.5	75.8
1968	1030.9	921.6	109.3	51.7	76.1
1969	1305.3	1052.4	252.9	65.4	79.6
1970	1271.8	1208.9	62.9	61.1	77.2

* 1950–1959, includes only large copper mining; 1960–1970, includes total copper exports.
Sources: Columns (1), (2), (3) and (5), 1950–1959, IEU; 1960–1970, Plan de la Economía Nacional. Column (4), 1950–1959, Mamalakis and Reynolds (1965); 1960–1970, Plan de la Economía Nacional: Antecedentes sobre el Desarrollo Chileno, 1960–1970, ODEPLAN, 1971.

mutatis mutandis one. With this limitation in mind, let us investigate specific subperiods of foreign trade activity.

From table 4.4, it can be seen that the acceleration in inflation occurring in 1954–1956 (see table 4.1) is associated with a favorable trade position (primarily through the improvement in copper prices), thereby damping the rate of inflation by allowing imports to increase.

During the acceleration in inflation that occurred in the last years of the Frei administration (1968–1970), the foreign trade surplus achieved its peak and so cannot be blamed for the ensuing inflation. The fact that imports did not increase more than they did was not because of the foreign trade situation but because of a deliberate policy of increasing foreign reserves pursued by the **Central Bank.**

From table 4.4 we find that during the last four years only one product (copper) has had a contribution of over 75% of the value of export from commodities. If the country has a comparative advantage in the production of copper, as most studies indicate, then this high share should be a matter of concern only in the sense of designing a system to stabilize copper earnings.

In addition, it is important to note that the foreign trade situa-

TABLE 4.5
Commodity terms of trade (indexes 1960 = 100.0).

Year	Export prices (1)	Import prices (2)	Terms of trade (3) = (1) : (2)
1950	75.6	94.0	80.4
1951	95.7	109.8	87.2
1952	110.4	115.2	95.8
1953	112.6	106.7	105.5
1954	100.8	105.8	95.3
1955	109.5	102.3	107.0
1956	125.9	103.9	121.2
1957	98.5	105.5	93.4
1958	87.0	104.9	82.9
1959	96.1	103.4	92.9
1960	100.0	100.0	100.0
1961	96.3	98.5	97.8
1962	97.0	93.8	103.4
1963	95.8	98.9	96.9
1964	101.8	99.2	102.6
1965	109.4	96.1	113.8
1966	130.9	94.1	139.1
1967	122.9	95.7	128.4
1968	126.6	95.3	132.8
1969	150.9	98.5	153.2
1970	154.5	100.8	153.3

Sources: see appendix B.

tion is very important as a source of tax revenue for the government and as a means of providing a continuous flow of imported raw materials, certain consumption goods (sugar, coffee, meat, etc.) and, above all, the bulk of the economy's capital goods.

From table 4.5 we see that this period was not characterized by a deterioration in the terms of foreign trade, but rather that the latter improved noticeably over the conditions that existed in 1950–1951. Consequently, the data do not support the Prebish thesis that a deterioration in the terms of foreign trade in developing countries is a result of their pattern of trade.

4.5. Distribution of income

In a neoclassical world where expectations are always fulfilled, the only distributional effect of inflation is the tax that it imposes on the holders of money. But in a world with price inflexibilities and non-instantaneous adjustment (even with presence of fulfilled ex-

TABLE 4.6
Income distribution (percentages).

Year	Wages, salaries and employer's social security contributions	Income of independent workers	Rent and profits	Rest	National income
1960	52.9	21.8	17.7	7.6	100.0
1961	51.8	21.5	17.2	9.5	100.0
1962	50.8	19.6	20.7	8.9	100.0
1963	48.5	17.8	24.2	9.5	100.0
1964	47.9	17.6	26.3	8.2	100.0
1965	52.0	18.4	21.6	8.0	100.0
1966	52.7	17.4	20.6	9.3	100.0
1967	52.8	16.1	22.3	8.8	100.0
1968	54.4	15.2	22.3	8.1	100.0
1969	53.1	14.3	24.5	8.1	100.0

Source: Plan de la Economía Nacional: Antecedentes sobre el Desarrollo Chileno, 1960–1970, ODEPLAN, 1971, Cuadro No. 30, p. 43.

pectations), some redistribution of income takes place between groups which have different bargaining powers. This redistribution usually flows from unorganized labor to organized labor.

When the aggregate data for the factorial distributions of income were analyzed, no major shift was detected during the 1960–1969 period (the only period for which data exist) with the exception of the decrease in the share of labor associated with the acceleration of inflation in the last years of the Alessandri administration (1963–1964). A similar situation existed during the acceleration of inflation in the last two years of the Frei administration (1969–1970). If more disaggregate data had been available, we could have tested the hypothesis that the lower share of labor payments in these sub-periods was due, in part, to the behavior of wages and salaries in the government sector, for government wages and salaries usually increased by a percentage equal to the previous year's inflationary rate.

4.6. Inflationary tax and other government taxes

Inflation is a tax on the holders of cash balances where the proceeds of the tax are collected by the monetary authority and the banking system. That part of the tax collected by the banking system is redistributed, via the banking system, within the private sector [4]. This redistribution can occur in one of two ways or a combination of them, namely: (1) a direct redistribution from the holders of demand deposit to the stockholders on the commercial banks; or (2) an indirect redistribution from the holders of demand deposits to some fortunate stockholder. The first of these exists when the commercial banks make their loans at a positive real rate of interest while the second exists when there are lucky stockholders who can obtain loans from the commercial banks at a real rate of interest below the real social rate of interest.

---

[4] In Chile, the monetary system is formed by the Central Bank and the commercial banks. The commercial banks are composed of all the private commercial banks plus the State Bank. The inflationary tax collected by the State Bank is redistributed to the private sector through a subsidy credit.

TABLE 4.7
Interest rates and the cost of credit (percentages).

Year	Current banking interest rate (1)	Maximum legal interest rate (2)	Nominal cost of credit (3)	Rate of change in retail prices (4)	Real cost of credit $\frac{(3)-(4)}{100+(4)}$
1950	10.7	15.6	27.6	16.7	0.0932
1951	11.7	16.8	38.8	22.3	0.0532
1952	12.1	18.1	30.1	21.6	0.0700
1953	12.3	17.1	29.1	26.2	0.0233
1954	13.2	15.3	27.3	56.2	−0.1852
1955	13.4	16.2	28.2	76.3	−0.2728
1956	13.3	16.3	28.3	65.8	−0.2264
1957	14.4	16.8	28.8	28.7	0.0007
1958	15.7	18.1	30.0	25.9	0.0323
1959	16.3	19.3	32.4	38.6	−0.0447
1960	16.6	19.8	33.1	11.6	0.1925
1961	15.6	19.6	27.6	7.7	0.1849
1962	14.4	17.9	25.7	13.9	0.1039
1963	14.3	17.0	24.5	44.3	−0.1371
1964	14.9	17.4	24.8	46.0	−0.1450
1965	15.6	18.2	28.9	28.8	0.0005
1966	15.8	19.0	34.4	22.9	0.0930
1967	16.2	19.0	32.6	18.1	0.1224
1968	17.9	19.9	36.2	26.6	0.0755
1969	19.8	23.2	40.7	30.3	0.0794
1970	20.0	24.0	42.0	32.8	0.0692

Sources: Columns (1), (2), (4), various issues MBCB. Column (3), 1950–1957, equals column (2) plus 10%; 1958–1969, Ffrench-Davis (1971, p. 338).

In order to obtain some idea of which of these two forms of redistribution predominates, the cost of credit is presented in table 4.7, from which we observe that for most of the period the redistribution took the second form.

In discussing the inflationary tax and the negative correlation observed between the rate of inflation and the real profits of commercial banks, Lüders (1968, pp. 163–164) says:

'In other words, although they lost some money as owners of a bank by pushing for rediscounts (adding heat to the inflation), they more than made up for these losses by way of the relatively low cost loans they were obtaining.'

TABLE 4.8

Government taxes (percentages of total taxes including inflationary tax).

Year	Personal taxes	Corporation taxes	Copper taxes	Property taxes	Import taxes	Other indirect taxes *	Total income from taxes	Inflationary taxes	Total taxes
1950	11.4	8.7	11.9	10.3	18.9	31.4	92.5	7.5	100.0
1951	10.5	7.6	15.3	9.1	20.0	29.4	91.9	8.1	100.0
1952	8.8	7.3	18.6	8.8	19.5	28.8	91.8	8.2	100.0
1953	9.8	8.7	11.0	8.0	15.7	35.2	88.4	11.6	100.0
1954	8.8	7.7	13.8	6.8	9.4	33.1	79.6	30.2	100.0
1955	6.5	5.0	15.5	6.7	10.9	33.1	77.7	22.3	100.0
1956	7.0	6.7	20.8	5.6	12.1	30.0	82.2	17.8	100.0
1957	7.4	9.4	16.1	4.3	17.3	37.3	91.8	8.2	100.0
1958	10.0	8.8	11.0	6.5	13.8	42.1	92.2	7.8	100.0
1959	7.2	7.6	14.8	5.1	14.8	40.4	89.8	10.2	100.0
1960	7.2	9.0	13.2	5.3	19.8	41.6	96.2	3.8	100.0
1961	6.8	12.2	9.7	6.0	21.5	41.0	97.1	2.9	100.0
1962	6.3	10.7	11.7	5.9	19.5	39.9	94.1	5.9	100.0
1963	7.1	7.3	11.0	5.6	16.9	36.5	84.3	15.7	100.0
1964	7.8	8.4	11.7	8.1	9.4	39.1	84.5	15.5	100.0
1965	8.3	10.5	12.1	9.6	10.3	39.6	90.5	9.5	100.0
1966	9.5	9.6	16.2	7.1	11.0	39.1	92.3	7.7	100.0
1967	10.7	10.4	14.4	6.5	10.3	41.4	93.6	6.4	100.0
1968	10.1	8.9	12.7	5.8	10.8	43.1	91.3	8.7	100.0
1969	10.1	8.0	14.6	4.1	10.5	43.3	90.6	9.4	100.0
1970	9.3	8.7	14.9	3.8	11.2	41.9	89.8	10.2	100.0

* Includes: retail sales tax, production tax, service tax, tax to legal acts, and other indirect taxes.

The inflationary tax collected by the government operates like any other tax levied on the private sector. We will define the inflationary tax as the product of average high-powered money [5] during the year and the inflation rate (measured by the retail price index). In table 4.8 we can see the share of different taxes in total taxes (including the inflationary tax). This table clearly shows that during most of the period the inflationary tax is more important than the personal tax, especially for those years where inflation was high.

Table 4.8 also shows that the other indirect taxes are the ones that have increased the most for the 20-year period we have studied. It is difficult to make any inference about the regressivity of this type of tax without carefully examining their structure. The sales tax (introduced massively in 1955) is the most important component of other indirect taxes and is levied at a different rate for different groups of commodities and services. This system of differential rates is usually higher for commodities and services with high income elasticities. Consequently, to study the effect of a sales tax on the distribution of income would entail a detailed investigation of the pattern of consumption by income levels and such an undertaking is beyond the scope of this book.

4.7. Fiscal expenditures, fiscal income and the fiscal deficit

A secular inflation of the magnitude of the Chilean one requires for its development a continuous 'financing' from the Central Bank. Until 1956, this 'financing' had mainly taken the form of discounting government documents at the Central Bank. From then on, additional financing was provided through the government borrowing foreign currency and selling it to the Central Bank to finance their operations. It is important to note that the continuous financing needed to perpetuate inflation does not imply that the solution to inflation is to cut off the 'financing' and

---

[5] We should use high-powered money adjusted by borrowed reserves, but we do not have this information.

Inflation in developing countries

TABLE 4.9

Fiscal expenditures, fiscal income and fiscal deficit (millions of current escudos).

Year	Fiscal expenditures	Rate of change	Fiscal current income	Rate of change	Deficit	Rate of change
1950	21.8	30.5	20.0	12.4	1.8	–
1951	29.1	33.5	27.4	37.0	1.7	-6.4
1952	43.9	50.9	38.1	39.1	5.8	241.2
1953	56.6	28.9	46.5	22.1	10.1	74.1
1954	84.6	49.5	75.9	63.2	8.7	-13.9
1955	161.6	91.1	141.2	86.1	20.4	134.5
1956	251.0	55.3	223.4	58.2	27.6	35.3
1957	355.4	41.6	301.1	34.8	54.3	96.7
1958	450.3	26.7	372.2	23.6	78.1	43.8
1959	707.6	57.1	569.4	53.0	138.2	77.0
1960	903.4	27.7	707.7	24.3	195.7	41.6
1961	1015.7	12.4	796.0	12.5	219.7	12.3
1962	1272.7	25.3	957.3	20.3	315.4	43.6
1963	1778.7	39.8	1353.8	41.4	424.9	34.7
1964	2496.2	40.3	1958.6	44.7	537.6	26.5
1965	4002.0	60.3	3209.1	63.8	792.9	47.5
1966	5686.5	42.1	4897.9	52.6	788.6	-0.5
1967	6870.9	20.8	6312.2	28.9	558.7	-29.2
1968	9682.3	40.9	8757.6	38.7	924.7	65.5
1969	13734.7	41.9	13068.6	49.2	666.1	-28.0
1970	21882.3	59.3	19614.9	50.1	2267.4	240.4

Sources: 1950–1959, IEU; 1960–1969, ODEPLAN (excluding from fiscal expenditures changes in cash holdings); 1970, February, 1972, issue of MBCB.

thereby eliminate the government deficit. Attempts to stop inflation in this manner will usually have important repercussions on the unemployment of labor and the under-utilization of capital stock (stemming from the downward inflexibility of prices and wages in the short run). However, meaningful and substantial swings in the rate of inflation can be accomplished via the money-creation role of the government deficit. This last consideration would make it interesting to pursue the relation between government deficit, high-powered money and the rate of inflation.

From table 4.9 we find that in all the years in which inflation exceeded 40% (except for 1965), the increase in the government deficit was a result of a higher expansion in government expenditures than in government current income. Once again, this reflects the fact that during most of the period it was easy to obtain a consensus to increase government expenditures but it was very difficult to obtain agreement on how to finance those expenditures. Hence, the door has always been open for the type of tax that is levied by default — the inflationary tax. Furthermore, tables 4.8 and 4.9 show that only during the first years of the Frei government was any major effort made to finance the budget without resorting to an inflationary tax. Increased tax revenues were financed by a real adjustment in the tax base used to compute income taxes and by the introduction of a wealth tax in 1965. Furthermore, the need to resort to other means of financing was alleviated to some extent by the increased tax revenues that were generated when the international price of copper increased.

4.8. Public sector and private sector obligations, foreign exchange operations and high-powered money

In an inflation of the magnitude of the Chilean one, with its major swings, an important role is played also by the behavior of the money supply. As we show in ch. 10, one of the main factors which determines the money supply is the level of high-powered money. In this section, we want to describe the behavior of this latter variable during the period 1950–1970. If we concentrate on the

TABLE 4.10

Public sector and private sector obligations, foreign exchange operations and high-powered money (millions of current escudos).

Year	Change in Public sector obligations (1)	Change in private sector obligations (2)	Change in foreign exchange obligations (3)	Change in other net obligations (4)	Change in high-powered money (5)	Rate of change in high-powered money
1950					1.1	15.1
1951					2.2	26.2
1952					4.6	43.4
1953					8.1	53.3
1954					9.2	39.5
1955					20.2	62.2
1956	11.1	15.4	-1.2	-4.3	21.2	40.2
1957	28.0	24.8	-18.6	-15.3	18.9	25.6
1958	23.3	1.4	-4.3	12.3	32.7	35.2
1959	-9.5	-25.4	69.6	22.1	56.5	45.0
1960	77.4	-10.1	50.4	-31.6	83.1	45.7
1961	117.4	10.2	-70.2	-28.7	28.7	10.8
1962	117.0	25.2	101.2	-36.1	207.3	70.6
1963	16.7	-18.7	-48.3	81.6	31.3	6.2
1964	-12.3	102.5	45.5	254.6	390.3	73.3
1965	129.7	-81.9	408.0	-76.8	359.0	38.9
1966	184.4	224.1	403.0	46.6	765.3	59.7
1967	238.6	229.0	-88.0	54.8	434.4	21.2
1968	41.4	240.9	862.0	-9.8	1134.5	45.7
1969	56.7	207.4	1314.0	-69.3	1508.8	41.7
1970	868.8	808.2	1754.9	165.8	3597.7	70.2

Sources: built with raw data from Ffrench-Davis (1971) and unpublished data from the Central Bank of Chile.

period 1956–1970, the only period for which we have disaggregate data, the following can be observed:

(1) The lowest rate of growth in high-powered money (10.8% in 1963) coincides with the third highest rate of inflation.

(2) The deceleration of inflation during 1960 coincides with an acceleration in the rate of growth of high-powered money.

(3) Only in 1967 is there a clear correspondence between the behavior of high-powered money and the rate of inflation. In this year the rate of unemployment had a major increase also in what was a traditional monetary cure to inflation, viz. a cut in the rate of growth in money supply.

(4) The acceleration in the inflation rate in the period 1968–1970 coincides with an expansion in high-powered money, due mainly to the monetary effect of the foreign exchange operations followed by a policy of building a stock of foreign reserves pursued by the Central Bank.

CHAPTER 5

A BASIC MACROMODEL OF THE CHILEAN ECONOMY

In this chapter, we develop a simple macroeconomic model of the Chilean economy, and in the following chapters it will be extended and estimated. The main objective of this chapter, and the next seven chapters, is to formulate explicitly the mechanism of interaction between the real and financial sectors. The understanding of these interactions is fundamental to the explanation of the inflationary process and to the design of a stabilization program. Therefore, most of the disaggregation that we undertake is directly related to this objective.

5.1. The working of the Chilean economy

In a Wicksell–Keynes–Patinkin–Modigliani model the interaction between the real and monetary sectors of the economy is twofold: first, through the rate of interest which is an argument in the demand for money and the demand for commodities; and second, through the real-wealth effect which also appears as an argument in the demand for money and the demand for commodities.

In the Chilean case, this mechanism deviates from that described above for two reasons. First, the rate of interest does not act as a price that rations the market. This is quite evident upon examination of one of the more important subperiods under study where we find that the real interest rate was negative and credit rationing was achieved, usually, by means of quotas. Secondly, the cost of holding money (which is always changing because of the changing level of inflation) and the weak nature of the financial market results in a money market that is not always in equilibrium. Therefore, in the formulation of our model we must make a distinction between the supply and the demand for money so that 'disequilibria' can be accommodated. Hence, we hypothesize that the mechanism of interaction between the monetary and real sector (in the Chilean economy) is as follows:

(1) The disequilibrium in the money market spills over to the commodity market. This is captured by including, *à la* Patinkin, the difference between real supply and real demand for money in the demand function of the commodity market.

(2) There is a credit rationing mechanism that makes the opportunity cost of borrowing more dependent on the amount of credit from the monetary system to the private sector than on the rate of interest. The credit rationing effect is captured by including real monetary sector credit to the private sector in the demand for durables and investment goods.

In addition to testing the above hypothesis, we will want to test three other important characteristics of the Chilean economy:

(1) The price formation mechanism. We will assume, as in ch. 3, that the price of commodities is determined by some kind of mark-up over average variable cost of production. This mark-up is affected by the amount of excess demand in the market for that type of commodity.

(2) The role of monetary policy. As stated before, monetary policy has not played an independent role during most of the period. On the contrary, the money base was adjusted to whatever level was necessary to finance the government deficit.

(3) Labor and employment. In our model, labor is treated as a quasi-fixed factor; therefore, we must distinguish between momentary employment (observed employment) and short-run employment (desired employment) with the former adjusting towards the latter through a Nerlove–Cagan adjustment mechanism.

5.2. The basic model

This section presents a simplified version of the model whose specification and estimation are presented later. We will concentrate on the interrelations between the variables of interest to us. Consequently, the justification of the specification presented and of the different lag patterns employed must be postponed temporarily until the next seven chapters.

The model is structured in four blocks, the first of which contains the equations of the expenditure sector and the market for labor. In the second block, we develop the price equations for goods and services and for labor. The third block specifies the government's tax and expenditure behavior (which will assist in explaining the government deficit), and the last block presents the money market relations.

5.2.1. List of variables

$*BTFR$ = borrowing of the treasury from abroad, annual change,
$*BTBS$ = borrowing of the treasury from banking system, annual change,
$*CK$ = price of capital services,
CP = real personal consumption,
CU = capacity utilization rate,
$*d$ = nominal credit from the monetary system to the private sector,
D = nominal government deficit,
$*E$ = real change in inventories,
$*FEO$ = nominal foreign exchange operations, annual change,
$*G$ = real government expenditures in national account,
GDI = real gross investment,
H = real imports,
I = opportunity cost of holding money,
$*J$ = real government expenditures in fiscal account,
$*K$ = stock of capital,
L = employment,
$*LFC$ = 'full employment' level of labor,
LR = labor requirements,
$*LCBP$ = lending from the Central Bank to the public, annual change,
$LCBT$ = lending from the Central Bank to the treasury, annual change,

* Indicates that the variable is exogenous in this simple model.

M = money supply,
MB = money base,
$(M/P)^d$ = real money demand,
*N = labor force,
P = price of commodities and services,
*PM = price of imports,
*$(\dot{P}/P)^e$ = expected rate of inflation,
Q = gross output,
Q_{FC} = full capacity gross output,
*r = real rate of interest,
T = real taxes,
U = unemployment rate,
W = wage rate,
*X = real exports.

5.2.2. The expenditure sector and the labor market

5.2.2.1. Production of goods and services and the labor requirements

The production function

$$Q(t) = F[L(t), CU(t) K(t)] . \tag{5.1}$$

Gross output $Q(t)$ is a function of employment $L(t)$ and the services of capital $CU(t)K(t)$ where $K(t)$ is the stock of capital in year t and $CU(t)$ is an index of utilization of capital services during year t.

Full capacity output

$$Q_{FC}(t) = F[L_{FC}(t), SK(t)] . \tag{5.2}$$

Full capacity gross output $Q_{FC}(t)$ is the same function as in (5.1) but with the 'full employment' level of labor $L_{FC}(t)$ and the

---

* Indicates that the variable is exogenous in this simple model.

'full employment' level of capital services $SK(t)$ as arguments. The symbol S is a full employment of capital coefficient.

Labor requirements in the short run

$$LR(t) = LR[CU(t) K(t), Q(t)] . \tag{5.1}'$$

Labor requirements in the short run are obtained by solving (5.1) for a given level of output and capital services.

Labor employment

$$L(t) - L(t-1) = \mu[LR(t) - L(t-1)] . \tag{5.3}$$

Employment adjusts towards the labor requirements in the short run via a Cagan–Nerlove adjustment mechanism where the parameter μ is the speed of adjustment.

Capacity utilization

$$CU(t) = \frac{Q(t)}{Q_{FC}(t)} . \tag{5.4}$$

Capacity utilization is equal to the ratio between output and full employment output.

Unemployment rate

$$U(t) = \frac{N(t) - L(t)}{N(t)} . \tag{5.5}$$

The unemployment rate $U(t)$ is equal to the difference between the total available labor force $N(t)$ and employment $L(t)$ as a proportion of the total available labor force.

5.2.2.2. Demand for goods and services

$$Q(t) = CP(t) + G(t) + GDI(t) + E(t) + X(t) - H(t) . \tag{5.6}$$

Gross product $Q(t)$ is equal to private consumption $CP(t)$ plus government consumption $G(t)$, gross domestic investment $GDI(t)$, the change in inventories $E(t)$, and the level of exports $X(t)$ minus the level of imports $H(t)$.

Private consumption

$$CP(t) = CP\left[YD(Q(t), T(t)), \ d(t)/P(t), \frac{M(t)}{P(t)} - \left(\frac{M(t)}{P(t)}\right)^d\right]. \quad (5.7)$$

Private consumption is a function of personal disposable income YD, which in turn is a function of gross output and taxation $T(t)$; real credit to the private sector $d(t)/P(t)$; and the difference between the existing real supply of money $M(t)/P(t)$ and the quantity of real balance that individuals desire to hold $(M(t)/P(t))^d$.

The main idea underlying (5.7) is that the nonbusiness private sector's best alternative to cash balances — in a framework in which there is no well developed market for financial assets and in which there are ceilings on the nominal rate of interest — is commodities, mainly durables. Hence, if the public end up with more money than they want to hold, then they will spend part of the difference to purchase consumption goods.

Gross domestic investment

$$GDI(t) = GDI\left[Q(t), \ d(t)/P(t), \frac{CK(t)}{P(t)} \ K(t)\right]. \quad (5.8)$$

Gross investment $GDI(t)$ is a function of gross output, credit from the monetary system to the private sector and the real value of capital services. In eq. (5.8), $CK(t)$ represents the nominal price of capital services.

Imports

$$H(t) = H\left[GDI(t), \ CP(t), \frac{PM(t)}{P(t)}\right]. \quad (5.9)$$

Imports are a function of gross domestic investment, private consumption and the relative price of imports $PM(t)/P(t)$.

5.2.3. Price equations

Price of commodities and services

$$\frac{\dot{P}(t)}{P(t)} = R_1 \left[\frac{\dot{W}(t)}{W(t)}, \frac{\dot{PM}(t)}{PM(t)}, CU(t) \right]. \tag{5.10}$$

The rate of change in the price of commodities and services $\dot{P}(t)/P(t)$ is a function of the rate of change in the wage rate $\dot{W}(t)/W(t)$, the rate of change in the price of imported raw materials $\dot{PM}(t)/PM(t)$ and capacity utilization.

Wage rate

$$\frac{\dot{W}(t)}{W(t)} = R_2 \left[U(t), \frac{\dot{P}(t)}{P(t)} \right]. \tag{5.11}$$

The rate of change in the wage rate $\dot{W}(t)/W(t)$ is a function of the rate of unemployment and the rate of change in the prices of commodity and services.

5.2.4. Government sector

Government deficit in real terms

$$\frac{D(t)}{P(t)} = J(t) - T(t). \tag{5.12}$$

Government deficit in real terms, $D(t)/P(t)$, is equal to the difference between govenment expenditures in the fiscal account $J(t)$ and total taxes in the fiscal account $T(t)$.

Total real taxes

$$T(t) = T \left[X(t), Q(t), \frac{\dot{P}(t)}{P(t)}, \frac{\dot{P}(t-1)}{P(t-1)} \right]. \tag{5.13}$$

Total taxes are a function of the level of exports (through taxation of copper), the level of gross domestic product (through taxation of imports and indirect taxation) and the rate of change of current year's prices and the previous year's prices (through the direct taxation of persons).

5.2.5. Money sector

Change in money base

$$\Delta MB(t) = LCBT(t) + LCBP(t) + FEO(t) \, . \tag{5.14}$$

The change in the monetary base $\Delta MB(t)$ is equal to the change in the lending from the Central Bank to the Treasury, $LCBT(t)$, plus the change in lending from the Central Bank to the banking system and the public, $LCBP(t)$, plus the net position of the foreign exchange operations, excluding the operations with the Treasury, $FEO(t)$. All the variables are in current units.

Change in lending from Central Bank to the Treasury

$$LCBT(t) = D(t) - BTFR(t) - BTBS(t) \, . \tag{5.15}$$

The change in lending from the Central Bank to the Treasury is equal to the government deficit $D(t)$ minus the change in lending to the Treasury from abroad $BTRF(t)$ and the change in lending to the Treasury from the banking system $BTBS(t)$.

Changes in money supply

$$\Delta M(t) = M[\Delta MB(t), I(t)] \, . \tag{5.16}$$

The change in the money supply $\Delta M(t)$ is a function of the change in the monetary base and the opportunity cost of holding money $I(t)$. The latter argument affects the money multiplier through the behavior of free reserves.

Demand for money

$$\left[\frac{M(t)}{P(t)}\right]^d = L[I(t), Q(t)] \, . \tag{5.17}$$

The demand for money $[M(t)/P(t)]^d$ is a function of the opportunity cost of holding money and the gross domestic product.

Opportunity cost of holding money

$$I(t) = \left[\frac{\dot{P}(t)}{P(t)}\right]^e + r(t) .$$ (5.18)

The opportunity cost of holding money is equal to the expected rate of inflation $[\dot{P}(t)/P(t)]^e$ plus the real interest rate, $r(t)$.

The system specified by (5.1)–(5.18) consists of 18 equations and 18 unknowns: Q, L, CU, Q_{FC}, LR, U, CP, GDI, H, P, W, D, T, MB, $LCBT$, M, I, and $(M/P)^d$. This model can be solved numerically for the unknown variables and in principle it can be solved in closed form as well (although one has to be cautious because of the non-linearities implicit in some of the equations).

CHAPTER 6

THE PRODUCTION PROCESS AND THE EMPLOYMENT
OF FACTORS

In this chapter, the technology of the economy will be investigated in order to determine the influence of its link with capacity output and the employment of factors[1]. Since we would expect differences in technology to exist between the sector producing commodities and the sector producing services, real expenditures in gross domestic product will be divided into expenditures in gross domestic product of commodities (QC) and expenditures in gross domestic product of services (QS)[2].

In preparation for our study, we will require some specification of the link between capacity output and the employment of factors. This is usually provided by means of a production function, but lately an increasing number of authors have questioned the theoretical existence of an aggregate production function even at the firm level (Fisher, 1965, pp. 263–288; 1968, pp. 391–412; 1969, pp. 553–577; Gorman, in Wolfe, 1968). However, we agree with Fisher (1969, pp. 571–572) that:

> 'Despite all this, there is, after all, considerable evidence that aggregate production functions may be appropriate approximations.... On the other hand, there is apparently nothing about the aggregation or estimation procedure involved in such studies which guarantees that the production function so estimated will give approximately the correct picture of factor shares. Yet clearly this is the case.'

[1] For an alphabetical list of the variables in this and the following chapters, see ch. 11.
[2] In this section, all variables are in real terms unless otherwise indicated.

6.1. The expenditure in gross domestic product

The expenditure in gross domestic product (Q) is equal to the gross product of commodities (QC) plus the gross product of services (QS).

$$Q(t) = QC(t) + QS(t) \, . \tag{6.1}$$

6.2. Gross domestic product of commodities

To start with, we will assume that in the sector producing commodities the technology is given by a constant elasticity of substitution (CES) production function on the utilized level of the primary factors. The advantage of this function is that it is general enough to include as special cases the Leontief and the Cobb–Douglas formulations (see Arrow et al., 1961).

We will also assume that the production function can be written as

$$QC(t) = \gamma \, \{\delta[CA(t)KC(t)]^{-\rho} + (1-\delta)[LC(t)]^{-\rho}\}^{-\nu/\rho} e^{u(t)} \, , \tag{6.2}$$

where CA = utilization rate of the capital stock, QC = expenditure in gross domestic product in the sector producing commodities, $KC(t)$ is the capital stock in plant and equipment in the sector producing commodities at the beginning of year t, LC is the employment in the sector producing commodities, $\sigma = 1/(1+\rho)$ is the elasticity of substitution, ν is the degree of homogeneity in $CA(t)KC(t)$ and $LC(t)$ of the function, u is the random error and γ is the efficiency parameter.

To have a positive marginal product for both factors, we require $\delta > 0$ and $1-\delta > 0$. Therefore, δ should be in the range $0 < \delta < 1$.

The condition for diminishing returns to one factor depends on the degree of returns to scale.

Specifically it can be shown (Brown, 1966, p. 47) that

$$\frac{\partial^2 QC(t)}{\partial LC^2(t)} \lesseqqgtr 0$$

when

$$\frac{(v+\rho)}{[\delta/(1-\delta)][v(t)]^{\rho}+1} \gtreqless 1/\sigma ,$$

where

$$v(t) = \frac{LC(t)}{CA(t)\,KC(t)} .$$

For the case of constant return to scale ($v = 1$), the condition of diminishing marginal returns to labor, $\partial^2 QC/\partial LC^2 < 0$, is immediately satisfied if $\sigma > 0$ and if the condition of positive marginal product is satisfied ($0 < \delta < 1$). Moreover, in this case $\sigma > 0$ is a necessary condition for diminishing marginal returns. (This can be easily shown by *reductio ad absurdum.*)

It can also be shown that the weaker condition of a strictly quasi-concave production function will be satisfied *for any value of v* provided that $1 + \rho > 0$.

In the estimation of a production function, there are two available methods. The first is to estimate it directly from a series on output and factor inputs. The alternative is to estimate it using the side conditions for profit maximization. With small countries such as Chile, the assumption of competitive behaviour is doubtful to say the least, especially when there exists important evidence of nonoptimizing behavior in the pricing of commodities and labor.

Furthermore, if one were to obtain poor estimation results using the side condition, one would not be able to discriminate between rejecting the technology assumption or the assumptions built in the first-order conditions for profit maximization (conditions on the markets for product and factors). Owing to the limited applicability of the second alternative, we will try to estimate (6.2) directly.

Estimation of (6.2) directly creates a problem, for it is highly nonlinear in its parameters and, therefore, requires a special estimation procedure. One procedure that has been suggested, now known as Kmenta's approximation, is to approximate the production function by a Taylor series expansion of the first- and second-order terms around $\rho = 0$ (Kmenta, 1967, pp. 180–189). Kmenta's approximation of (6.2) is given by

$$\ln QC(t) = \ln \gamma + \nu\delta \ln CA(t) \, KC(t) + \nu(1-\delta) \ln LC(t)$$

$$- \tfrac{1}{2} \rho\nu\delta(1-\delta)[\ln CA(t)KC(t) - \ln LC(t)]^2 + u(t). \quad (6.3)$$

Although the parameters of (6.3) can be estimated without major difficulties (Kmenta, 1967), it is hazardous to attempt to compute the coefficients of (6.2) from the estimated coefficients of (6.3).

The difficulty lies in the fact that, as we have shown in appendix C, eq. (6.3) is in most cases a better approximation (in the sense that it has a smaller remainder) to another well known production function – the variable elasticity of substitution production function VES (Hildebrand and Liu, 1957). Since we cannot distinguish between a CES and a VES production function, we will estimate (6.2) directly using a nonlinear estimation procedure rather than Kmenta's approximation.

Before proceeding to estimate (6.2) directly, let us consider the special case in which $\nu = 1, \rho = 0$. By a limiting process we obtain, from (6.2), the Cobb–Douglas function with constant returns to scale.

For this case, the production function can be written (Arrow et al., 1961, p. 374) as

$$\ln QC(t) = \ln \gamma + \delta \ln CA(t)KC(t) + (1-\delta) \ln LC(t) + u(t),$$

and can be rewritten as

$$\ln \frac{QC(t)}{LC(t)} = \ln \gamma + \delta \ln \frac{CA(t)KC(t)}{LC(t)} + u(t).$$

When this function was estimated adding a Hicks neutral technical change parameter, the following values were obtained:

$$\ln \frac{QC(t)}{LC(t)} = \underset{(2.502)}{2.862} + \underset{(5.270)}{0.619} \ln \frac{CA(t) \, KC(t)}{LC(t)} + \underset{(5.488)}{0.016t}. \quad (6.4)$$

$$\rho = -0.78 \quad SS_e = 0.013 \quad DW = 2.18 \quad T = 9$$

Instruments:

$$C, t, \ln \frac{G(t)}{PO(t)}, \ln \frac{XC(t)}{PO(t)}, \ln \frac{QC(t-1)}{LC(t-1)}, \ln \frac{CA(t-1)\,KC(t-1)}{LC(t-1)}.$$

This function implies an elasticity of output with respect to utilized capital of 0.619 and with respect to labor of 0.381. It also implies a rate of Hicks neutral technical change of 1.6% per year.

All the coefficients here are significant at a 2% level. More importantly, the point estimate of δ is 0.619, a number which makes a lot of empirical sense if we consider what other authors have obtained for the elasticity of output with respect to capital. In a perfectly competitive model where capital is paid its marginal product, this parameter will be equal to the share of capital in total output.

Now we will proceed to estimate (6.2) directly. As pointed out previously, the problem with (6.2) is that it is nonlinear in its parameters. Therefore, we will use a nonlinear estimation procedure.

Taking the logs of (6.2) and adding a Hicks neutral technical change parameter we have, for the case of constant returns to scale:

$$\ln \frac{QC(t)}{LC(t)} = \ln \gamma - \frac{1}{\rho} \ln \left\{ \delta \left[\frac{CA(t)\,KC(t)}{LC(t)} \right]^{-\rho} + (1-\delta) \right\} + \lambda t + u(t).$$

$$(6.5)$$

This equation is nonlinear in δ and ρ. Therefore, we will need to use some nonlinear method of estimation. The estimation procedure that we will employ is the following:

(1) For given values of δ and ρ (δ_0, ρ_0) generate the new variable:

$$V(t, \delta_0, \rho_0) = \frac{1}{-\rho_0} \ln \left\{ \delta_0 \left[\frac{CA(t)\,KC(t)}{LC(t)} \right]^{-\rho_0} + (1-\delta_0) \right\}.$$

(2) Next, generate the following variable:

$$\text{RHS}(t, \delta_0, \rho_0) = \ln \frac{QC(t)}{LC(t)} - V(t, \delta_0, \rho_0) .$$

(3) Now run the following regression:

$$\text{RHS}(t, \delta_0, \rho_0) = \ln \gamma + \lambda t + u(t) . \tag{6.6}$$

(4) Finally, select the pair (δ, ρ) that minimizes the residual sum of squares in (6.6).

If this process converges, then the estimation procedure is equivalent to ordinary least squares appropriately adjusted for the nonlinearities.

In the iteration procedure, δ was constrained to the interval $(0, 1)$ and the elasticity of substitution to the interval $(1/2, \infty)$. The constraint on δ was discussed above while the elasticity of substitution was derived from accumulated empirical evidence. Specifically. it is assumed that $-1 < \rho < 1$.

By estimating (6.5) with the above procedure, we can obtain the following results for those values of δ and ρ that minimize the residual sum of squares.

$$\ln \frac{QC(t)}{LC(t)} = \underset{(319.89)}{2.909} - 1/0.05 \ln \left\{ 0.66 \left[\frac{CA(t) KC(t)}{LC(t)} \right]^{-0.05} + 0.34 \right\}$$

$$+ \underset{(12.50)}{0.017t} . \tag{6.7}$$

$$R^2 = 0.946 \qquad\qquad T = 11$$

The elasticity of substitution estimated for this production function was 0.952 and is very close to 1.00, the constraint value that we used when estimating the Cobb–Douglas production function. Hence, one would not expect to find substantial differences in the parameters of (6.7) and (6.4) and, indeed, this is the case for the point estimates, for $\ln\gamma$ and δ are very similar.

Consequently, we will use eq. (6.4) in our model for it is easier to operate than (6.7). Our results show that, in Chile, there exists a sufficient degree of substitution between labor and capital in the production process. It follows that those who indiscriminately use a Harrod—Domar growth model to describe the technology of countries like Chile should be more cautious. Furthermore, our results are atypical of the traditional description of underdeveloped countries. A traditional description usually runs along the following lines (Eckaus, 1955, p. 545):

'There have been frequent comments which describe certain features of underdeveloped and overpopulated areas as essentially the result of limited variability in the coefficients of production.'

Eckaus concludes (1955, p. 565) that, 'If the technical substitutability of factors is limited, as is suggested here, the possibility of labor redundancy arises'.

Therefore, our results clearly show that Chile does not come under the traditional description of a developing country's technology.

6.3. Full capacity level of gross domestic product of commodities

The full capacity level of gross domestic product of commodities (QCF) is the same function as defined in (6.4). Here we use the 'full employment' level of labor (NCF) and the 'full employment' level of capital (KCF) rather than the actual level of labor and capital. Specifically, we have

$$\ln \frac{QCFE(t)}{NCF(t)} = 2.862 + 0.619 \ln \frac{KCF(t)}{NCF(t)} + 0.016\, t. \tag{6.8}$$

$$\hat{\rho} = 0.78$$

6.4. Gross domestic product of services

In the sector producing services, we include commerce, government services, personal services, and owner-occupied houses.

We assume that in these sectors there are no capacity limitations, and, therefore, the level of output (QS) is entirely determined by demand. Furthermore, we assume that the level of demand is a linear function of real expenditure in gross domestic product of commodities and the relative price of services. When the equation was estimated, the following values were obtained:

$$QS(t) = \begin{array}{c} -3093.2 \\ (-1.053) \end{array} + \begin{array}{c} 1.165 \\ (6.063) \end{array} QC(t) \begin{array}{c} -1573.4 \\ (-1.172) \end{array} \frac{PS(t)}{PC(t)} . \qquad (6.9)$$

$\hat{\rho} = 0.654 \qquad DW = 2.75 \qquad$ years: 1962–1970
outside equation instruments: $AUTX(t), AUTX(t-1)$.

6.5. Desired employment and desired capital stock in the sector producing commodities

To derive the factor requirements functions, we will assume that the sector producing commodities is organized so that, at the aggregate level, the desired level of employment of labor and the desired level of capital stock are determined through the side conditions for cost minimization. We prefer to assume cost minimization rather than the stronger assumption of profit maximization since there exists strong evidence for mark-up pricing, as shown in ch. 3.

For a sector that faces fixed expected prices of factors – $W^e(t)$ for labor and $C^e(t)$ for capital – and whose technology can be characterized by a Cobb–Douglas function of the form

$$QC(t) = A[LC(t)]^\alpha [KC(t) \, CA(t)]^\beta e^{\lambda t} , \qquad (6.10)$$

we have as first-order conditions for cost minimization at a given value of output (6.10) and

$$\frac{W^e(t)}{C^e(t)} = \frac{\alpha}{\beta} \frac{KC(t)}{LC(t)} . \qquad (6.11)$$

The values of $KC(t)$ and $LC(t)$ that satisfy (6.10) and (6.11) generate a global minimum if the production function given in (6.10) is strictly quasi-concave [3]. Solving (6.10) and (6.11) for $KC(t)$ and $LC(t)$ and employing the constant returns to scale assumption, we

---

[3] A sufficient condition for strict quasi-concavity is given by $\alpha, \beta > 0$.

obtain what we call the desired level of capital and employment in the sector producing commodities.

$$LC^*(t) = \left(\frac{\beta}{1-\beta}\right)^{-\beta} A(t)^{-1} QC(t) \left[\frac{W^e(t)}{C^e(t)}\right]^{-\beta} [CA(t)]^{-\beta} e^{-\lambda t}, \quad (6.12)$$

$$KC^*(t) = \left(\frac{\beta}{1-\beta}\right)^{1-\beta} A(t)^{-1} QC(t) \left[\frac{W^e(t)}{C^e(t)}\right]^{1-\beta} [CA(t)]^{-\beta} e^{-\lambda t}, \quad (6.13)$$

where $A(t)$ is related to the auto-regressive transformation in (6.4) (see ch. 11).

6.5.1. Employment

Now we need only to link the desired level of employment (6.12) with the actual level of employment. We will treat labor as a quasi-fixed factor of production; that is, employment adjusts toward the desired level following some adjustment pattern. The justification in treating labor as a quasi-fixed factor lies in the high cost of hiring and re-hiring, especially where skilled labor is concerned (Kuh, 1965, pp. 1–12; Dhrymes, in Duesenberry et al., 1969). In this framework, firms adjust with a lag to the equilibrium level of the factor use. We will also assume that labor use moves toward the desired level following a geometric lag. Thus, we can write

$$LC(t) = \sum_{i=0}^{\infty} \delta(1-\delta)^i LC^*(t-i). \qquad (6.14)$$

Performing a Koyck transformation on (6.14), we obtain

$$LC(t) = \delta LC^*(t) + (1-\delta) LC(t-1). \qquad (6.15)$$

Therefore, the labor employment can be written as

$$LC(t) = \delta_0 + \delta_1 LC^*(t) + \delta_2 LC(t-1), \qquad (6.16)$$

with the constraint that $\delta_1 + \delta_2 = 1$.

The estimation of (6.16) can be done by either of two methods. The first is to substitute (6.12) in (6.16) and to estimate δ_0, δ_1, δ_2, β and A and λ by a nonlinear procedure. The alternative is to take the values of β, A and λ from the production function, compute $LC^*(t)$ from (6.12) and proceed to estimate (6.16). Because of the major nonlinearities involved in the first procedure, we opt for the second alternative.

For the purpose of estimation, we assume that $W^e(t)/C^e(t)$ is a simple average of the current year's and the previous year's wage–rental ratio. We will estimate (6.16) directly, and thereafter, we will test the hypothesis that $\delta_1 + \delta_2 = 1$. The results of estimating (6.16) are

$$LC(t) = 0.193 + 0.132\ LC^*(t) + 0.731\ LC(t-1). \qquad (6.17)$$
$$\quad\ \ (1.410)\quad (1.745)\qquad\quad (4.593)$$

$\hat{\rho} = 0.099$ $DW = 1.53$ years: 1962–1970
Outside equation instruments: $XC(t)$, $XC(t-1)$.

From our estimated equation, we observe that all the coefficients have the expected signs and that the average lag in the adjustment is fairly long, around 2.7 years (taking the coefficient of $LC(t-1)$ as an estimate of $(1 - \delta)$. Upon testing the null hypothesis that the sum of the coefficients equals unity, we found that the null hypothesis could be accepted at a 5% level of significance.

It would have been interesting to study the impact of the immobility law of 1965 on employment but, unfortunately, we did not have enough observations to pursue this problem.

6.6. Employment in the service sector

Since we previously specified that the service sector is not constrained by capacity limitations, we will assume that the production function for services is of a Leontief type with labor as the limiting factor. On this assumption, we have a desired labor requirement as a constant proportion of the level of output.

Once again, we assume that actual employment is a geometrical-ly distributed lag of desired employment. Performing a Koyck transformation on the distributed lag expression, we obtain actual employment as a linear function of actual output in the sector and the previous year's employment. The estimated equation was

$$LS(t) = -0.075 + 0.000026 \ QS(t) + 0.857 \ LS(t-1) . \quad (6.18)$$
$$ (-1.565) \quad (1.279) \quad\quad\quad (3.493)$$

$\hat{\rho} = -0.386$ $\quad\quad\quad$ $DW = 2.30$ $\quad\quad\quad$ years: 1963–1970

Outside equation instruments: $G(t)$, $XC(t)$.

The average lag in this equation is six years and is clearly too long. The fixed coefficient for desired labor requirements is 0.00018. This means that, for each million escudos (at 1965 prices) of output by the service sector, 180 wage-earners were required.

CHAPTER 7

AGGREGATE EXPENDITURES

In this chapter, the expenditure side of the gross domestic product of output will be developed[1]. We will start with the definition of real expenditure in gross domestic product and then go on to the specification and estimation of the equations for its different components.

7.1. Aggregate demand

Expenditure in gross domestic product (Q) is equal to private consumption expenditures (CP) plus government consumption expenditures (G) plus gross domestic investment in fixed capital (GDI) plus the change in inventories (DEE) plus exports (X) minus imports (H).

$$Q(t) = CP(t) + G(t) + GDI(t) + DEE(t) + X(t) - H(t) . \qquad (7.1)$$

7.2. Consumption expenditures

The only existing official statistics referring to consumption for the complete period of analysis are total consumption expenditures. As most of the literature on consumption function has shown, the mechanism that explains the expenditures in non-

---

[1] All variables in this chapter are defined at constant prices, unless otherwise indicated.

durables differs from the one for expenditures in durables, so we will have to split the consumption expenditures series into these two components. For the period 1960–1969, the Oficina de Planificacion Nacional (ODEPLAN) has computed a series for expenditures in non-durables and services. Using this information, the weights from the 1962 input–output table, and the indexes of production of durables and imports of durables, an index was built of the supply of durables for the period 1950–1960. (For details, see appendix B.) Employing this index and the absolute value of expenditures on durables in the year 1960, we can create an estimated series for expenditures on durables for the period 1950–1969. Subtracting this series from the total expenditures in consumption series, we obtain the consumption of non-durables and services.

Unfortunately, we do not have price information for these two types of consumption goods over the sample period considered. Hence, in our formulation of the consumption function, we are forced to leave out the relative price variable.

Now our consumption equation is developed, as follows:

$$CP(t) = CND(t) + CD(t) . \tag{7.2}$$

Private consumption expenditures are divided into private expenditures in non-durables and services (CND) and private expenditures in durables (CD).

7.3. Expenditures in non-durables and services

We will assume at the outset that expenditures in non-durables and services are a distributed lag function of personal disposable income:

$$CND(t) = a \sum_{i=0}^{\infty} w_i \, YD(t-i) + u(t) . \tag{7.3}$$

Given that we are working with an annual model, it can be expected, in general, that $w_i < w_{i-1}$ for $i > 0$. The simplest function that generates this pattern for the w's is a geometric function, and so it is assumed that $w_i = \lambda(1-\lambda)^i$, $\lambda \geqslant 0$. The average lag for this function is given by $(1-\lambda)/\lambda$.

Substituting the expression for w_i in (7.3) and taking a Koyck transformation, we obtain

$$CND(t) = a\,\lambda\,YD(t) + (1-\lambda)CND(t-1) + u(t) - (1-\lambda)u(t-1)\,.$$

The equation that will be estimated is

$$CND(t) = b_1 + b_2\,YD(t) + b_3\,CND(t-1) + \psi(t)\,.$$

In the estimation of this equation, it is assumed that the $\psi(t)$ follows a Markov first-order autoregressive process and we will employ Fair's method in estimating the equation.

After estimating this model, the following values were obtained:

$$CND(t) = \underset{(2.477)}{1062.5} + \underset{(2.212)}{0.285\ YD(t)} + \underset{(2.319)}{0.507\ CND(t-1)}\,. \qquad (7.4)$$

$\hat{\rho} = -0.148 \qquad\qquad DW = 2.02 \qquad\qquad$ years: 1952–1970
Outside equation instruments: $G(t)$, $G(t-1)$, $XC(t)$, $XC(t-1)$.

Performing our tests with the asymptotic standard errors yields coefficients that are all statistically significant. The average lag in

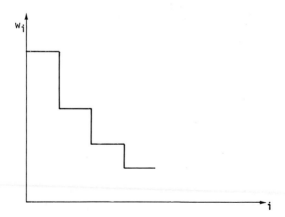

Fig. 7.1. Lag distribution of non-durable consumption and services.

the response of consumption to income is a little over one year, which seems reasonable. The marginal propensity to consume non-durables and services is 0.285 in the short run and 0.578 in the long run.

The implicit lag structure is given by

$$w_i = 0.493 \, (0.507)^i; \quad i = 0, 1, \ldots .$$

Plotting the *w*s yields the lag structure illustrated in fig. 7.1. In view of the fact that we are working with an annual model, this lag is quite reasonable.

7.4. Expenditures in durables

In this section, we will develop a stock adjustment model to explain expenditures in durables. We begin by assuming that the desired level of demand for services of durables (SD^*) is a linear function of a distributed lag in gross personal disposable income. The lag structure will begin in the previous period and extend backwards in time for *m* periods.

$$SD^*(t) = b_0 + b_1 \sum_{i=1}^{m} YD(t{-}i)$$

In addition, it is also assumed that the desired stock of durables at the beginning of the period *t*, i.e. $KD^*(t)$, is proportional to the desired level of services from durables. (This is similar to a production function.)

$$KD^*(t) = d \, SD^*(t). \tag{7.5}$$

The actual level of stock in durables $[KD(t)]$ moves toward the equilibrium level following a Cagan–Nerlove partial adjustment process with a response parameter of ϕ, i.e.

$$NCD(t) = KD(t{+}1) - KD(t) = \phi \, [KD^*(t{+}1) - KD(t)] \, ,$$

where *NCD* is the net expenditures in durables.

Substituting (7.5) in the previous equation and assuming that the replacement of durables is a constant proportion θ of the stock of durables, we obtain

$$CD(t) = NCD(t) + \theta \, KD(t) = \phi b_0 d + \phi b_1 d \sum_{i=0}^{m} YD(t-i)$$

$$-(\phi - \theta) \, KD(t) \, .$$

To this demand for durables originating on the income side, we will add the demand originating from the adjustment process in the money market. As pointed out in ch. 5, there is no instantaneous clearing in the money market, mainly because a well developed financial market does not exist, and so the nominal interest rate is not allowed to move freely. Consequently, we will assume that the disequilibrium in the money market spills over to the commodity market.

Now, it is very difficult to obtain a measure of the disequilibrium in one market, for the mere existence of a disequilibrium means that it is possible to observe only the smaller of the two values for quantity supplied and quantity demanded, at a given set of prices. Even the more recent developments in econometric techniques for dealing with disequilibrium situations (Fair and Jaffee, 1970) cannot be applied here because we do not have a price whose movements can be followed.

Thus, in our estimations, we will measure the disequilibrium in the money market by the estimated residuals from the demand for money equation. These residuals will have a random component and, therefore, the measurement of the disequilibrium in the money market will include an error in measurement. Introducing the disequilibrium in the money market into the previous equation yields the final equation:

$$CD(t) = \phi b_0 d + \phi b_1 d \sum_{i=0}^{m} YD(t-i) - (\phi - \theta) \, KD(t) + cZM(t) \, ,$$

where

$$ZM(t) = \frac{M(t)}{P(t)} - \left(\frac{M(t)}{P(t)} \right)^d ,$$

$$\left(\frac{M(t)}{P(t)}\right)^d = \text{fitted real money demanded},$$

and

$$\frac{M(t)}{P(t)} = \text{real money supply}.$$

Unfortunately, it is not possible to estimate an equation of this type because we cannot construct a series for the stock of durables. We could have used a procedure similar to the one used for capital stock in the sector producing commodities, if we had a way of obtaining an estimate of the stock of capital in a given year. On the other hand, we can avoid this problem by extending the expenditures in durables series to include observations before 1950 in such a way that the initial value of the stock of capital is less important but, unfortunately, lack of sufficient data makes this impossible.

When this equation was estimated, excluding the stock of capital variable and assuming that the weights of the income variable followed a second-degree polynomial (Hall, 1967), the following values were obtained:

$$CD(t) = \begin{matrix} -3363.3 + & 0.840 \ ZM(t) + & 0.097 \ YD(t) \\ (-3.705) & (1.523) & (1.457) \end{matrix}$$

$$\begin{matrix} + & 0.202 \ YD(t-1) + & 0.170 \ YD(t-2) \, . \\ & (6.232) & (3.627) \end{matrix} \qquad (7.6)$$

mean lag 1.155   sum of lag coefficients = 0.469
        (4.29)   (7.82)
$\hat{\rho} = 0.834$ $R^2 = 0.989$ years: 1954–1960

This equation was estimated by ordinary least squares, for it was not considered worthwhile to undertake the investment necessary to generalize the polynomial distributed lag procedure for the case of instrumental variables.

Eq. (7.6) was also estimated by including a variable representing the total flow of real credit from the banking system to the private sector but, in most cases, this variable was not significant and had the wrong sign. Alternative specifications could have been attempted, but a better measure of credit conditions in the market for durable goods did not exist. From the results, we can observe that the coefficient of $ZM(t)$ indicates that, for each escudo of excess supply of money at constant prices, 0.84 escudo is spent on durables.

7.5. Gross personal disposable income

Given the fact that depreciation allowances seem to be overestimated in the national accounts, we will work with gross personal disposable income.

Gross personal disposable income in current escudos (NYD) is equal to gross personal income in current escudos (NYP), plus net transfers received by persons from the government and from abroad net of interest paid by persons in current escudos ($NNETTR$), less direct taxes to persons in current escudos (NTP), and less total social security contributions paid by persons (TSS), where this last variable is multiplied by the cost of living index.

$$NYD(t) = NYP(t) - NTP(t) + NNETTR(t) - P(t)TSS(t) . \quad (7.7)$$

7.6. Gross personal income

Gross personal income in current escudos is composed of the total wage bill in current escudos (TW), plus employers' social security contributions in current escudos, plus profits net of taxes in current escudos ($NPROF$), plus depreciation, income of self-employed and imputed rent for owner-occupied homes (RES).

$$NYP(t) = TW(t) + P(t)ERSS(t) + NPROF(t) + RES(t) . \quad (7.8)$$

7.7. Employers' social security contributions

We assume that employers' social security contributions in constant escudos (*ERSS*) are a linear function of the total real wage bill (where the latter does not include the former contribution). When this relation was estimated, the following was obtained:

$$ERSS(t) = -174.5 + 0.201 \frac{TW(t)}{P(t)} \ . \tag{7.9}$$
$$(-2.193) \quad (19.642)$$

$\hat{\rho} = 0.263 \qquad DW = 1.57 \qquad \text{years: } 1961-1970$

Outside equation instruments: $XC(t)$, $G(t)$.

If this equation is compared with eq. (7.16), we observe that the results are very reasonable. The coefficient of the wage bill variable is 50% higher for total social security contributions (employers plus employees) than for employers' contributions.

7.8. Direct taxes on persons in national accounts

Until 1964 the tax base consisted of personal income and personal wealth of the previous year. From 1965 onwards this base was modified to include an escalator factor to correct for inflation. The escalator allowed for 0.5 of the previous year's inflation in 1965, 0.8 in 1966, and 1.0 thereafter.

We will assume that in the period before 1965, the nominal tax can be specified as a linear function homogeneous to the first degree in the lagged values of prices, nominal income and nominal wealth. Specifically,

$$NTP(t) = v_1 P(t-1) + \kappa_1 NYP(t-1) + \omega_1 NW(t-1) + P(t-1)u^1(t)$$

$$t \leqslant 1964 \tag{7.10}$$

where

$NTP(t)$ = nominal tax to persons in the year t,
$P(t)$ = cost of living index in the year t,
$NYP(t)$ = nominal personal income in the year t, and
$NW(t)$ = nominal wealth in the year t.

Furthermore, we assume that $NYP(t) = \eta_1 NW(t)$. Therefore, (7.10) can be written as

$$NTP(t) = \nu_1 P(t-1) + \bar{\kappa}_1 NYP(t-1) + P(t-1)u^1(t)$$

$$t \leqslant 1964 \qquad\qquad (7.11)$$

where

$$\bar{\kappa}_1 = \kappa_1 + \omega_1/\eta_1 .$$

For the period from 1965 on, we assume that the nominal tax is a linear function homogeneous in lagged prices, the adjusted tax base (taking care of previous year inflation) and a dummy variable equal to one in 1965 to allow for the lower escalator in this year. Specifically, we can write

$$NTP(t) = \nu_2 P(t-1) + \bar{\kappa}_1 \frac{NYP(t-1)P(t-1)}{P(t-2)} + \psi dv(t)P(t-1)$$

$$+ P(t-1)u^2(t) . \qquad\qquad (7.12)$$

$$t \geqslant 1965$$

Now, (7.11) can be written as

$$\frac{NTP(t)}{P(t-1)} = \nu_1 + \bar{\kappa}_1 \frac{NYP(t-1)}{P(t-1)} + u^1(t) . \qquad\qquad (7.13)$$

$$t \leqslant 1964$$

Eq. (7.12) can be written as

$$\frac{NTP(t)}{P(t-1)} = \nu_2 + \bar{\kappa}_1 \frac{NYP(t-1)}{P(t-2)} + \psi dv(t) + u^2(t) . \qquad\qquad (7.14)$$

$$t \geqslant 1965$$

Now, (7.13) and (7.14) can be written in matrix form as

$$V = \left[\frac{NTP}{P(-1)}\right] = [i \ du \ Rd\upsilon] \begin{bmatrix} \nu_1 \\ \nu_2 - \nu_1 \\ \overline{\kappa}_1 \\ \psi \end{bmatrix} + u_{12} \ ,$$

where

$V = \dfrac{NTP}{P(-1)}$ = vector of order $(T_1 + T_2) \times 1$,

i = vector of order $T \times 1$ with only ones,

du = vector of order $(T_1 + T_2) \times 1$ with the first T_1 elements equal to zero and the last T_2 equal to one,

$$R = \begin{bmatrix} YP(-1) \\ NYP(-1) \\ \hline P(-2) \end{bmatrix} ,$$

$d\upsilon$ = vector of index $T \times 1$ with a component of value unity in 1965 and zero elsewhere,

$YP(-1)$ = vector of order $T_1 \times 1$,

$\dfrac{NYP(-1)}{P(-2)}$ = vector of order $T_2 \times 1$,

$$u_{12} = \begin{bmatrix} u^1 \\ u^2 \end{bmatrix} = \text{vector of order } (T_1 + T_2) \times 1 \ .$$

When we estimated this equation, we obtained

$$V(t) = -172.4 + 97.900 \ DU(t) + 0.037 \ R(t) - 156.7 \ d\upsilon(t).$$
$$(-2.484) \quad (1.587) \qquad\qquad (5.630) \qquad\qquad (-5.007)$$

$$(7.15)$$

$\hat{\rho} = 0.614 \qquad DW = 2.43 \qquad$ years: 1952–1970

Outside equation intruments: $XC(t), XC(t-1), G(t), G(t-1)$.

7.9. Social security contributions in national accounts

The employer's social security contributions and the employee's security contributions are based on the level of wages; therefore, it is natural to assume that they are a function of total wages (excluding employer's social security contributions).

When such a function was estimated, the following values were obtained:

$$TSS(t) = \underset{(-2.169)}{-243.0} + \underset{(20.267)}{0.289} \frac{TW(t)}{P(t)} , \qquad (7.16)$$

where $TW(t)$ is the nominal wage bill in the economy.

$\hat{\rho} = 0.312 \qquad DW = 1.78 \qquad$ years: $1961-1970$

Outside equation instruments: $XC(t), G(t)$.

Using the asymptotic standard errors, a one-tail test of the coefficient of the total wage bill variable proved to be significant even at a 0.5% level. Furthermore, the order of magnitude of the coefficient is what we would have expected *a priori*.

7.10. Gross domestic investment in fixed capital

Gross domestic investment in fixed capital is equal to net domestic investment in plant and equipment (IM), plus gross domestic investment in housing ($IHOU$), plus replacement investment in plant and equipment (REP):

$$GDI(t) = IM(t) + IHOU(t) + REP(t). \qquad (7.17)$$

7.11. Net domestic investment in plant and equipment

Owing to the expected differences in technology, it would be advantageous, in the specification of the model, to separate the total investment in plant and equipment between the copper industry and the rest of the commodity-producing sector. Unfortunately, if this is attempted, we cannot make any progress. The problem encountered was that investment series for the copper industry compatible with the one included in the national accounts could not be obtained for the entire sample period and attempts to build one were unsuccessful. Thus, an aggregate investment equation for the whole sector producing commodities was estimated.

Following the developments in the last chapter, we assume that the desired capital stock is the stock of capital that equalizes the marginal rate of substitution between labor and capital with the wagenrental ratio.

Specifically, we had in the last chapter the following:

$$KC^*(t) = \left(\frac{\beta}{1-\beta}\right)^{1-\beta} A^{-1} QC(t) \left(\frac{W^e(t)}{C^e(t)}\right)^{1-\beta} [CA(t)]^{-\beta} e^{-\lambda t}. \quad (7.18)$$

Once again, we need to link the desired capital stock with the level of investment.

Following Jorgenson and his associates[2], we will assume that net investment is a distributed lag on the desired changes in the stock of capital:

$$IM(t) = \sum_\tau w_\tau \Delta KC^*(t-\tau),$$

where

$$\Delta KC^*(t) = KC^*(t+1) - KC^*(t).$$

Specially, we assume a rational distributed lag of the form

$$IM(t) = \frac{\sum r_\tau \Delta KC^*(t-\tau)}{1 - b_1 L}, \quad (7.19)$$

where L is a linear operator defined as $X(t-i) = L^i X(t)$ and the r_τ falls along a second-degree polynomial.

---

[2] Hall and Jorgenson (1967, pp. 391–414); Jorgenson and Stephenson (1967a, pp. 169–220; 1967b, pp. 16–27).

Therefore, using (7.18), we obtain

$$IM(t) = \frac{1}{1-bL}\left(\frac{\beta}{1-\beta}\right)^{1-\beta} A^{-1}\left\{\sum r_\tau\left[QC(t-\tau)\left(\frac{W^e(t-\tau)}{C^e(t-\tau)}\right)^{1-\beta}\right.\right.$$

$$\times [CA(t-\tau)]^{-\beta}e^{-\lambda(t-\tau)} - QC(t-\tau-1)\left(\frac{W^e(t-\tau-1)}{C^e(t-\tau-1)}\right)^{1-\beta}$$

$$\left.\left.\times [CA(t-\tau-1)]^{-\beta}e^{-\lambda(t-\tau-1)}\right]\right\}.$$

Employing the definition of the lag operator, we obtain

$$IM(t) = \left(\frac{\beta}{1-\beta}\right)^{1-\beta} A^{-1}\left\{\sum r_\tau\left[QC(t-\tau)\left(\frac{W^e(t-\tau-1)}{C^e(t-\tau-1)}\right)^{1-\beta}\right.\right.$$

$$\times [CA(t-\tau)]^{-\beta}e^{-\lambda(t-\tau)} - QC(t-\tau-1)\left(\frac{W^e(t-\tau-1)}{C^e(t-\tau-1)}\right)^{1-\beta}$$

$$\left.\left.\times [CA(t-\tau-1)]^{-\beta}e^{-\lambda(t-\tau-1)}\right]\right\} + bIM(t-1). \qquad (7.20)$$

We can see that the parameters A, β and λ were previously encountered and also appear in (7.20). This suggests an estimation procedure in which we form the likelihood function of (7.20) and maximize it with respect to the parameters involved. Unfortunately, this procedure becomes very complicated because there are many nonlinearities involved. *In our estimation, we will take the values of A, β and λ that were estimated in ch. 6 and estimate the r's and b conditioned on the values of A, β and λ.*

Before performing this estimation it was allowed a shift in the function related to the credit.

Estimating the equation, we have

$$IM(t) = 163.3 + 0.876\ IM(t-1) - 0.23\ \frac{\Delta MB(t)}{P(t)}$$
$$\quad\ (1.322)\quad (5.232)\qquad\qquad (-0.839)$$

$$+\ 0.012\ \Delta KC^*(t)$$
$$\quad\ (0.266)$$

$$+ \; 0.055 \Delta KC^*(t-1) + \; 0.051 \; \Delta KC^*(t-1).$$
$$(1.632) \qquad\qquad\qquad (1.423)$$

$R^2 = 0.85$ $DW = 1.96$ years: 1953–1969

This equation was estimated by ordinary least squares for the same reason as given in the estimation of the expenditure in durables function.

We can see from this result that the coefficient of $\Delta MB(t)/P(t)$ has the wrong sign although it is not significant. Therefore we estimated (7.20) without correction for credit conditions. Upon performing this estimation, the following values were obtained:

$$IM(t) = \; 168.1 \; + \; 0.797 \; IM(t-1) + \; 0.012 \; \Delta KC^*(t)$$
$$(1.378) \quad (5.815) \qquad\qquad\quad (0.268)$$

$$+ \; 0.052 \; \Delta KC^*(t-1) + \; 0.048 \; \Delta KC^*(t-2). \qquad (7.21)$$
$$(1.581) \qquad\qquad\qquad (1.373)$$

$R^2 = 0.84$ $DW = 1.98$ years: 1953–1969

This is one of the weaker equations in our model because of the long lag in the response. Any better estimation would require splitting the investment series into copper and no copper; the first component being an autonomous component (but changing through time), and the second an endogenous component. This equation was again estimated by ordinary least squares, for the same reason as given in the estimation of the expenditure in durables function.

7.12. Cost of capital services

The cost of capital services is equal to the product of the price of capital goods (IPK) and the gross rate of return before taxes. This last variable is defined as the real rate of profit (RA) plus the depreciation rate (DE), divided by one minus the effective tax rate on corporate profit (UTK).

$$CK(t) = IPK(t)\left(\frac{RA(t) + DE}{1 - UTK(t)}\right). \tag{7.22}$$

7.13. Gross domestic investment in plant and equipment

Gross domestic investment in plant and equipment (GIM) is equal to net domestic investment in plant and equipment plus replacement investment in plant and equipment (REP):

$$GIM(t) = IM(t) + REP(t). \tag{7.23}$$

7.14. Replacement investment in plant and equipment

Investment in plant and equipment for replacement in the sector producing commodities is a proportion of the stock of machinery and equipment (KC) where the proportionality factor is assumed equal to 0.035:

$$REP(t) = 0.035 \, KC(t). \tag{7.24}$$

7.15. Capital stock of plant and equipment

The capital stock in plant and equipment in the sector producing commodities at the beginning of the year t is equal to the capital stock in plant and equipment at the beginning of the year $(t-1)$ plus the net investment in plant and equipment in that sector in the year $(t-1)$:

$$KC(t) = KC(t-1) + IM(t-1). \tag{7.25}$$

7.16. Change in inventories

We will assume that the desired level of inventories $[E^*(t)]$ is a linear function of the expected sales and the opportunity cost of holding inventories. Similarly, we assume that expected sales are proportional to a distributed lag in real gross domestic product and that the opportunity cost of holding inventories can be measured by the real rate of profit.

Our inventory model is

$$E^*(t) = \alpha_0 + \alpha_1 \sum_i w_i Q(t-i) + \alpha_2 RA(t) . \tag{7.26}$$

In addition, we will also assume that the actual level of inventories adjusts towards the desired level following a Cagan–Nerlove partial adjustment model with a response parameter of δ.

Based on the above, we have the following relation between the actual and the desired level of inventories:

$$E(t) - E(t-1) = \delta \left[E^*(t) - E(t-1) \right] . \tag{7.27}$$

From (7.26) and (7.27), we obtain

$$DEE(t) = \delta \alpha_0 + \delta \alpha_1 \Sigma w_\tau Q(t-\tau) + \delta \alpha_2 RA(t) - \delta E(t-1), \tag{7.28}$$

where $DEE(t)$ is the change in inventories.

We cannot estimate eq. (7.28) because we do not have a series for $E(t-1)$. Consequently, we proceed to estimate (7.28) excluding $E(t-1)$ and this, of course, will yield biased coefficients for the variables $\Sigma w_\tau Q(t-\tau)$ and $RA(t)$.

From Theil's specification error theorem, we can expect an upward bias in the coefficient of $\Sigma w_\tau Q(t-\tau)$ and a downward bias in the coefficient of $RA(t)$ [3].

In the estimation the values of w_τ were restricted to those on a second-degree polynomial. Furthermore, the annual characteristic of the model necessitates the use of only one lagged value for $Q(t)$.

Estimating (7.28) by ordinary least squares, yielded

---

[3] This is so because a regression of $E(t-1)$ against $\Sigma w_\tau Q(t-\tau)$ and $RA(t)$ should yield a positive coefficient for the first variable and a negative coefficient for the second.

$$DEE(t) = -893.4 + 0.584\ Q(t) - 0.528\ Q(t-1) \qquad (7.29)$$
$$(-5.498) \quad (5.286) \qquad (-4.645)$$

$$-2360.0\ RA(t).$$
$$(-1.490)$$

$$\hat{\rho} = -0.752 \qquad R^2 = 0.85 \qquad \text{years: } 1961-1970$$

7.17. Total imports

In general, one would expect that the different components of imports could be explained by different economic variables. Therefore, we will divide imports into four groups: imports of raw materials (HI), imports of consumption goods (HC), imports of capital goods (HKM) and imports of services and others (HS).

Algebraically, we have

$$H(t) = HI(t) + HC(t) + HKM(t) + HS(t)\ . \qquad (7.30)$$

In an economy where there are given quantitative restrictions on trade in commodities and services, one would expect, in general, that the flow of trade for the various types of goods would be determined by aggregate demand (expenditures in gross domestic product, consumption, investment) and by relative prices.

Chile, during the last 20 years, has undergone major changes in the quantitative controls placed on imports. In general, the whole period has been characterized by movements back and forth between quantitative controls (via quotas and prohibitions) and price controls (via devaluations and tariffs). It is these 'structural changes' that make the specification of stable import equations difficult.

In our model, the impact of devaluations and tariffs are captured through the price variable which is expressed in domestic currency inclusive of tariffs. To capture the impact of quotas and prohibitions, we will use an index built by Ffrench-Davis (1971) in which he tries to capture the restrictions to trade of the different trade regulations. The index that we will use is the reciprocal of an index that orders the restrictions to trade in a scale from one to ten, increasing with the relaxation of restrictions. Ffrench-Davis himself added one hundred to this index before using it. Furthermore, to account for the substantial increase in imports in the last quarter of 1970, connected with the change in administration, we will include a dummy variable that takes a value of one in 1970 and zero elsewhere.

7.18. Imports of raw materials

It is assumed that imports of raw materials are a linear function of gross domestic product of commodities and of the relative prices of imported raw materials in domestic currency (*RPI*). (In all of the imports equations, the adjective 'relative' refers to the implicit deflator of gross domestic product of commodities.)

This equation is derived by assuming some kind of linear technology for the import of raw materials with respect to the level of production. The coefficients are affected by the relative prices of this type of import. In the Chilean case, we would expect the price variable to reflect only substitution on the technological side (among labor, capital and raw materials) where raw materials that are not competitive with domestic production are involved. For competitive raw materials, we would expect the price variable to be more important since it would reflect technological substitution and demand substitution[4].

In Chile, most raw materials are non-competitive, and so we would expect the price variable to indicate mainly substitution on the technological side.

Estimating the regression, excluding the change in quantitative controls, we have

$$HI(t) = 48.3 + 0.143 \, QC(t) - 260.7 \, RPI(t) + 147.3 \, sa(t) .$$
$$(0.082) \quad (4.481) \quad (-1.009) \quad (1.220)$$
$$(7.31)$$

$$\hat{\rho} = 0.736 \qquad DW = 1.82 \qquad \text{years: } 1952-1970$$

[4] In the estimation of all the import equations, we treat relative price variables as endogenous.

Outside equation instruments: $XC(t)$, $XC(t-1)$, $G(t)$, $G(t-1)$.

Including the quantitative restrictions, we obtain the equation

$$HI(t) = \underset{(0.321)}{133.3} + \underset{(5.499)}{0.144\ QC(t)} - \underset{(-1.812)}{273.6\ RPI(t)}$$

$$\underset{(-1.396)}{-444.6\ FDV(t)} + \underset{(1.253)}{137.5\ sa(t)}\ . \qquad (7.32)$$

$\hat{\rho} = 0.338$ $\qquad$ $DW = 1.75$ $\qquad$ years: 1953–1970

Outside equation instruments: $XC(t)$, $XC(t-1)$, $G(t)$, $G(t-1)$.

$FDV(t)$ is the liberalization of trade variable, and $sa(t)$ is the dummy variable, equal to unity in 1970 and zero otherwise.

Comparing eqs. (7.31) and (7.32), we see that the coefficient of $QC(t)$ is very similar for both equations. This marginal coefficient of 0.144 compares very well with the average coefficient of 18.6% obtained from the 1962 input–output matrix (ODEPLAN).

As a result of the inclusion of the trade liberalization variable in the regression, the estimated asymptotic standard error of the coefficient of the price variable decreased. Therefore we have some evidence to show that this is a better specification of the equation. The low t-ratio for the trade liberalization variable is due to the fact that restrictions to trade in raw materials are less strong than restriction to trade in consumption and capital goods.

The operation of the import system in Chile is characterized, on the average, by a lag of six months between the approval of an application for imported commodities and their entry into the country. Unfortunately, we cannot verify this lag on the basis of annual data. However, this may be partially explained by a shorter-than-average lag in the approval of applications for imports of raw materials.

7.19. Imports of consumption goods

Assuming that imports of consumption goods are a linear function of personal consumption and the relative prices [5] (in domestic currency) of imported consumption goods (*RPC*), we estimated the equations that appear in table 7.1.

Examining the results of table 7.1, we find no evidence, judging by the value of the *t*-statistics for the different variables, of a lag in the response of imports of consumption goods to the level of consumption, relative prices and quantitative controls. As we pointed out in the last section, there should be a lag with two components. First, there is a lag associated with the approval of applications for imports by the Central Bank (this is a variable lag that depends on the discretion of the Central Bank). Second, there is a lag that begins with the confirmation of the approval to import and terminates when the imported goods enter the country. (This is a more stable lag and is primarily determined by the amount of time required to transport the goods to the country.)

Where consumption goods are involved, one would expect the first lag to be longer than the first lag where raw materials are involved. Unfortunately, these lags were not revealed by our annual data.

7.20. Imports of capital goods

Here, we will assume that the imports of capital goods are a linear function of gross investment in plant and equipment and the relative price of imported capital goods in domestic currency (*RPK*). This last variable enters through substitution in the production process between capital, labor and raw materials. We do not expect substitution on the demand side because imported capital goods do not have substitutes in the domestic economy. The results of the various equations estimated appear in table 7.2.

Examining table 7.2 reveals that eq. (7.39) is clearly 'the best'

---

[5] The role of relative prices enters via substitution on the demand side between imported and domestically produced consumption goods.

TABLE 7.1
Imports of consumption goods.

Equation	Constant	CP(t)	CP(t-1)	RPC(t)	RPC(t-1)	FDV(t)	sa(t)	FDV(t-1)	T	DW	$\hat{\rho}$	R^2
(7.33)	-31.3 (-0.116)	0.045 (3.543)		-183.7 (-1.187)			125.3 (2.079)		18	1.76	0.552	
(7.34)	124.4 (0.763)	0.033 (5.036)		-176.6 (-1.284)		-379.8 (-3.025)	217.2 (3.876)		18	1.97	-0.061	
(7.35)	60.74 (0.358)		0.036 (4.474)		-88.643 (-0.948)		222.9 (3.338)	-244.0 (-2.200)	18	2.01		0.907

Note: Eqs. (7.33) and (7.34) have outside equation instruments of $XC(t)$, $XC(t-1)$, $G(t)$ and $G(t-1)$. Eq. (7.35) was estimated by ordinary least squares because the right-hand side of the equation contains only predetermination variables.

TABLE 7.2
Imports of capital goods.

Equation	Constant	GIM(t)	GIM(t-1)	RPK(t)	RPK(t-1)	FDV(t)	sa(t)	FDV(t-1)	T	DW	$\hat{\rho}$	R^2
(7.36)	514.1 (0.759)	0.318 (2.479)		-539.6 (-1.038)			-23.09 (-0.155)		19	1.56	0.586	
(7.37)	-366.3 (-1.056)	0.420 (3.762)		93.55 (0.488)		-300.4 (-1.219)	-15.91 (-0.163)		17	1.96	0.725	
(7.38)	487.9 (2.175)		0.228 (3.553)		-214.6 (-1.607)		111.5 (118.3)	-576.3 (-2.789)	17	1.98	0.319	0.872

Note: In eqs. (7.36) and (7.37), the outside equation instruments were $XC(t)$, $XC(t-1)$, $G(t)$ and $G(t-1)$. Eq. (7.38) was estimated by ordinary least squares (see note in table 7.1).

in terms of the t-statistics. These results strongly support a lag in the response of imported capital goods to prices, investment and the relaxation of quantitative controls.

The low marginal import coefficient (0.228) in eq. (7.39) confirms the fact that, although Chile lacks a heavy capital goods industry, investment requires (in addition to imported capital goods) the concurrence of domestic inputs; namely, the labor cost associated with the installation of the capital goods and the domestic input consumed in the installation (cement, steel, etc.).

This result also shows that imported capital goods are far more sensitive to quantitative controls than consumption goods or raw materials. This is logical because imported capital goods can easily be postponed in the short run.

Furthermore, the results show that imports of capital goods respond to their determinant variables with a lag of a year.

CHAPTER 8

PRICES AND WAGES

In this chapter, we will draw heavily on the extensive developments of ch. 3 concerning prices and wages in the industrial sector.
Equations will be developed here for the price of commodities,
price of services, cost of living, wages in the commodity sector,
and wages in the service sector.

8.1. Price of commodities

As in ch. 3, it will be assumed that, while the rate of change in
commodity prices $P\dot{C}(t)/PC(t)$ is a linear function of both the rate
of change in unit labor cost $UL\dot{C}C(t)/ULCC(t)$ and the rate of
change in the price of imported raw materials $P\dot{R}M(t)/PRM(t)$, the
expression will also include a non-linear term $1/[g-CUC(t)]$ for
capacity utilization. In the last expression, g is a parameter to be
estimated.

$$CUC(t) = \frac{QCF(t)}{QCFE(t)},$$

where $QCF(t)$ is the estimated level of output derived from the
production function when the actual level of employment and the
actual level of capital stock were employed, and $QCFE(t)$ is the
estimated level of output derived from the production function
when unemployment was assumed to be 3% and the stock of
capital was assumed to be fully employed.

Specifically, we have

$$\frac{\dot{PC}(t)}{PC(t)} = \alpha_0 + \alpha_1 \frac{U\dot{L}CC(t)}{ULCC(t)} + \alpha_2 \frac{\dot{PRM}(t)}{PRM(t)} + \alpha_3 \frac{1}{g-CUC(t)} . \qquad (8.1)$$

In the estimation of (8.1), we have available only 10 observations for $U\dot{L}CC(t)/ULCC(t)$ and $CUC(t)$. As discussed in ch. 3, we expect *a priori* that $\alpha_1 + \alpha_2 = 1$. Therefore, in order to gain one additional degree of freedom, we will impose this restriction on the coefficients of (8.1).

Upon estimating this equation with the restriction that $\alpha_1 + \alpha_2 = 1.0$, we get the following results for the minimum value of the residual sum of squares:

$$\frac{\dot{PC}(t)}{PC(t)} = \frac{-0.028}{(-2.009)} + \frac{0.767}{(23.678)} \frac{U\dot{L}CC(t)}{ULCC(t)} + \frac{0.233}{(7.766)} \frac{\dot{PRM}(t)}{PRM(t)} \qquad (8.2)$$

$$+ \frac{0.0023}{(3.205)} \frac{1}{(0.82-CUC(t))} .$$

$\hat{\rho} = 1.0 \qquad DW = 2.91 \qquad \text{years: } 1963-1970$

Outside equation instruments: $\dfrac{\dot{LPR}(t)}{LPR(t)}, G(t).$

If we compare eq. (8.2) with eq. (3.21) i.v.', we can see that the coefficient of the imported raw materials variable is substantially lower in the first equation (obviously the contrary occurs for the coefficient of the labor cost variable). This result can be explained by the difference in the cost structure of the industrial sector as compared to the commodity sector. In fact, the industrial sector's share of imports in total cost — exclusive of domestic raw materials — is 18.8%, while the corresponding share is only 9.6% for the rest of the commodity sector. For the commodity sector as a whole, this share is 14.3% [1].

---

[1] These coefficients were computed using the Chile, ODEPLAN, 'Cuadro de transacciónes intersectotiales para la economía Chilena, 1962'.

From (8.2) we find that demand pressures disappear when $CUC(t)$ stays at a constant value given by $-0.028 + 0.0023 \times [1/0.82 - CUC(t)] = 0$. The value for $CUC(t)$ that we obtained was 0.738; and this looks very reasonable if we compare it with the average of the capacity utilization variable which was 0.743 for the period used in the estimation.

The most important conclusion to be drawn from (8.2) is that labor costs play a substantial role in the determination of prices and this role is more important in the sector producing commodities than in the industrial sector alone.

8.2. Price of services

In the specification of the price equation for the sector producing services, we will exclude demand pressures on existing capacity as an independent variable. This assumption is in accordance with the assumption that was made in ch. 6; namely, that the output of services is entirely determined by demand.

In the case of the services sector (commercial services, government services, personal services and owner-occupied houses), one would expect labor costs to be the most important component in determining price, and this is clearly so for government services but holds to a lesser extent for commercial and personal services.

When the prices of services equation was estimated, restricting the sum of the coefficients of the cost variables to unity, we obtained the following results:

$$\frac{\dot{PS}(t)}{PS(t)} = \frac{-0.023}{(-1.728)} + \frac{0.846}{(11.409)} \frac{\dot{ULCS}(t)}{ULCS(t)} + \frac{0.154}{(2.078)} \frac{\dot{PRM}(t)}{PRM(t)}. \quad (8.3)$$

$\hat{\rho} = -0.076$ $\qquad$ $DW = 2.21$ $\qquad$ years: 1963–1970

Outside equation instruments: $\dfrac{\dot{LPR}(t)}{LPR(t)}, \dfrac{\dot{LPR}(t-1)}{LPR(t-1)}$.

$\dot{PS}(t)/PS(t)$ is the annual rate of change in the price of services, and $\dot{ULCS}(t)/ULCS(t)$ is the annual rate of change in the unit labor cost of the sector producing services.

Comparing the coefficients of the unit labor cost variable in equations (8.2) and (8.3), we find that the unit labor cost coefficient is higher in the last equation, which is as expected *a priori.*

8.3. Cost of living

The only price that remains is the cost of living. To close our system, we will assume that the rate of change in the cost of living is a linear function of the rates of change in the price of commodities and in the price of services. Although this equation can be considered as a weighting procedure between two components of a price model, it may be interpreted as a structural equation of the mark-up type with a specification error because we are leaving out the non-available unit cost of labor in the retail industry. Here we consider the first interpretation and therefore the equation is estimated by ordinary least squares.

Upon estimating the equation using ordinary least squares, the following results were obtained:

$$\frac{\dot{P}(t)}{P(t)} = \frac{0.120}{(1.355)} + \frac{0.688}{(3.469)} \frac{\dot{PC}(t)}{PC(t)} + \frac{0.489}{(1.507)} \frac{\dot{PS}(t)}{PS(t)}. \tag{8.4}$$

$$\hat{\rho} = 0.511 \qquad DW = 2.87 \qquad \text{years: } 1963-1970$$

8.4. Wages in the commodity sector

Following the developments of ch. 3, we will assume some type of Phillips curve for the behavior of wages in the commodity sector.

We will start our study of the wage equation by testing the hypothesis that the rate of change in the wage rate is a linear function of the reciprocal of the unemployment rate and of the rate of change in the cost of living index. When an equation was estimated according to this specification, the following results were obtained:

$$\frac{W\dot{R}C(t)}{WRC(t)} = \frac{0.075}{(0.561)} + \frac{0.013}{(1.292)} \frac{1}{UC(t)} + \frac{0.614}{(3.455)} \frac{\dot{P}(t)}{P(t)}. \qquad (8.5)$$

$\hat{\rho} = 0.587 \qquad DW = 2.02 \qquad \text{years: } 1963-1970$

Outside equation instruments: $G(t), \dfrac{P\dot{R}M(t-1)}{PRM(t-1)}$.

Eq. (8.5) would be sufficient except that policy programs during 1965–1967 led to certain effects that have not been accounted for. Therefore, we will digress momentarily to consider this point.

The blame for the failure of the stabilization intent during the Frei administration is placed usually on the behavior of wage-earners. It is said that wage-earners did not wish to accept an increase in real wages closest to the increase in labor productivity.

Hence, we find in the writings of economists, who were working for the government during the Frei administration, various statements concerning the 1965–1967 period, such as the following (Ffrench-Davis, 1971, pp. 48 and 49):

> 'Despite the apparently generalized successful results, actual outcome differed from what was planned in one major respect – a substantial divergence between programmed and effective wage increases.'

> 'The wages of organized workers (which includes both public and private-sector workers) increased substantially over the official or programmed increases in all three years. But the average for the private sector also substantially exceeded the targets.'

To take care of these increases in the aggressiveness of trade unions, we added a dummy variable to the coefficient of the cost of living variable in the wage equation. The dummy variable $[dw(t)]$ took on a value of 1.0 from 1965 onwards. However, the direct estimation of this equation presents a problem. Estimating the equation by Fair's method, with correction for autocorrelation in the error term, leaves only two observations before 1965; and as a result, a strong collinearity develops in the sample between $\dot{P}(t)/P(t)$ and $[\dot{P}(t)/P(t)]dw(t)$. It was decided that it would be more important to take into account the change in the coefficient of the cost of living variable than to correct for autocorrelation in the error terms, and so the equation was estimated directly using instrumental variables without correcting for autocorrelation. By so doing, two additional observations were gained for the period before 1965.

The equation finally estimated was

$$\frac{W\dot{R}C(t)}{WRC(t)} = \frac{0.005}{(0.077)} + \frac{0.0057}{(1.245)} \frac{1}{UC(t)} + \frac{0.787}{(11.381)} \frac{\dot{P}(t)}{P(t)}$$

$$+ \frac{0.405}{(6.418)} dw(t) \frac{\dot{P}(t)}{P(t)}. \qquad\qquad (8.6)$$

$DW = 1.79$ years: 1961—1970

Instruments:

$$\frac{P\dot{R}M(t)}{PRM(t)} dw(t), \quad \frac{L\dot{P}R(t)}{LPR(t)} dw(t), \quad \frac{P\dot{R}M(t)}{PRM(t)}, \quad \frac{P\dot{R}M(t-1)}{PRM(t-1)},$$

$$\frac{L\dot{P}R(t)}{LPR(t)}, \quad G(t), \quad \frac{1}{UC(t-1)}, \quad C.$$

We now find that the coefficient of the unemployment variable is lower but the coefficient of the cost of living variable has increased substantially. Furthermore, the coefficient of the dummy variable has the correct sign. Thus, our results imply that, from 1965 onwards, the increase in wages was higher than the change in the cost of living. This result is apparently in contradiction with the one in ch. 3 and can be explained by the different composition of the sectors considered. The commodity sector included, in addition to the industrial sector, agriculture, transportation, mining and construction sectors. Since the last two sectors had substantial increases in wage rates during the 1965—1970 period, this could explain the differing wage equations.

Before concluding, we should note again that, as in ch. 3, we obtain far better results (in terms of *t*-statistics and correct signs) when we consider the cost of living variable without lags.

8.5. Wages in the service sector

In estimating the wage equation for the service sector, we will again begin with an equation in which the rate of change in the wage rate is a linear function of the reciprocal of the unemployment rate in the service sector and of the rate of change in the cost of living index.

The estimated equation under this specification follows:

$$\frac{\dot{WRS}(t)}{WRS(t)} = \frac{0.061}{(0.132)} + \frac{0.0115}{(0.643)} \frac{1}{US(t)} - \frac{0.122}{(-0.175)} \frac{\dot{P}(t)}{P(t)}. \tag{8.7}$$

$$\hat{\rho} = 0.118 \qquad DW = 1.96 \qquad \text{years: } 1963-1970$$

Outside equation instruments: $G(t), \dfrac{\dot{PRM}(t-1)}{PRM(t-1)}$.

Eq. (8.7) does not fare well, since the *t*-values are very small and the coefficient of the cost of living variable enters with the wrong sign.

When we introduce a dummy variable for the period 1965–1970, the results again improve quite substantially. As before, instrumental variables were used to gain two additional observations and to obtain the following results:

$$\frac{\dot{WRS}(t)}{WRS(t)} = \frac{-0.282}{(-0.829)} + \frac{0.0128}{(1.186)} \frac{1}{US(t)} + \frac{0.465}{(1.853)} \frac{\dot{P}(t)}{P(t)}$$

$$+ \frac{0.599}{(2.492)} dw(t) \frac{\dot{P}(t)}{P(t)}. \tag{8.8}$$

$$DW = 1.77 \qquad \text{years: } 1961-1970$$

Instruments: the same as (8.6).

As in (8.6), the increase in the cost of living coefficient is substantial for the period 1965–1970.

CHAPTER 9

GOVERNMENT TAXES AND THE GENERATION OF THE GOVERNMENT DEFICIT

In this chapter, we will pursue the generation of the government deficit in fiscal account. In order to investigate the impact of the government deficit in the generation of the money supply, we need to work with the concept of a government deficit in fiscal account rather than the concept utilizing the national accounts.

There are differences between the fiscal accounts and the national accounts classification of government revenues and expenditures; therefore, some of the variables already defined in previous chapters will appear again with different adjectives.

9.1. Government deficit in the fiscal account

The government deficit in the fiscal account in real terms (De/PT) is equal to the difference between total government expenditures in real terms (J) and government revenues in real terms (T). The last two terms have been taken from the fiscal account.

$$\frac{De(t)}{PT(t)} = J(t) - T(t), \tag{9.1}$$

where $PT(t)$ is the implicit deflator of taxes, and will be defined in ch. 11.

9.2. Decomposition of taxes in the fiscal account

Total real taxes in the current account are equal to: direct taxes to non-copper corporations in the fiscal account (*TNCF*), plus direct taxes to persons in fiscal accounts (*TPF*), plus taxes on imports in fiscal accounts (*TMF*), plus taxes on copper in fiscal accounts (*TCF*), plus other taxes in fiscal accounts (*TRF*) [1].

$$T(t) = TNCF(t) + TPF(t) + TMF(t) + TCF(t) + TRF(t) . \qquad (9.2)$$

9.3. Direct taxes to non-copper corporations in the fiscal account

We will formulate again a model similar to the one used for taxes to persons in national accounts and presented in ch. 7.

Specifically, we will assume that, during the period 1950–1964, taxes in current escudos are a linear function homogeneous of first degree in the previous year's prices and the previous year's corporate profits in current escudos.

$$NTNCF(t) = \alpha_1 P(t-1) + \alpha_2 NPROF(t-1), \qquad (9.3)$$

for $t < 1965$

where $NTNCF(t)$ is the taxes to non-copper corporations in current escudos, $P(t)$ is the cost of living index, and $NPROF(t)$ is the profits of non-copper corporations in current escudos.

For the years 1965–1970, we will keep the specification under (9.3) but we will adjust the tax base by the previous year's inflation and allow for a different constant. Furthermore, we will add a dummy in 1965 to allow for an escalator lower than previous year's inflation on the tax base of that year.

---

[1] Where the price deflators in the same order are: cost of living index, cost of living index, implicit price deflator of imports, implicit price deflator of exports, implicit price deflator of gross domestic product.

So, for the years 1965–1970, we have

$$NTNCF(t) = \alpha_1 P(t-1) + \alpha_2 \frac{NPROF(t-1)P(t-1)}{P(t-2)}$$

$$+ \alpha_3 P(t-1)dv(t), \tag{9.4}$$

for $t \geqslant 1965$

where $dv(t) = 1$ in 1965 and 0 elsewhere.

Dividing both sides of (9.3) and (9.4) by $P(t-1)$, we obtain

$$\left[TNCF \times \frac{P}{P(-1)} \right] = \begin{bmatrix} i_1 & 0 & F_1 \\ i_2 & i_2 & F_2 \end{bmatrix} dv \begin{bmatrix} \alpha'_1 \\ \alpha_1 \\ \alpha_2 \\ \alpha_3 \end{bmatrix} = \alpha'_1 i + \alpha_1 du + \alpha_2 F$$

$$+ \alpha_3 dv(t), \tag{9.5}$$

where

$dv = a(T_1 + T_2) \times 1$ vector with unit value in 1965 and zero elsewhere,

$F_1 = \dfrac{NPROF(-1)}{P(-2)}$ is a vector of order $T_1 \times 1$,

$F_2 = \dfrac{NPROF(-1)}{P(-2)}$ is a vector of order $T_2 \times 1$,

$i_1 = aT_1 \times 1$ vector of unit components,

$i_2 = aT_2 \times 1$ vector of unit components, and

$F = \begin{bmatrix} F_1 \\ F_2 \end{bmatrix}, i = \begin{bmatrix} i_1 \\ i_2 \end{bmatrix}, du = \begin{bmatrix} 0 \\ i_2 \end{bmatrix}.$

Upon estimating (9.5), we obtained the following results:

$$TNCF(t) \frac{P(t)}{P(t-1)} = 71.025 + 0.093\,F(t) - 132.3\,dv(t)$$
$$\phantom{TNCF(t) \frac{P(t)}{P(t-1)} = } (1.861) \quad (5.922) \quad (-3.894)$$
$$+ 60.6\,du(t). \tag{9.6}$$
$$ (1.183)$$

$\hat{\rho} = 0.447 \qquad DW = 1.84 \qquad$ years: 1953–1970

Outside equation instruments: $XC(t)$, $XC(t-1)$, $G(t)$, $G(t-1)$.

9.4. Direct taxes to persons in the fiscal account

There are only minor differences between this variable and the one considered in ch. 7; consequently, we will utilize the same specification here. The only difference is that here we are forcing the constant to be the same in both periods. We find that we cannot estimate an equation with different constants because there is too much collinearity among the regressors in the sample.

The estimated equation is

$$TPF(t) \times \frac{P(t)}{P(t-1)} = -128.2 + 0.034\ R(t) -171.3\ dv(t).$$
$$\qquad\qquad\qquad (-2.208)\quad (10.160)\quad (-4.768)\quad\quad (9.7)$$

$\hat{\rho} = 0.609$ $\qquad\qquad$ $DW = 1.73$ $\qquad\qquad$ years: 1953–1970
Outside equation instruments: $XC(t)$, $XC(t-1)$, $G(t)$, $G(t-1)$.

If we compare eq. (7.15) from ch. 7 with eq. (9.7), we can appreciate the close agreement of the results, which is as it should be.

9.5. Taxes on imports in the fiscal account

Most of the taxes on imports are *ad valorem* taxes levied with differential rates and depend closely on the type of imported goods (raw materials, consumption goods, capital goods). Therefore, from a specification viewpoint, it would be more convenient to have taxes classified by the type of good taxed; unfortunately, this information is not available, and so we have to work with aggregate data.

In the specification of the taxes on import equations, we will assume that taxes on imports, in current escudos, are a linear function homogeneous of first degree in the implicit deflator of imports (PM) and the value of imports in current escudos (NH).

Estimating this equation in real terms, yielded

$$TMF(t) = 75.7 + 0.139\ H(t). \qquad (9.8)$$
$$(1.028)\quad (4.602)$$

$\hat{\rho} = 0.513$ $\qquad$ $DW = 1.54$ $\qquad$ years: 1952–1970

Outside equation instruments: $XC(t)$, $XC(t-1)$, $G(t)$, $G(t-1)$.

From 1964 on, the imports made by the public sector were excluded from import taxes; therefore, we would expect that the marginal tax rate on the total value of import to be substantially lower for the period 1964–1970. To take care of this 'institutional change' we add a dummy variable to the coefficient of total imports.

When we estimate the taxes on imports equation with this change in the specification, we obtain the result

$$TMF(t) = -105.3 + 0.265\ H(t)\ -0.079\ H(t)d_m(t), \qquad (9.9)$$
$$(-1.887)\quad (8.149)\quad\ (-4.549)$$

where $d_m(t)$ is a dummy variable (equal to 1 for $t \geqslant 1964$ and zero otherwise).

$\hat{\rho} = 0.343$ $\qquad$ $DW = 2.11$ $\qquad$ years: 1952–1970

Outside equation instruments: $XC(t)$, $XC(t-1)$, $G(t)$, $G(t-1)$.

Comparing (9.8) and (9.9) we find that, besides any cost in terms of inefficiencies in resource allocation, the elimination of the import tax decreases the marginal tax rate on imports by 7.9 percentage points. Furthermore, the quality of the equation improved substantially in terms of the t-statistics.

In passing, it is important to note that this is not the only tax on imports; but it is the only tax collected by the treasury. Besides the other import taxes, at various times in the history of the Chilean economy the government also required import deposits which are additional costs to the price of imports [2]. However, this additional cost was taken into account in the definition of the relative price of imports in ch. 7.

---

[2] For a good description of the foreign trade policy of Chile in the period 1952–1970, see Ffrench-Davis (1971, ch. 4).

9.6. Taxes on copper in the fiscal account

Most of the taxes on copper are corporate income taxes and therefore we should attempt to specify them as a function of the profits in the copper industry. Unfortunately, we do not have information for this variable and so we must work with exports of copper
as a proxy for profits.

Taxation on copper has almost always been based on the principle of giving an incentive to its production. The incentive usually
takes the form of marginal tax rates lower than the average. The
problem we face is that the system of taxation has changed a
number of times in our sampling period. As an average behavior,
we will assume that the unit tax on copper (per unit of export of
copper) is a linearly decreasing function of the export of copper,
i.e.

$$\frac{TCF(t)}{XC(t)} = \beta_0 + \beta_1 XC(t) \quad \text{with } \beta_1 < 0 . \tag{9.10}$$

At the beginning of the Frei government, there were major
changes in the treatment of the copper industry that culminated in
Chile being brought in as a partner in the previously foreign-owned
copper companies. In order to incorporate the higher tax revenues
generated by the copper industry as a result of this institutional
change, we introduce a dummy variable in (9.10).

Estimating our final equation with *TCF* as the dependent variable, we have

$$TCF(t) = \underset{(3.965)}{0.326\ XC(t)} - \underset{(-0.717)}{0.00005\ XC^2(t)} + \underset{(2.937)}{0.091\ d_c(t)\ XC(t)} ,$$

$$\tag{9.11}$$

$DW = 1.72 \qquad \text{years: } 1951-1970$

where $d_c(t)$ is a dummy variable (equal to one for $t \geqslant 1965$ and
zero otherwise).

In (9.11), all the right-hand-side variables are exogenous; therefore, the equation was estimated by ordinary least squares. Analyz-

ing the residuals from this equation, it is clear that the equation is not too good. We will return to it in ch. 12.

9.7. Other taxes in the fiscal account

This item includes: indirect taxes, property taxes and other taxes. The indirect taxes are mainly sales taxes; therefore, we will assume that they are closely related to the level of sales measured by gross domestic product. Unfortunately, we do not have a measure of the value of the property subject to taxation. To close our model, we will assume that the property taxes and other taxes are also related to the gross domestic product.

Specifically, we assume that nominal taxes in this category are a linear function, homogeneous of first degree in the implicit price deflator of expenditures in gross domestic product and the nominal value of gross domestic product.

The estimated function is

$$TRF(t) = -997.5 + 0.158\ Q(t)\ . \qquad (9.12)$$
$$(-2.552)\quad (7.204)$$

$\hat{\rho} = 0.711 \qquad\qquad DW = 1.74 \qquad\qquad$ years: 1952–1970

Outside equation instruments: $XC(t)$, $XC(t-1)$, $G(t)$, $G(t-1)$.

CHAPTER 10

THE MONETARY SECTOR

One of the most interesting theoretical problems facing an economy without a well developed financial market is that of connecting the real sector to the monetary sector. As we saw in ch. 2, most studies of Chilean inflation do not investigate the explicit connection between the monetary and real sectors of the economy. In fact, most of these authors assume that commodity prices respond instantaneously to clear the money market (see Deaver, 1961) or that commodity prices adjust, according to a certain distributed lag, to changes in the money supply (see Harberger, 1963, Behrman, 1970) but none of them presents the mechanism by which the two sets of variables interact.

This chapter is divided into two parts. In the first, we will study the demand for money and devote a considerable amount of time to investigating the alternative specifications of this function. In the remaining part, we will study the generation of the money supply within a reduced form model of a simplified monetary system.

10.1. Demand for money

On the demand side it will be assumed that, in an economy with a high rate of inflation, money is clearly dominated in the portfolio by other assets. Therefore, we assume that the principal role of money is to function as a medium of exchange and as a temporal means of holding reserves in between income payments.

In the specification that follows, we will use the Neo-Fisherian hypothesis of B. Friedman (1968). The Neo-Fisherian hypothesis assumes that there is a desired demand for money which is a function of the level of economic activity (measured by gross domestic product) and the opportunity cost of holding money.

The usual way of measuring the opportunity cost of holding money, in an economy with a high inflation, has been through the expected rate of inflation. This last variable has traditionally been defined as some weighted average of the present and past inflation rates [1]. In this approach, given the level of output from the effective demand side, the only role that the money market process plays is to determine the rate of inflation (Johnson, 1967). In our work, we assume that prices are determined by a kind of mark-up equation (with demand pressures affecting the mark-up coefficient). In addition to the expected rate of inflation, we include the expected real rate of interest as a component of the cost of holding money and in this way we obtain an additional connection between the real and monetary sectors of our model.

The properties of an estimator of expected prices that follows the Cagan–Nerlove adjusting expectational model were studied by Muth (1960). Interpreting Muth's results in terms of a model that forms expectations on the basis of the rate of inflation, he proved that if we assume:

(1) actual inflation (P_t) is equal to expected inflation (P^*_t) plus a random error (η_t), where η_t is independently distributed with zero mean and a variance of σ^2_η;

(2) expected inflation is defined by

$$P^*_t = P^*_{t-1} + \epsilon_t,$$

where the ϵ_t is a random variable with zero mean and a variance of σ^2_ϵ;

(3) η_t is independent of ϵ_t (this, however, is not an essential assumption);

---

[1] This way of measuring the expected rate of inflation was first rationalized in an adjusting expectation model by Cagan (1956). In Chile, this approach has been used by Deaver (1961); Cortes and Tapia (1970, pp. 51–100); Ffrench-Davis (1971, pp. 328–336).

then $\Sigma_{i=1}^{\infty} \lambda(1-\lambda)^i P_{t-i}$ is the optimal predictor of $P*_t$. This predictor is optimal in the sense that it minimizes the error variance defined as $V = E[P_t - P*_t]^2$ where E is the expected value operator.

In view of this result, it becomes necessary to investigate the second condition of Muth's theorem. For periods in which inflation is either accelerating or decelerating, it becomes difficult to justify the naive hypothesis that next year's expected inflation will be equal to this year's expected inflation plus a random error with zero expected value and a constant variance. Furthermore, during periods of acceleration or deceleration in the rate of inflation, any average of past inflation will be a very poor prediction of actual inflation, even if we include current inflation.

With these considerations in mind, the expected rates of inflation employed in various studies of the demand for money in Chile were computed and compared with the actual rates of inflation. Others have devised various schemes for predicting expected inflation, of which the more notable are the following:

(1) Deaver (1961, p. 26) employed the following 'arbitrary' weighting pattern, starting with the current rate of inflation:

$$\frac{64}{63} \frac{1}{2}, \frac{64}{63} \frac{1}{4}, \frac{64}{63} \frac{1}{8}, \frac{64}{63} \frac{1}{16}, \frac{64}{63} \frac{1}{32}, \frac{64}{63} \frac{1}{64}.$$

(2) Ffrench-Davis (1971, p. 330) used 'arbitrary' weights of (0.35, 0.35, 0.20, 0.10) and also started with the current rate of inflation.

(3) Cortes and Tapia (1970, pp. 74 and 85) interpreted their results as coming from a Cagan–Nerlove adjusting expectational model with an adjustment parameter of 0.158 in one case and 0.134 in another.

Table 10.1 presents the expected rates of inflation generated from the studies and the actual rates of inflation. The results strongly support our contention that, for economies with important swings in the rate of inflation, a prediction obtained by use of a weighted average of past inflation will be a very poor one. From table 10.1, we find that the r.m.s. errors were over 25% of the

TABLE 10.1

	Actual inflation (1)	Ffrench-Davis expected inflation	Deaver expected inflation	Cortes–Tapia expected inflation I (adjusting parameter 0.158)	Cortes–Tapia expected inflation II (adjusting parameter 0.134)
1950	0.1672	0.1935	0.1830	0.1281	0.1156
1951	0.2230	0.1921	0.2041	0.1375	0.1243
1952	0.2159	0.2058	0.2104	0.1457	0.1322
1953	0.2616	0.2284	0.2354	0.1565	0.1418
1954	0.5624	0.3539	0.4019	0.2048	0.1818
1955	0.7629	0.5377	0.5870	0.2845	0.2509
1956	0.6584	0.6361	0.6266	0.3347	0.2963
1957	0.2871	0.5397	0.4573	0.3192	0.2869
1958	0.2593	0.3992	0.3587	0.2992	0.2723
1959	0.3860	0.3491	0.3733	0.3027	0.2769
1960	0.1162	0.2563	0.2412	0.2608	0.2426
1961	0.0769	0.1707	0.1536	0.2051	0.1929
1962	0.1387	0.1373	0.1420	0.1584	0.1483
1963	0.4428	0.2305	0.2037	0.1721	0.1555
1964	0.4596	0.3513	0.3782	0.2040	0.1822
1965	0.2884	0.3642	0.3325	0.2050	0.1837
1966	0.2287	0.3172	0.2815	0.1904	0.1709
1967	0.1814	0.2417	0.2323	0.1835	0.1666
1968	0.2664	0.2313	0.2503	0.1929	0.1762
1969	0.3035	0.2586	0.2758	0.2038	0.1865
1970	0.3280	0.2924	0.3009	0.2025	0.1838
Root mean square error		0.1175	0.0866	0.1841	0.1988
r^2		0.7329	0.8782	0.4670	0.4213
Theil's inequality coefficient		0.1694	0.1248	0.3167	0.3549
Fraction of error due to:					
(a) bias		0.0024	0.0027	0.3015	0.3719
(b) difference of regression coefficient from unity		0.0002	0.0900	0.0121	0.0089
(c) residual variance		0.9974	0.9073	0.6865	0.6192

mean of the inflation rate. The quality of the predictions would have been better if a higher weight was given to the current inflation. This evidence, however, does not answer the question of how expectations regarding price changes are formed; but it does throw some doubt on the use of procedures which take expected inflation as a weighted average of past inflation, in countries where major changes in economic policy cause the rate of inflation to follow a cyclical behavior[2] .

It is only natural to think that an annual model would include enough information about the present situation so that expected inflation would not be too far from actual inflation. Another measure of expected inflation could also be obtained from nominal wage negotiations of some sector of the economy possessing stable bargaining power.

In our study, we will assume that the expected cost of holding money (whose main component is the expected rate of inflation) is equal to the actual cost of holding money plus a random error component. Specifically, we will assume that $I^*(t) = I(t) [1 + \eta(t)]$, where $I(t)$ is the cost of holding money and $[I(t) \eta(t)]$ is the forecast error which is proportional to the actual cost of holding money. Furthermore, $\ln[1 + \eta(t)]$ is a random error with a constant expected value and a constant variance.

Before continuing, we will pause to discuss how to measure the opportunity cost of holding money. The opportunity cost of holding money is usually defined as having two components: the real interest foregone and the rate of inflation. The real interest foregone is equal to the real yield on the best alternative investment that might have been made. The problem is simple in theory; but in practice there are numerous assets which possess different combinations of yields and risk premiums, and therefore these complicate the problem of distinguishing the alternatives to money holdings. In Chile, the situation is even worse, for it is difficult to pick up the correct real rate of interest. However, we are fortunate that the major component of the opportunity cost of holding money is

---

[2] For an analysis of the different public policies associated with the cyclical behavior of the inflation rate, see Ffrench-Davis (1971).

not the real rate of interest, but the rate of inflation. In our work, we measure the real rate of interest for the business sector by the average real rate of profit after tax. (See appendix B for the definition of this variable.) For the household sector, we assume that only a portion of the households have access to financial assets which yield a real rate of interest (those households connected with the business sector) and that the remainder have as their main alternative to holding money, the storing of commodities which yield a zero real rate of interest (we are neglecting storage costs).

Since recent figures on the distribution of money holdings between businesses and households does not exist, we will employ the distribution estimated by Sunkel (1953) at the beginning of the 50's; namely, that 2/3 of cash balances were owned by firms and that the remaining 1/3 were owned by households. Furthermore, it will be assumed that 10% of the money held by households could also have been invested at the real rate of profit.

10.1.1. The long run demand for money

We will assume that the long run demand for money is given by the function

$$M^*(t) = L[P(t) Q(t), P(t), PO(t), I^e(t)],$$

where $M^*(t)$ = desired demand for nominal money balances, $P(t)$ = price level, $Q(t)$ = real expenditure in gross domestic product, $PO(t)$ = population, and $I^e(t)$ = expected cost of holding money. In addition, we assume that the function L is homogeneous to the first degree in nominal output and prices.

Solving for the desired demand for real money balances yields

$$\frac{M^*(t)}{P(t)} = L[Q(t), 1, PO(t), I^e(t)], \qquad \frac{M^*(t)}{P(t)} = \overline{L}[Q(t), PO(t), I^e(t)].$$

At this point, it is necessary to assume that $\overline{L}$ is homogeneous of degree one in $PO(t)$. On the basis of this assumption, we can now write the desired per capita demand for real money balances as

$$\frac{M^*(t)}{P(t)\,PO(t)} = L^*\left[\frac{Q(t)}{PO(t)}, I^e(t)\right].$$

In the specification of the function L^*, it will be assumed also that the elasticities with respect to both arguments are constant. Thus, the final function is given as

$$\frac{M^*(t)}{P(t)\,N(t)} = \phi_0\left[\frac{Q(t)}{PO(t)}\right]^{\phi_1} [I^e(t)]^{\phi_2}\, e^{u(t)},$$

where $u(t)$ = a random error.

Earlier, we hypothesized $I^e(t) = I(t)\,[1 + \eta(t)]$. Substituting this in the previous equation and taking the natural logs of the demand for money equation, we obtain

$$\ln m^*(t) = \phi_0' + \phi_1 \ln q(t) + \phi_2 \ln I(t) + u'(t),$$

where

$$m^*(t) = \frac{M^*(t)}{P(t)\,PO(t)},$$

$$q(t) = \frac{Q(t)}{PO(t)},$$

$$\phi_0' = \ln \phi_0,$$

$$u'(t) = u(t) + \phi_2 \ln (1 + \eta(t)).$$

It is assumed further that $u'(t)$ has an expected value of μ_u and a variance of σ_u^2.

10.1.2. The short run demand for money

The problem that we now face is that $M^*(t)$ is not observable for a market in which there is no instantaneous clearing, as is the case for an economy without a well developed financial market and where price changes are stably related to both cost changes and demand pressures. In this situation, a person who desires to decrease the level of his nominal balances finds that he cannot obtain the commodities or financial assets necessary to do so. However, instead of prices increasing instantaneously to clear the money market (the demand pressures do not transform themselves to higher prices), initially the length of the queues and/or the level of inventories increase. We will approximate this lag in adjustment with a Cagan–Nerlove partial adjustment mechanism (Cagan, 1956, p. 33). Therefore, we have

$$\ln m(t) - \ln m(t-1) = \gamma(\ln m^*(t) - \ln m(t-1)) \; .$$

It is important to note that $m(t)$ in our model is an endogenous variable, so the question of how $m^*(t)$ adjusts to a change in $m(t)$ is meaningless because both are endogenous variables. Therefore, the critique of Starleof (1970) concerning the incorrect implications of demand responses to changes in the supply does not apply to this specification.

Introducing the long run demand for money into this last expression, we obtain

$$\ln m(t) = \phi_0' \gamma + \phi_1 \gamma \ln q(t) + \phi_2 \gamma \ln I(t) + (1-\gamma) \ln m(t-1)$$

$$+ \gamma \, u'(t) \; .$$

Upon estimating this equation by employing the technique of instrumental variables, the equations found in table 10.2 were obtained.

One of the results (eq. 10.1) which deserves special attention is the high elasticity of the demand for real balances per capita with respect to real expenditures in gross domestic product per capita (1.451 in the short run and 3.134 in the long run). A possible explanation for this high elasticity is that with the increase in the level of income per capita there has simultaneously been a change in the structure of output in favor of sectors that are more monetarized. (This occurred mainly through the decrease in agricul-

TABLE 10.2

Equation	Constant (1)	$\ln q(t)$ (2)	$\ln I(t)$ (3)	$SHA(t)$ (4)	$d(t)$ (5)	$\ln m(t-1)$ (6)	SS_e (7)	$\hat{\rho}$ (8)	DW (9)	T (10)
10.1	-8.723 (-2.669)	1.451 (2.705)	-0.087 (-1.703)			0.537 (2.417)	0.0587	0.645	1.786	16
10.2	-3.766 (-0.758)	0.735 (1.023)	-0.086 (-1.745)	-0.026 (-0.805)		0.690 (3.114)	0.0564	0.545	1.64	16
10.3	-4.545 (-1.506)	0.861 (1.836)	-0.084 (-2.389)		0.146 (2.894)	0.586 (3.711)	0.0411	0.701	1.36	16
10.4	5.000 (2.114)	-0.453 (-1.483)	-0.082 (-3.504)	-0.045 (-2.671)	0.183 (4.978)	0.768 (9.373)	0.0320	0.039	1.50	16

Note: All of the above equations were estimated by instrumental variables ensuring that the instruments chosen satisfy Fair's criteria. The basis set of instruments used were: C, $\ln q(t-1)$, $\ln q(t-2)$, $\ln m(t-1)$, $\ln m(t-2)$, $\ln I(t-1)$, $\ln I(t-2)$, $\ln I(t-3)$, $\ln gxci(t)$, $\ln gxci(t-1)$, $\ln gxci(t-2)$. In eq. 10.2, we added $SHA(t)$ as an instrument. In eq. 10.3, we added $d(t)$ and in equation 10.4, $SHA(t)$ and $d(t)$.

ture's share of output.) If this were the case, the effect of leaving out the structure of output, i.e. share of agriculture output in total output (*SHA*), in the regression will be to cause an upward bias in the income coefficient. This bias could explain the high income coefficient that was obtained. Furthermore, we would expect that this specification error causes only a minor bias in the coefficients of $\ln I(t)$ and $\ln m(t-1)$, since the regression coefficients of these variables should be nearly zero in a regression with *SHA* as a dependent variable.

When the share of agriculture was included in the regressions, eq. 10.2 in table 2 was obtained. In eq. 10.2 the coefficient of the share of agriculture in gross product has the expected sign but is not significantly different from zero. What is important to note from eq. 10.2 is that now the coefficient of $\ln q(t)$ is reduced to almost half of its original value, and its ratio to the asymptotic standard error is below 2. What is even more important is that the other coefficients (excluding the constant) are fairly stable, in particular the cost elasticity of cash balances. The minor changes in these coefficients confirm our contention that the specification error of eq. 10.1 (table 2) should not substantially affect the coefficients of $\ln I(t)$ and $\ln m(t-1)$.

During 1965, there were some important institutional changes that could have caused a once and for all shift in the demand for money. Ffrench-Davis (1971, p. 142), then a high-ranking official at the Central Bank, stated:

> 'Usually the approach to monetary policy is to estimate the increase in the demand for money and, then, try to manipulate the supply accordingly. In addition to the regulation of the supply of money, the economic authorities of Chile explored and successfully exploited another device: that of a policy-induced positive shift in the demand for money.'

Continuing, he describes the institutional changes (1971, pp. 143 and 144; italics in original).

> 'First, until April, 1965, holders of checking accounts were permitted by the banks to overdraw, whenever they pleased, up to a given amount agreed to by the depositor and the bank. Interest was paid only when the account was actually overdrawn.

Thus, account holders could regard as part of their cash balances the overdraft *authorized* and not utilized. However, the overdraft privileges were not reflected either in deposit or in credit accounts. The amount of such overdrafts was sizeable when the reform was made: they represented over 8 per cent of the current supply of money. In addition, actual overdrafts by "large" enterprises sometimes exceeded the amounts authorized by their banks. (The checks were cashed by the banks for "fear of losing important customers".) The reform in April, 1965, eliminated such overdraft privileges except when the amount did not exceed E° 100. Thereafter an overdraft in an amount larger than E° 100 was to be counted both as an interest-bearing credit and as a deposit for the bank, against which the bank must hold reserves. Simultaneously, checking account holders lost a form of liquidity and had to replenish the loss (up to its new equilibrium point) paying the going cost of credit or whatever the (private) opportunity cost of funds was.'

'Second, until 1964, up to 50 percent of the legal minimum wages of agricultural workers could be paid in kind. Starting in 1965, however, no more than 25 percent could be paid in kind. Thus, this measure forced some additional monetization of the countryside.
'Third, before 1966 an account holder A could write a check in favor of B, B then could deposit the check in his account at a second bank and, because of the regulations of the clearing house, A had until noon of the next day to make a deposit sufficient to balance his account. Starting in March of 1966, it was required that each check must be covered on the day of arrival at the second bank. This measure forced account holders to keep higher cash balances than otherwise.'

To take care of this shift in the demand for money, we will introduce a dummy variable [$d(t)$] that has a value of unity for the period 1965–1970 and zero elsewhere. Thus the dummy variable enters into eq. 10.1 with the expected sign and is significant. Furthermore, a permanent upward shift in the demand for per capita real money balances of 15.8% is implied from 1965 onwards. This estimate is somewhat higher than the Central Bank estimate of 11.7% (Ffrench-Davis, 1971, p. 144). The coefficients of ln $m(t-1)$ and of ln $I(t)$ are fairly stable again and the t-ratio of both increases. The coefficient of income once again decreases (with respect to eq. 10.1) and its t-value decreases slightly. The difficulty encountered in estimating the coefficient of the income variable could be due in part to the characteristics of the sample with which we are working. For the period of analysis, there is not enough variation in the natural log of real output per capita to make it possible to measure its contribution to $\ln m(t)$ accurately. The coefficient of variation of $\ln q(t)$ is only 0.015. Furthermore, $\ln q(t)$ is highly correlated with the dummy variable $r = 0.863$.

Finally, in eq. 10.4, we have added to eq. 10.1 both the dummy variable and the change in output structure. Again, all variables have fairly stable coefficients with the exception of the income variable that now enters with the wrong sign.

Let us now work with a model in which the expected cost of holding money is a geometric distribution of the actual cost of holding money.

In this model, the assumption is that the expectation with respect to the cost of holding money is adjusted following a Cagan–Nerlove mechanism. Specifically, the assumption is

$$I^*(t) - I^*(t-1) = \beta[I(t) - I^*(t-1)] .$$

From the above, we can obtain

$$I^*(t) = \sum_{i=0}^{\infty} \beta(1-\beta)^i I(t-i) .$$

This method of measuring the expected cost of holding money has usually been introduced in a demand for money equation in which the cost elasticity is proportional to the expected cost of holding money.

The model employed which was originally developed by Cagan (1956) and since then has been applied to Chile by a long list of authors (Cortes and Tapia, 1970; Hynes, 1967) is

$$m^*(t) = b_0 (q(t))^{b_1} e^{b_2 I^*(t) + u(t)} .$$

Taking the logs of both sides yields

$$\ln m^*(t) = \ln b_0 + b_1 \ln q(t) + b_2 I^*(t) + u(t) .$$

In this model, the long-run cost elasticity of the demand for money is a variable equal to $b_2 I^*(t)$.

If we substitute in the previous equation the expressions

$$I^*(t) = \sum_{i=0}^{\infty} \beta(1-\beta)^i I(t-1),$$

$$\ln m(t) - \ln m(t-1) = \gamma[\ln m^*(t) - \ln m(t-1)],$$

we obtain

$$\ln m(t) = \beta\gamma \ln b_0 + b_1\gamma \ln q(t) - b_1(1-\beta)\gamma \ln q(t-1)$$

$$+ b_2\beta\gamma I(t) + [(1-\beta) + (1-\gamma)] \ln m(t-1)$$

$$- (1-\beta)(1-\gamma) \ln m(t-2) + \gamma u(t) - (1-\beta)\gamma u(t-1) .$$

This equation is over-identified: we will proceed to its estimation without taking into account the over-identifying restrictions in the parameters and then check the results for these restrictions.

In the regression, a variable will be included also to take care of the change in the structure of output (*SHA*) and a dummy variable to account for the institutional changes that took place in 1965.

The results in table 3 reveal that once again the low variability in $\ln q(t)$ and $\ln q(t-1)$ have created a sticky problem. This low variability makes it impossible to estimate the coefficients of these two variables accurately. However, the coefficients of $\ln m(t-1)$ and $\ln m(t-2)$ in the regressions are informative. The coefficient of $\ln m(t-1)$ has the correct sign and it is fairly stable from regression to regression but the coefficient of $\ln m(t-2)$ is very nearly zero in most of the regressions and its estimated t-ratio is never greater than unity. Furthermore, in one out of the four cases, the latter coefficient fails to have the correct sign. This last evidence casts some doubt on the relevance of the model used. (We also studied the case in which the cost of holding money included only the rate of inflation but the results were similar to the one presented in table 10.3.)

Based on the above results, eq. 10.3 was selected as the demand for money function in the model. Eq. 10.3 implies an average lag

TABLE 10.3

Equation	Constant	$\ln q(t)$	$\ln q(t-1)$	$I(t)$	$SHA(t)$	$d(t)$	$\ln m(t-1)$	$\ln m(t-2)$	SS_e	$\hat{\rho}$	DW
10.5	-8.119 (-2.456)	1.932 (2.090)	-0.548 (-0.588)	-0.101 (-0.505)			0.595 (1.811)	-0.054 (-0.192)	0.064	0.439	1.83
10.6	-1.953 -0.632	1.136 (1.937)	-0.632 (-0.994)	-0.123 (-0.938)		0.151 (2.662)	0.726 (3.144)	-0.095 (-0.482)	0.044	0.436	1.06
10.7	-9.779 (-1.251)	2.627 (1.226)	-1.152 (-0.795)	-0.099 (-0.441)	0.032 (0.513)		0.646 (1.642)	0.013 (0.039)	0.073	0.229	1.91
10.8	5.868 (1.488)	-0.545 (-0.718)	0.029 (0.055)	-0.171 (-1.702)	-0.052 (-2.036)	0.175 (3.795)	0.868 (4.333)	-0.133 (-0.761)	0.036	0.274	1.20

Note: All of the above regressions were run on 15 observations. The same set of instruments listed in table 10.2 were employed here, substituting $\ln I(t)$ for $I(t)$.

in the adjustment of per capita money balance of a little less than one-and-a-half years. This makes sense for an economy with a high cost of holding money and in which there is a high penalty for being outside of equilibrium. The income elasticity of the demand for money from this equation is 0.861 in the short run and 1.86 in the long run. The cost elasticity from this equation is −0.084 in the short run and −0.181 in the long run.

10.2. The supply of money

10.2.1. Introduction[3]

The monetary system in Chile is composed of the Central Bank, the commercial banks and the State Bank.

The Central Bank was created in 1925 and started to operate in January of 1926. The creation of the Central Bank in 1925 was the culmination of a long list of projects drafted between 1913 and 1925, but never approved by Congress. The need for a Central Bank stemmed from increasing public pressures to control the persistent inflation which at that time dated back to 1878, when Chile suspended convertibility.

Curiously enough, the Central Bank was established as a mixed institution. Its capital was subscribed by the government, the national commercial banks, the foreign commercial banks and the general public. Linked to the property structure, the board of directors was composed of 10 members: 3 designated by the President of the Republic; 2 designated by the national commercial banks; 1 by the foreign commercial banks; 1 by the general public; 1 by the private agricultural, mining and industrial development institutes; 1 by the Chamber of Commerce and the Nitrate Corporation; and 1 by the labor unions.

The main functions given to the newly created Central Bank were:

(1) monopoly of the bill issue in the country,
(2) to buy and sell gold and foreign currencies,
(3) to make loans to the Treasury, and
(4) to make loans to the private sector.

[3]This introduction draws heavily from appendix A of Lüders (1968).

The Central Bank was required to have a minimum reserve ratio of 50% against its deposits and bills issued.

Parallel to the creation of the Central Bank, a new banking law was enacted. The main characteristics of this law were as follows.

(1) Paid-in capital and reserves could not be less than 25% of deposits.

(2) The banks were required to hold reserves against their demand deposits (a 20% ratio) and their time deposits (8% ratio).

Another important feature of the organization of the banking system in Chile is that, by special laws, the Central Bank is obligated to rediscount documents to the Treasury. Therefore, the Central Bank is not only the lender of last resource for the Commercial Banks and the State Bank, but also for the Treasury.

The behavior of the money supply in this fractional system will be the main concern of the rest of this chapter.

Now, we will develop a simplified model to explain the behavior of the money supply. Our main interest is to connect the money supply with the high-powered money and the latter with the government deficit.

The specification that follows is conditioned on available information. We do not have data on the composition of reserves (between reserves on demand deposits and reserves on time deposits) and so we are forced to work only with total reserves.

10.2.2. Asset components of the money base

The money base (MB) is composed of the credits from the Central Bank to the Treasury ($CCBT$), plus credits from the Central Bank to the banking system and the rest of the private sector ($CCBP$), plus the net monetary effect of foreign exchange operations ($CCBFX$):

$$MB(t) = CCBT(t) + CCBP(t) + CCBFX(t). \qquad (10.9)$$

10.2.3. Net flow of Central Bank credits to the Treasury

The net flow of Central Bank credits to the Treasury is equal to the difference between the government deficit and the flow of Treasury borrowing from other sources (*FTBO*):

$$CCBT(t) - CCBT(t-1) = De(t) - FTBO(t). \qquad (10.10)$$

10.2.4. Liability components of the money base

The money base (*MB*) is composed of the currency held by the public (*CUP*), plus the reserves held by the banking system (*RESV*):

$$MB(t) = CUP(t) + RESV(t). \qquad (10.11)$$

10.2.5. Supply of money

We define the money supply at the end of the year (*MF*) to be private demand deposits plus currency held by the public:

$$MF(t) = DDP(t) + CUP(t). \qquad (10.12)$$

From (10.11) and (10.12), we obtain

$$MF(t) = MB(t) \left[\frac{1 + \dfrac{CUP(t)}{DDP(t)}}{\dfrac{CUP(t)}{DDP(t)} + \dfrac{RESV(t)}{DDP(t)}} \right]. \qquad (10.13)$$

The term in brackets is the money multiplier.

Taking natural logs in (10.13) and differentiating with respect to time, we obtain

$$\frac{\dot{MF}(t)}{MF(t)} = \frac{\dot{MB}(t)}{MB(t)} + b_1 \frac{\left(\dfrac{\dot{CUP}(t)}{DDP(t)} \right)}{\dfrac{CUP(t)}{DDP(t)}} + b_2 \frac{\left(\dfrac{\dot{RESV}(t)}{DDP(t)} \right)}{\dfrac{RESV(t)}{DDP(t)}}, \qquad (10.14)$$

where

$$b_1 = \frac{\dfrac{CUP(t)}{DDP(t)}\left(\dfrac{RESV(t)}{DDP(t)} - 1\right)}{\left(1 + \dfrac{CUP(t)}{DDP(t)}\right)\left(\dfrac{CUP(t)}{DDP(t)} + \dfrac{RESV(t)}{DDP(t)}\right)} < 0,$$

and

$$b_2 = -\frac{\dfrac{RESV(t)}{DDP(t)}}{\dfrac{CUP(t)}{DDP(t)} + \dfrac{RESV(t)}{DDP(t)}} < 0.$$

Taking b_1 and b_2 as constants, we can estimate (10.14) directly. The estimation of (10.14) using instrumental variables was tried but it was not possible to find instruments correlated with the last two right-hand side variables; so, finally, ordinary least-squares estimation was used. When (10.14) was estimated by ordinary least squares and without constraining the coefficient of $M\dot{B}(t)/MB(t)$ to be unity, the following results were obtained:

$$\frac{M\dot{F}(t)}{MF(t)} = \underset{(1.100)}{0.036} + \underset{(12.450)}{0.959} \frac{M\dot{B}(t)}{MB(t)} - \underset{(-1.563)}{0.234} \frac{\left(\dfrac{C\dot{U}P(t)}{DDP(t)}\right)}{\dfrac{CUP(t)}{DDP(t)}}$$

$$- \underset{(-11.881)}{0.523} \frac{\left(\dfrac{RE\dot{S}V(t)}{DDP(t)}\right)}{\dfrac{RESV(t)}{DDP(t)}}. \tag{10.15}$$

$$R^2 = 0.94 \qquad DW = 2.18 \qquad \text{years: } 1953–1970$$

An explanation was also sought within the model for the behavior of $CUP(t)/DDP(t)$ and of $RESV(t)/DDP(t)$ but the attempt was unsuccessful. The negative result with respect to the last variable is due in part to the continuous changes in quantitative restrictions on Commercial bank operations during the period under study. In this framework, banking reserves do not maintain a stable relationship to variables such as reserve requirements and the cost of holding them.

Finally, it was decided to take $RESV(t)/DDP(t)$ and $CUP(t)/DDP(t)$ as exogenous variables in the model.

CHAPTER 11

AN ANNUAL MACROECONOMIC MODEL OF THE CHILEAN ECONOMY

In this chapter we present a complete macroeconomic model of the Chilean economy. The model consists of the different equations studied in chs. 6–10 together with the identities and miscellaneous equations required to complete the model.

The chapter is divided into seven sections. In the first five, we examine the equations given respectively in chs. 6–10. The additional identities and equations mentioned earlier are included in section 11.6. Finally, in section 11.7 we examine in alphabetical order a list of the endogenous variables, exogenous variables and the instruments used in the model.

The equations have been renumbered to facilitate counting but, in the right-hand corner of each. the equation number used in previous chapters has been included for convenience.

11.1. The production process and the employment of factors

Equivalent to
previous equation

(1) $Q(t) = QC(t) + QS(t),$ (6.1)

(2) $\ln \dfrac{QCF(t)}{LC(t)} = -0.78 \ln \dfrac{QCF(t-1)}{LC(t-1)} + 5.094$ (6.4)

$\qquad + \underset{(5.270)}{0.619} \left(\ln \dfrac{CA(t)KC(t)}{LC(t)} + 0.78 \ln \dfrac{CA(t-1)KC(t-1)}{LC(t-1)} \right)$

Equivalent to
previous equation

$$+ \; 0.016 \; [t + 0.78(t-1)],$$
$$(5.488)$$

(3) $\ln \dfrac{QCFE(t)}{NCF(t)} = -0.78 \ln \dfrac{QCFE(t-1)}{NCF(t-1)} + 5.094$ (6.8)

$$+ \, 0.619 \left(\ln \frac{KCF(t)}{NCF(t)} + 0.78 \ln \frac{KCF(t-1)}{NCF(t-1)} \right)$$

$$+ \, 0.016[t + 0.78(t-1)],$$

(4) $QS(t) = 0.6887 \, QS(t-1) - 357.2$ (6.9)

$$+ \quad 0.557 \; [Q(t) - 0.6887 \, Q(t-1)]$$
$$(12.397)$$

$$-1425.7 \left(\frac{PS(t)}{PQ(t)} - 0.6887 \frac{PS(t-1)}{PQ(t-1)} \right),$$
$$(-1.200)$$

(5) $LC^*(t) = \left(\dfrac{0.619}{0.381} \right)^{-0.619} (A(t))^{-1} QC(t) \left(\dfrac{W^e(t)}{C^e(t)} \right)^{-0.619}$ (6.12)

$$\times \; [CA(t)]^{-0.619} \, e^{-0.016t},$$

(6) $KC^*(t) = \left(\dfrac{0.619}{0.381} \right)^{0.381} (A(t))^{-1} QC(t) \left(\dfrac{W^e(t)}{C^e(t)} \right)^{0.381}$ (6.13)

$$\times \; [CA(t)]^{-0.619} \, e^{-0.016t},$$

(7) $LC(t) = 0.099 \, LC(t-1) + 0.174$

$$+ 0.132[LC^*(t) - 0.99 \, LC^*(t-1)]$$ (6.17)

$$+ \; 0.731 \; [LC(t-1) - 0.099 \, LC(t-2)],$$
$$(4.593)$$

(8) $LS(t) = -0.386 \, LS(t-1) - 0.104$ (6.18)

$$+ \; 0.000026 \; [QS(t) + 0.386 \, QS(t-1)]$$
$$(1.279)$$

$$+ 0.857[LS(t-1) + 0.386 \, LS(t-2)],$$
$$(3.493)$$

Equivalent to
previous equation

(9) $Q(t) = CP(t) + G(t) + GDI(t) + DEE(t) + X(t) - H(t)$.   (7.1)

11.2. Aggregate expenditures

(10) $CP(t) = CND(t) + CD(t)$,   (7.2)

(11) $CND(t) = -0.148\ CND(t-1) + 1219.8$ (7.4)

$$+\ 0.285\ [YD(t) + 0.148YD(t-1)]$$
$$(2.212)$$

$$+\ 0.507\ [CND(t-1) + 0.148CND(t-2)],$$
$$(2.319)$$

(12) $CD(t) = 0.843CD(t-1) - 527.9$ (7.6)

$$+\ 0.840\ [ZM(t) - 0.843ZM(t-1)]$$
$$(1.523)$$

$$+\ 0.097\ [YD(t) - 0.843YD(t-1)]$$
$$(1.457)$$

$$+\ 0.202\ [YD(t-1) - 0.843YD(t-2)]$$
$$(6.232)$$

$$+\ 0.170\ [YD(t-2) - 0.843YD(t-3)],$$
$$(3.627)$$

(13) $NYD(t) = NYP(t) - P(t)TSS(t) - NTP(t) + NNETTR(t),$ (7.7)

(14) $NYP(t) = TW(t) + P(t)ERSS(t) + NPROF(t) + RES(t),$ (7.8)

(15) $ERSS(t) = 0.263\ ERSS(t-1) - 128.64$

$$+ 0.201 \left[\frac{TW(t)}{P(t)} - 0.263\ \frac{TW(t-1)}{P(t-1)} \right],$$ (7.9)

$$(19.642)$$

Equivalent to
previous equation

$$(16)\ NTP(t) = 0.614 \frac{NTP(t-1)P(t-1)}{P(t-2)} - 66.5\ P(t-1)$$

$$+\ 0.037P(t-1)[R(t) - 0.614R(t-1)]$$
$$(7.207)$$

$$-\ 156.7P(t-1)[dv(t) - 0.614dv(t-1)] \qquad (7.15)$$
$$(-5.007)$$

$$+\ 97.9P(t-1)[du(t) - 0.614du(t-1)],$$
$$(1.587)$$

$$(17)\ TSS(t) = 0.312\,TSS(t-1) - 167.2 \qquad (7.16)$$

$$+\ \underset{(20.267)}{0.289} \left[\frac{TW(t)}{P(t)} - 0.312\,\frac{TW(t-1)}{P(t-1)}\right],$$

$$(18)\ GDI(t) = IM(t) + IHOU(t) + REP(t), \qquad (7.17)$$

$$(19)\ IM(t) = 168.1 \quad +\ 0.797\ IM(t-1) +\ 0.012 \qquad (7.21)$$
$$(1.378) \qquad (5.815) \qquad\qquad (0.268)$$
$$\times\ [KC^*(t+1) - KC^*(t)] +\ 0.052\ [KC^*(t) - KC^*(t-1)]$$
$$(1.581)$$

$$+\ 0.048\ [KC^*(t-1) - KC^*(t-2)],$$
$$(1.373)$$

$$(20)\ CK(t) = IPK(t)\left[\frac{RA(t) + 0.035}{1 - UTK(t)}\right], \qquad (7.22)$$

$$(21)\ GIM(t) = IM(t) + REP(t), \qquad (7.23)$$

$$(22)\ REP(t) = 0.035\ KC(t), \qquad (7.24)$$

$$(23)\ KC(t) = KC(t-1) + IM(t-1), \qquad (7.25)$$

Equivalent to
previous equation

(24) $DEE(t) = -0.752DEE(t-1) - 1565.2$ (7.29)

$+ 0.584 [Q(t) + 0.752Q(t-1)] - 0.528 [Q(t-1)$
(5.286)   (−4.645)

$+ 0.752Q(t-2)] - 2360.0 [RA(t) + 0.752RA(t-1)]$,
(−1.490)

(25) $H(t) = HI(t) + HC(t) + HKM(t) + HS(t)$,   (7.30)

(26) $HI(t) = 0.338HI(t-1) + 88.2 + 0.144 [QC(t)$
(5.499)

$- 0.338QC(t-1)] - 273.6 \left[\dfrac{PRM(t)(1+UTXM(t))}{PQ(t)}\right.$ (7.32)
(−1.812)

$\left. - 0.338\dfrac{PRM(t-1)(1+UTXM(t-1))}{PQ(t-1)}\right] - 444.6 [FDV(t)$
(−1.396)

$- 0.338FDV(t-1)] + 137.5 [sa(t) - 0.338sa(t-1)]$,
(1.253)

(27) $HC(t) = -0.061HC(t-1) + 131.9 + 0.033 [CP(t)$ (7.34)
(5.036)

$+ 0.061CP(t-1)] - 176.6 \left[\dfrac{PCN(t)(1+UTXM(t))}{PQ(t)}\right.$
(−1.284)

$\left. + 0.061\dfrac{PCN(t-1)(1+UTXM(t-1))}{PQ(t-1)}\right] - 379.8 [FDV(t)$
(−3.025)

$+ 0.061FDV(t-1)] + 217.2 [sa(t) + 0.061sa(t-1)]$,
(3.876)

(28) $HKM(t) = 0.319HKM(t-1) + 332.5 + 0.228 [GIM(t-1)$
(3.553)

$-0.319GIM(t-2)] - 214.6 PK(t-1)[1+UTXM(t-1)]/$
(−1.607)

Equivalent to
previous equation

$$PQ(t-1) - 0.319PK(t-2)[1+UTXM(t-2)/PQ(t-2)]$$

$$\underset{(-2.789)}{-} \quad 576.32[FDV(t-1) - 0.319FDV(t-2)]$$

$$\underset{(1.183)}{+ 111.31} [sa(t) - 0.319sa(t-1)]. \tag{7.38}$$

11.3. Prices and wages

$$(29) \quad \frac{PC(t) - PC(t-1)}{PC(t-1)} = -\frac{PC(t-1) - PC(t-2)}{PC(t-2)} - 0.0554 \tag{8.2}$$

$$\underset{(23.678)}{+ \quad 0.767} \left[\frac{ULCC(t) - ULCC(t-1)}{ULCC(t-1)} + \frac{ULCC(t-1)-ULCC(t-2)}{ULCC(t-2)} \right]$$

$$\underset{(7.766)}{+ 0.233} \left[\frac{PRM(t)-PRM(t-1)}{PRM(t-1)} + \frac{PRM(t-1) - PRM(t-2)}{PRM(t-2)} \right]$$

$$\underset{(3.205)}{+ 0.0023} \left[\frac{1}{0.82-CUC(t)} + \frac{1}{0.82-CUC(t-1)} \right],$$

$$(30) \quad \frac{PS(t) - PS(t-1)}{PS(t-1)} = -0.076\frac{PS(t-1) - PS(t-2)}{PS(t-2)} - 0.025 \tag{8.3}$$

$$\underset{(11.409)}{+ \quad 0.846} \left(\frac{ULCS(t) - ULCS(t-1)}{ULCS(t-1)} \right.$$

$$+ 0.076 \frac{ULCS(t-1) - ULCS(t-2)}{ULCS(t-2)} \Bigg) + \underset{(2.078)}{0.154}$$

$$\times \left(\frac{PRM(t) - PRM(t-1)}{PRM(t-1)} + 0.076\frac{PRM(t-1)-PRM(t-2)}{PRM(t-2)} \right),$$

$$(31) \quad \frac{P(t) - P(t-1)}{P(t-1)} = 0.511\frac{P(t-1)-P(t-2)}{P(t-2)} - 0.059 \tag{8.4}$$

Equivalent to
previous equation

$$+ 0.688 \left(\frac{PC(t)-PC(t-1)}{PC(t-1)} - 0.511 \frac{PC(t-1)-PC(t-2)}{PC(t-2)} \right)$$
(3.469)

$$+ 0.489 \left(\frac{PS(t)-PS(t-1)}{PS(t-1)} - 0.511 \frac{PS(t-1)-PS(t-2)}{PS(t-2)} \right),$$
(1.507)

(32) $\dfrac{WRC(t) - WRC(t-1)}{WRC(t-1)} = 0.005 + 0.0057 \dfrac{1}{UC(t)}$ (8.6)
(1.007)   (1.245)

$$+ 0.787 \frac{P(t) - P(t-1)}{P(t-1)} [1 + 0.405 \; dw(t)],$$
(6.418)

(11.381)

(33) $\dfrac{WRS(t) - WRS(t-1)}{WRS(t-1)} = -0.282 + 0.0128 \dfrac{1}{US(t)}$ (8.8)
(−0.829)   (1.186)

$$+ 0.465 \frac{P(t) - P(t-1)}{P(t-1)} [1 + 0.599 \; dw(t)].$$
(1.853)   (2.492)

11.4. Government taxes and the generation of the government deficit

(34) $\dfrac{De(t)}{PT(t)} = J(t) - T(t),$ (9.1)

(35) $T(t) = TNCF(t) + TPF(t) + TMF(t) + TCF(t) + TRF(t),$ (9.2)

(36) $\dfrac{TNCF(t)P(t)}{P(t-1)} = 0.447 \dfrac{TNCF(t-1) \, P(t-1)}{P(t-2)} + 39.25$ (9.6)

$$+ 0.093 \; [F(t) - 0.447F(t-1)] + 60.6 \quad [du(t)$$
(5.922)   (1.183)

$$- 0.447du(t-1)] - 132.3 \; [dv(t) - 0.447dv(t-1)],$$
(−3.894)

Equivalent to
previous equation

(37) $\dfrac{TPF(t)P(t)}{P(t-1)} = 0.609\,\dfrac{TPF(t-1)P(t-1)}{P(t-2)} - 50.1$ (9.7)

$$+ \quad 0.034\ [R(t) - 0.609R(t-1)]$$
$$(10.160)$$

$$- \quad 171.3\ [dv(t) - 0.609dv(t-1)],$$
$$(-4.768)$$

(38) $TMF(t) = 0.343\,TMF(t-1) - 69.2$ (9.9)

$$+ \quad 0.265\ [H(t) - 0.343H(t-1)]$$
$$(8.149)$$

$$- \quad 0.079\ [H(t)dm(t) - 0.343H(t-1)dm(t-1)],$$
$$(-4.599)$$

(39) $TCF(t) = \quad 0.326\ XC(t) - 0.00005\,XC^2(t)$ (9.11)
$$(3.965)(-0.717)$$

$$+ \quad 0.091\ dc(t)XC(t),$$
$$(2.937)$$

(40) $TRF(t) = 0.771\,TRF(t-1) - 228.4$ (9.12)

$$+ \quad 0.158[Q(t) - 0.771Q(t-1)].$$
$$(7.204)$$

11.5. The monetary sector

(41) $\ln\left[\dfrac{M(t)}{P(t)PO(t)}\right]^d = -1.358 + 0.861\left(\ln\dfrac{Q(t)}{PO(t)}\right.$ (10.3)
$$\phantom{(41)\ \ln\left[\dfrac{M(t)}{P(t)PO(t)}\right]^d = -1.358 + }(1.836)$$

$$-\ 0.701\ \ln\dfrac{Q(t-1)}{PO(t-1)}\Bigg)\ -\ 0.084[\ln I(t) - 0.701\ \ln I(t-1)]$$
$$\phantom{-\ 0.701\ \ln\dfrac{Q(t-1)}{PO(t-1)}\Bigg)\ }(-2.389)$$

$$+\ 0.146\ [d(t) - 0.701d(t-1)] + 0.586\left(\ln\dfrac{M(t-1)}{P(t-1)PO(t-1)}\right.$$
$$(2.894)(3.71)$$

$$-\ 0.701\ \ln\dfrac{M(t-2)}{P(t-1)PO(t-1)}\Bigg)\ +\ 0.701\ \ln\dfrac{M(t-1)}{P(t-1)PO(t-1)}\ ,$$

Equivalent to
previous equation

(42) $MB(t) = MB(t-1) + FCCBT(t) + FCCBO(t),$ (10.9)

(43) $FCCBT(t) = De(t) - FTBO(t),$ (10.10)

(44) $\dfrac{MF(t) - MF(t-1)}{MF(t-1)} = 0.036$ (10.15)
$\qquad\qquad\qquad\quad (1.100)$

$$+ \underset{(12.450)}{0.959} \frac{MB(t) - MB(t-1)}{MB(t-1)} - \underset{(-1.563)}{0.234} \left[\frac{\dfrac{CUP(t)}{DDP(t)} - \dfrac{CUP(t-1)}{DDP(t-1)}}{\dfrac{CUP(t-1)}{DDP(t-1)}} \right]$$

$$\underset{(-11.881)}{-0.523} \left[\frac{\dfrac{RESV(t)}{DDP(t)} - \dfrac{RESV(t-1)}{DDP(t-1)}}{\dfrac{RESV(t-1)}{DDP(t-1)}} \right] .$$

11.6. Some miscellaneous equations and identities

11.6.1. Total wage bill

The total wage bill (TW) is equal to wages paid in the commodity sector (WC), together with the wages paid in the service sector (WS), less the employers' social security contributions ($ERSS\cdot P$):

(45) $TW(t) = WC(t) + WS(t) - ERSS(t)P(t).$ (11.1)

11.6.2. Wages in the commodity sector

Total wages paid in the commodity sector are equal to the product of the wage rate in the commodity sector and the employment level in that sector:

(46) $WC(t) = WRC(t)LC(t).$ (11.2)

11.6.3. Unit labor cost of commodities

The unit labor cost of commodities is equal to the ratio between total wages in the commodity sector and the level of output in that sector:

$$(47) \ ULCC(t) = \frac{WC(t)}{QC(t)} \ .$$ (11.3)

11.6.4. Wages in the service sector

Total wages paid in the service sector are equal to the product of the wage rate in the service sector and the employment level in that sector:

$$(48) \ WS(t) = WRS(t)LS(t).$$ (11.4)

11.6.5. Unit labor cost of services

The unit labor cost of services is equal to the ratio between total wages in the service sector and the level of output in that sector:

$$(49) \ ULCS(t) = \frac{WS(t)}{QS(t)}$$ (11.5)

11.6.6. Utilization rate of the capital stock

There are no good statistics for utilization of capital stock. What is available is some data for capacity utilized in 1961 which corresponds mainly to use of capital stock. What is assumed in our work is that the utilization rate of the capital stock in the sector producing commodities (CA) is equal to one, less three times the unemployment rate of labor in that sector. When this criterion was used, it was possible to reproduce closely the utilization rate of capital stock for 1961. Furthermore, the results were not too sensitive to other equally reasonable values for the coefficient of the unemployment rate.

(50) $CA(t) = 1 - 3\,UC(t)$. (11.6)

11.6.7. Capacity utilization in the commodity sector

Capacity utilization is defined as

(51) $CUC(t) = \dfrac{QCF(t)}{QCFE(t)}$, (11.7)

where *QCF* is the fitted value of output from the production function

11.6.8. Implicit price deflator of gross domestic product

The implicit price deflator of gross domestic product (*PQ*) is a weighted average of the price of commodities and the price of services, where the weights are the gross output of the respective sectors:

(52) $PQ(t) = \dfrac{PC(t)QC(t) + PS(t)QS(t)}{QC(t) + QS(t)}$. (11.8)

11.6.9. Implicit price deflator of taxes

The implicit price deflator of taxes (*PT*) is a weighted average of the price deflators of the different tax components:

(53) $PT(t) = \dfrac{P(t)TNCF(t)+P(t)TPF(t)+PM(t)TMF(t)+PX(t)TCF(t)+PQ(t)TRF(t)}{TNCF(t)+TPF(t)+TMF(t)+TCF(t)+TRF(t)}$.

(11.9)

11.6.10. Excess demand for real money

This is defined as the difference between the existing supply of money and the fitted demand for money, where both are given in real terms:

$$(54)\ ZM(t) = \frac{M(t)}{P(t)} - PO(t)\left(\frac{M(t)}{P(t)PO(t)}\right)^d . \qquad (11.10)$$

11.6.11. Opportunity cost of holding money

In accordance with our discussion in ch. 10, the opportunity cost of holding money is defined as the sum of the actual rate of change in the cost of living index and 0.7 times the real rate of profits corrected by the inflation rate:

$$(55)\ I(t) = \frac{P(t) - P(t-1)}{P(t-1)} + 0.7RA(t)\left(1 + \frac{P(t) - P(t-1)}{P(t-1)}\right). \qquad (11.11)$$

11.6.12. Unemployment rate in the commodity sector

The unemployment rate in the commodity sector is equal to the ratio between the level of unemployment in the commodity sector and the labor force in that sector:

$$(56)\ UC(t) = \frac{NC(t) - LC(t)}{NC(t)} . \qquad (11.12)$$

11.6.13. Unemployment rate in the service sector

The unemployment rate in the service sector is equal to the ratio between the level of unemployment in the service sector and the labor force in that sector:

$$(57)\ US(t) = \frac{NS(t) - LS(t)}{NS(t)} . \qquad (11.13)$$

11.6.14. Full employment labor force in the commodity sector

We define the full employment labor force in the commodity sector as the total labor force in that sector less 3% to account for frictional unemployment:

(58) $NCF(t) = 0.97 NC(t)$. (11.14)

11.6.15. Full employment utilization rate of capital stock in the commodity sector

We assume that the full employment utilization rate of capital is equal to unity.
Therefore,

(59) $KCF(t) = KC(t)$. (11.15)

11.6.16. Expected wage—rental ratio in the commodity sector

The expected wage—rental ratio in the commodity sector is defined as the simple average of the wage—rental ratios for the previous year and the current year:

(60) $\dfrac{W^e(t)}{C^e(t)} = \dfrac{1}{2}\left(\dfrac{WRC(t-1)}{CK(t-1)} + \dfrac{WRC(t)}{CK(t)}\right)$. (11.16)

11.6.17. Relation between average of end of the month money supply and end of the year money supply

In our model there are two variables which refer to the money supply, and we need some way to relate them to each other. Hence, we will make the average of end of the month money supply a linear function of the simple average of the end of the year money supply.

This is not a structural equation, therefore we will estimate it using ordinary least squares. The estimated equation is

$$(61)\ M(t) = 20.21 + 0.955 \left(\frac{MF(t) + MF(t-1)}{2}\right).$$

$$(1.214)\quad(180.656)$$

$$R^2 = 0.997 \qquad\qquad \text{years: } 1960{-}1970$$

(11.17)

11.6.18. Price of imports

In our model, we have as variables the implicit price deflator of imports and the price deflators for the different types of imported commodities. Here the implicit price deflator of imports will be related to the prices of the different types of imports.

We are not trying to estimate a structural equation; we wish only to get the weight of the different price indexes in the price of imports. Therefore, in the estimation we will use ordinary least squares. The estimated equation is

$$(62)\ PM(t) = -0.049 + 0.192\,PRM(t) + 0.186\,PCN(t)$$

$$(-1.583)\quad(0.988)\qquad\quad(0.864)$$

$$+\ 0.675\,PK(t).$$

$$(3.149)$$

$$R^2 = 0.9986 \qquad\qquad \text{years: } 1960{-}1970$$

(11.18)

11.6.19. Nominal profits

Nominal profits are defined as the product of a price index, the real rate of profits and the stock of capital:

$$(63)\ NPROF(t) = P(t)RA(t)KC(t).$$

(11.19)

11.6.20. Price of consumption goods

We relate the price of consumption goods to the price of commodities and the prices of services. Again we estimate this equation by ordinary least squares and obtain the result

(64) $PCON(t) = 0.044 + 0.434\ PC(t) + 0.504\ PS(t)$. (11.20)
$\qquad\quad$ (4.148)$\quad$ (3.958) $\qquad$ (4.415)

$\qquad R^2 = 0.998$ $\qquad\qquad\qquad$ years: 1960--1970

11.6.21. Price of capital goods

Finally we assume that the price of capital goods is a linear function of the price of imported capital goods and the implicit price deflator for gross domestic product.

The ordinary least-square estimated equation is

(65) $IPK(t) = -0.0015 + 0.552\ PK(t) + 0.430\ PQ(t)$. (11.21)
$\qquad\quad$ (−0.071)$\quad$ (4.053) $\qquad$ (3.624)

$\qquad R^2 = 0.999$ $\qquad\qquad\qquad$ years: 1960−1970

11.6.22. Other definitions

(66) $R(t) = \dfrac{NYP(t-1)}{P(t-1)}$, $\qquad\qquad$ for $t \leqslant 1964$ $\qquad$ (11.22)

$\qquad\quad = \dfrac{NYP(t-1)}{P(t-2)}$, $\qquad\qquad$ for $t > 1964$

(67) $F(t) = \dfrac{NPROF(t-1)}{P(t-1)}$, $\qquad\quad$ for $t \leqslant 1964$ $\qquad$ (11.23)

$\qquad\quad = \dfrac{NPROF(t-1)}{P(t-2)}$, $\qquad\quad$ for $t > 1964$

(68) $YD(t) = \dfrac{NYD(t)}{PCON(t)}$, $\qquad\qquad\qquad\qquad\qquad$ (11.24)

(69) $A(t) = -0.77965\ \ln\left[\dfrac{QC(t-1)}{LC(t-1)}\right] + 5.0942$ $\qquad\qquad$ (11.25)

$\qquad\quad + 0.4828\ \ln\left[\dfrac{CA(t-1)\,KC(t-1)}{LC(t-1)}\right] + 0.0126(t-1)$,

$$(70) \ U(t) = \frac{NC(t) + NS(t) - LC(t) - LS(t)}{NC(t) + NS(t)} \ . \tag{11.26}$$

11.7. List of variables[1]

A	= See eq. (69) in this chapter.
$^*AUTX$	= Autonomous expenditures (government expenditures, investment in housing and copper exports), in millions of 1965 escudos.
CA	= Utilization rate of the capital stock in the sector producing commodities, as a percentage.
CD	= Personal consumption of durables, in millions of 1965 escudos.
CK	= Price index of capital services, in current escudos per escudos of capital in plant and equipment at 1965 prices.
CND	= Personal consumption of non-durables, in millions of 1965 escudos.
CP	= Personal consumption, in millions of 1965 escudos.
CUC	= Capacity utilization in sector producing commodities, as a percentage.
$^*CUP$ DDP	= Ratio between currency held by the public and demand deposits, as a percentage.
$^*dc$	= Dummy variable for taxes on copper, dc equal to one for the years 1965–1970 and zero elsewhere.
De	= Government deficit in fiscal account, in millions of current escudos.
$^{**}DE$	= Depreciation rate of the stock of capital in plant and equipment, as a percentage.
DEE	= Change in inventories, in millions of 1965 escudos.
$^*dm$	= Dummy variable for change in the tax base of import taxes, dm equal to one for the years 1964–1970 and zero elsewhere.

[1] An asterisk in front of a variable indicates an exogenous variable of the model and/or an instrument used in the estimation of the equations. A double asterisk indicates a parameter.

$*du$	= Dummy variable for personal taxes and direct taxes to non-copper corporations, du equal to one from 1965 to 1970 and zero elsewhere.
$*dv$	= Dummy variable for personal taxes and direct taxes to non-copper corporations, dv equal to one in 1965 and zero elsewhere.
$*dw$	= Dummy variable for upward pressures in wages during the Frei administration, dw equal to one during years 1965–1970 and zero elsewhere.
$ERSS$	= Employers' social security contributions, millions of 1965 escudos.
F	= See eq. (9.5).
$*FCCBO$	= Flow of credit from the Central Bank to others (commercial banks, private sector and foreign exchange operations), in millions of current escudos.
$FCCBT$	= Flow of credit from the Central Bank to the Treasury, in millions of current escudos.
$*FDV$	= Liberalization of trade variable, index with range 0.1 to 1.0.
$*FTBO$	= Flow of Treasury borrowing from other sources, in millions of current escudos.
$*G$	= Government expenditures in national accounts, in millions of 1965 escudos.
GDI	= Gross domestic investment in fixed capital, in millions of 1965 escudos.
GIM	= Gross domestic investment in plant and equipment, in millions of 1965 escudos.
H	= Imports of goods and services, in millions of 1965 escudos.
HC	= Imports of consumption goods, in millions of 1965 escudos.
HI	= Imports of raw materials, in millions of 1965 escudos.
HKM	= Imports of capital goods, in millions of 1965 escudos.
$*HS$	= Imports of services, in millions of 1965 escudos.
I	= Cost of holding money, as a percentage.

IHOU = Gross domestic investment in housing, in millions of 1965 escudos.

IM = Net investment in plant and equipment, in millions of 1965 escudos.

IPK = Price index for stock of capital in plant and equipment, 1965 = 1.00.

J = Government expenditures in fiscal account, in millions of 1965 escudos.

KC = Capital stock in plant and equipment in the sector producing commodities at the end of the year, in millions of 1965 escudos.

KC^* = Desired capital stock in plant and equipment in the sector producing commodities at the end of the year, in millions of 1965 escudos.

KCF = Full employment level of capital stock in plant and equipment in the sector producing commodities, in millions of 1965 escudos.

LC = Employment in the sector producing commodities, in millions of workers.

LC^* = Desired employment in the sector producing commodities, in millions of workers.

ln gxci = Natural log of $(AUTX/PO)$.

LPR = Lending from commercial banks to the private sectors, in millions of current escudos.

LS = Employment in the sector providing services, in millions of workers.

M = Money supply, average of end of the month figures, in millions of current escudos.

$\left(\dfrac{M}{P.PO}\right)^d$ = Real money demanded, in millions of 1965 escudos.

MB = High-powered money, in millions of current escudos.

MF = Money supply, at the end of the year, in millions of current escudos.

NC = Labor force in the sector producing commodities, in millions of workers.

NCF = Full employment of labor in the sector producing commodities, in millions of workers.

*NNETTR = Net transfer to persons less interest paid by person, in millions of current escudos.

NPROF = Nominal profits, in millions of current escudos.

*NS = Labor force in the sector producing services, in millions of workers.

NTP = Taxes to persons in national accounts, in millions of current escudos.

NYD = Gross personal disposable income, in millions of current escudos.

NYP = Gross personal income, in millions of current escudos.

P = Cost of living index, 1965 = 1.00.

PC = Implicit price deflator for gross domestic product of commodities, 1965 = 1.00.

*PCN = Price index of imported consumption goods, 1965 = 1.00.

PCON = Implicit price deflator of consumption goods, 1965 = 1.00.

*PK = Price index of imported capital goods, 1965 = 1.00.

PM = Implicit price deflator for imports, 1965 = 1.00.

*PO = Population, in millions of persons.

PQ = Implicit price deflator for gross domestic product, 1965 = 1.00.

*PRM = Price index of imported raw materials, 1965 = 1.00.

PS = Implicit price deflator for gross domestic product of services, 1965 = 1.00.

PT = Implicit price deflator for taxes, 1965 = 1.00.

*PX = Implicit price deflator for exports, 1965 = 1.00.

Q = Expenditure in gross domestic product, in millions of 1965 escudos.

QC = Gross domestic product of commodities, in millions of 1965 escudos.

QCF = Gross domestic product fitted using eq. (6.4), in millions of 1965 escudos.

QCFE = Full employment level of gross domestic product of commodities, in millions of 1965 escudos.

QS = Gross domestic product of services, in millions of 1965 escudos.

R	= See eq. (66) in this chapter.
*RA	= Real rate of profit, escudos of 1965 per unit of capital stock at 1965 prices.
REP	= Depreciation of capital stock, in millions of 1965 escudos.
*$\dfrac{RESV}{DDP}$	= Ratio between reserves held by the banking system, and demand deposits, as a percentage.
*sa	= Dummy variable, equal to one in 1970 and zero elsewhere.
*SHA	= Share of agriculture in gross domestic product, as a percentage.
*t	= Time in years, 1960 = 1.
T	= Total taxes in fiscal accounts, in millions of 1965 escudos.
TCF	= Taxes on copper in fiscal accounts, in millions of 1965 escudos.
TMF	= Taxes on imports in fiscal accounts, in millions of 1965 escudos.
$TNCF$	= Direct taxes to non-copper corporations in fiscal account, in millions of 1965 escudos.
TPF	= Taxes to persons in fiscal accounts, in millions of 1965 escudos.
TRF	= Other taxes in fiscal accounts, in millions of 1965 escudos.
TSS	= Total social security contributions, in millions of 1965 escudos.
TW	= Total wage bill excluding employers' social security contributions, in millions of current escudos.
U	= Unemployment rate, as a percentage.
UC	= Unemployment rate in the sector producing commodities, as a percentage.
$ULCC$	= Unit labor cost of commodities, current escudos per worker.
$ULCS$	= Unit labor cost of services, current escudos per worker.
US	= Unemployment rate in the sector producing services, as a percentage.
*UTK	= Unit profit tax to corporation, as a percentage.

$\dfrac{W^e}{C^e}$ = Expected wage–rental ratio in the sector producing commodities.

WC = Total wages paid in the commodity sector, in millions of current escudos.

WRC = Wage rate in the sector producing commodities, in current escudos per worker.

WRS = Wage rate in the sector producing services, in current escudos per worker.

WS = Total wages paid in the service sector, in millions of current escudos.

$^*X$ = Exports of goods and services, in millions of 1965 escudos.

YD = Gross personal disposable income, in millions of 1965 escudos.

ZM = Disequilibrium in the money market, in millions of 1965 escudos.

CHAPTER 12

SOME SIMULATION EXPERIMENTS

In chs. 6−10 we studied the specification and the estimation of the different equations of the Chilean model. In those chapters, only individual tests were performed on each of the equations. In the present chapter, we will test the model estimated in chs. 6−10 and listed in ch. 11, by analyzing its performance as a whole, and by using it to study the consequences of alternative policies that could have been followed in the period 1965−1970. If the model were linear, the performance of the model and the consequences of alternative policies could be studied using its reduced form, but the model of the Chilean economy that we are working with is highly non-linear and therefore the reduced form approach is not applicable. Owing to the non-linearity of this model, the derivation of an explicit analytical solution for the endogenous variables as a function of predetermined variables and parameters can become cumbersome, if not impossible, and hence it becomes necessary to use some alternative analytical technique to study the performance of the model. In this chapter, we describe the results obtained by solving the model with an iterative procedure using the Troll system.

The chapter is divided into four sections. In the first section, we describe the performance of the model through a backcast of the period 1963−1970 (the maximum backcasting period considering the lags of the model and the limitations imposed by the non-availability of data for the endogenous variables); in this section we describe in detail the chief difficulties that were encountered using the model of ch. 11, and their possible causes. In the second section, we study the results of an experiment in which it is assumed that for a constant unemployment rate the real wage rate in the commodity sector is constant. In the third section, we discuss the results of an experiment in which it is assumed that the Central Bank does not accumulate foreign exchange during the period 1965–1970, but instead keeps a level of foreign reserves equal to the average of the period 1962–1964 and uses the surplus for buying additional competitive imports which are sold subsequently in the domestic market. Finally, in the last section, we examine the results of an experiment in which we assume that the Central Bank sells the foreign exchange in the open market and finances an expansion in public investment in machinery and equipment, with the proceeds of the sale of foreign exchange.

12.1. Model backcast properties

When the model of ch. 11 was used to solve for the endogenous variables in the period 1963–1970, the solution was found to be non-existent. Part of this problem was due to the poor performance of the three equations involving *DEF*, *TCF* and *WRS*. We see in table 12.1 the percentage simulation errors made with each of these equations considered separately. Let us now analyze these results one by one.

The bad performance of the equation for *DEE* may be the result of errors with non-constant variance, occurring in the measurement of this variable. However, since this variable is very small in relation to the other components of the aggregate demand equation, and it does not enter into the other equations of the model,

TABLE 12.1
Percentage errors in the simulated variables*.

	DEE	*TCF*	*WRS*
1963	6.19	10.26	3.26
1964	−42.92	−1.44	−3.63
1965	−11.46	18.48	−9.74
1966	4.65	−11.55	−5.83
1967	−10.94	−2.19	1.75
1968	11.23	5.43	4.55
1969	−29.64	2.86	2.04
1970	81.06	−9.36	0.85

* Percentage error = 100 × (simulated value − actual value)/(actual value).

no major errors are committed in considering this variable as exogenous both in the solution of the model and in the subsequent simulations.

With respect to taxes on copper (*TCF*), further complications arise since the bad performance of this equation carries over along the chain of endogenous variables: government revenues, fiscal deficit financing from the Central Bank to the Treasury and the money supply. Therefore, because of the structure of the model, small errors in *TCF* spill over into a set of other important variables. Fortunately, this variable depends mainly on other variables that are not explained in the model of the Chilean economy, such as volume of exports of copper, price of copper, and tax regulations on the copper industry. Therefore, in our simulations of the Chilean economy in the period 1963–1970, we can take this variable as exogenous. If we want to use the model to make forecasts, the above-mentioned procedure cannot be used and therefore it would be necessary to explain taxes on copper. To obtain a better explanation for taxes on copper would require the obtaining of statistics on profits of the copper industry and a close study of the innumerable changes in the tax regulations.

In the case of *WRS*, although the percentage errors are small for the equation taken by itself, owing to the crucial role that all prices play in the model, small errors in prices propagate through the structure of the model and create major errors in other endogenous variables. The bad performance of this variable may be due in part to the poor statistics on unemployment in the service sector. The unemployment statistics available refer to unemployment in metropolitan Santiago. As far as its production structure is concerned, metropolitan Santiago may be a good sample for the sector producing commodities, but this is not so for the sector producing services since most government offices are located in Santiago. Therefore, the unemployment in the service sector is heavily influenced by the unemployment in the government sector, which is not so for the country as a whole. One of the consequences of this measuring problem is the fact that there is almost no variability in the unemployment rate in services during the period used for the estimations. In the simulations that we are about to consider, this variable was taken as exogenous.

Taking the variable discussed above as exogenous, the model did

TABLE 12.2
Percentage errors in the simulation.

	PC*	PC**	PM
1963	0.69	4.18	−3.56
1964	0.36	0.31	14.33
1965	−2.04	−5.97	0.40
1966	1.04	−5.68	0.23
1967	−2.41	−3.18	0.78
1968	3.03	19.71	1.24
1969	−4.24	8.02	−0.17
1970	3.42	18.16	−0.78

   * Using eq. (29).
  ** Using eq. (29′).

have a solution but there were important forecast errors for some of the endogenous variables. After some experimentation with the model, it was discovered that the equation for PC was the one which was giving trouble. As we can appreciate from table 12.2, although eq. (29) used alone performs quite well, small errors from any one year accumulate throughout the simulation period, owing to the autoregressive characteristic of this equation. Owing to this problem it was decided to re-estimate eq. (29) without making a correction for autocorrelation in the errors. The results obtained were

(29)′

$$\frac{PC(t) - PC(t-1)}{PC(t-1)} = \underset{(-1.257)}{-0.1415} + \underset{(9.745)}{0.821} \; \frac{ULCC(t) - ULCC(t-1)}{ULCC(t-1)}$$

$$+ \underset{(2.131)}{0.179} \; \frac{PRM(t) - PRM(t-1)}{PRM(t-1)} + \underset{(1.346)}{0.028} \; \frac{1}{0.94 - CUC(t-1)} \;.$$

DW = 3.04   years: 1962−1970

Instruments: $\dfrac{\dot{PRM}(t)}{PRM(t)}, \; \dfrac{\dot{PRM}(t-1)}{PRM(t-1)}, \; \dfrac{\dot{LPR}(t)}{LPR(t)}, \; \dfrac{1}{0.94 - CUC(t-1)},$

$G(t), C.$

Although this equation is worse than eq. (29) from the last

chapter, in terms of *t*-statistics, when it was put into the model
with a constant adjustment for 1968, the former performed better
because of its non-autoregressive structure. A better estimation
for eq. (29) would require a longer time series.

Another problem arises with the equation for *PM*. This equation
performs quite well for most of the sampling period, with the
exception of 1964. Because of this, a constant adjustment was
made for that year.

The final problem arises with eq. (19) for investment in plant
and equipment. In this equation, we have a lead in *KC**, and this
cannot be handled when the model is simulated. Therefore, it is
necessary to work with the weaker equation which includes only
current and lagged endogenous variables. The equation obtained
in this case was

$$IM(t) = 207.08 + \underset{(3.533)}{0.755} \ IM(t-1) + \underset{(0.439)}{0.136} \ \frac{\Delta MB(t)}{P(t)}$$

$$+ \underset{(0.735)}{0.0338} \ [KC^*(t) - KC^*(t-1)]$$

$$+ \underset{(1.054)}{0.0391} \ [KC^*(t-1) - KC^*(t-2)]$$

$$+ \underset{(0.718)}{0.0278} \ [KC^*(t-2) - KC^*(t-3)].$$

$\hat{\rho} = -0.142$ DW = 1.98   years: 1955–1970

After this discussion of the problems faced in the simulation, let
us analyze the backcasts for the period 1963–1970. From tables
12.3, 12.4 and 12.5, we can appreciate that the model performs
quite well for the period 1963–1970. The biggest errors occur in
the government deficit which is a difference between two endogenous variables and therefore includes the difference in the errors
of both. The errors are important also for investment in plant and
equipment, but as stated above this is due to the weaker equation
with which we had to work. Also, there are major errors in *FCCBT*
and *ZM*, mainly due to the small absolute value of those variables.

TABLE 12.3
True values of endogenous variables.

	A	w^e/C^e	CA	CD	CK
1963	2.862	20031.5	0.824	2381.0	8.364E-02
1964	2.869	17957.5	0.804	2499.0	0.135
1965	2.856	19161.5	0.815	2613.0	0.160
1966	2.875	21610.3	0.819	3024.0	0.213
1967	2.864	21285.7	0.770	3445.0	0.292
1968	2.846	21242.0	0.782	3759.0	0.382
1969	2.871	21080.2	0.728	4158.0	0.585
1970	2.849	20065.0	0.740	4709.0	0.870

	CND	CP	CUC	De	ERSS
1963	9292.0	11673.0	0.783	425.52	834.6
1964	9813.0	12312.0	0.777	537.954	912.4
1965	9950.0	12563.0	0.775	792.900	1110.0
1966	10911.0	13935.0	0.784	788.145	1336.0
1967	10968.0	14413.0	0.751	557.449	1396.7
1968	11100.0	14859.0	0.733	924.187	1518.0
1969	11074.0	15232.0	0.702	667.371	1736.7
1970	11472.0	16181.0	0.683	2266.29	1950.3

	F	FCCBT	GDI	GIM	H
1963	2526.1	11.5	2834.0	2245.0	2195.0
1964	3018.2	−14.2	2735.0	2253.0	2287.0
1965	5007.8	70.1	2859.0	2347.0	2369.0
1966	3933.4	102.4	2900.0	2372.0	3005.0
1967	4031.0	213.8	2941.0	2443.0	2912.0
1968	4622.8	−3.4	3166.0	2594.0	3159.0
1969	5275.2	1.0	3313.0	2664.0	3533.0
1970	6626.2	257.0	3561.0	2921.0	3824.0

	HC	HI	HKM	I	IM
1963	292.1	871.3	478.5	0.560	1333.4
1964	239.7	871.2	478.7	0.588	1294.7
1965	249.9	1201.6	497.9	0.384	1343.4
1966	418.4	1550.9	639.3	0.323	1321.4
1967	422.0	1499.2	697.2	0.285	1346.1
1968	437.1	1374.4	748.7	0.379	1450.0
1969	574.3	1462.7	902.4	0.439	1469.3
1970	727.0	1661.4	954.5	0.483	1674.8

TABLE 12.3 (continued)

	IPK	KC	KCF	KC*	LC
1963	0.516	26046.7	26046.7	29515.5	1.127
1964	0.785	27380.1	27380.1	29744.5	1.151
1965	1.000	28674.8	28674.8	31274.2	1.174
1966	1.301	30018.2	30018.2	33659.0	1.188
1967	1.611	31339.5	31339.5	35915.1	1.189
1968	2.101	32685.7	32685.7	35999.8	1.192
1969	2.893	34135.7	34135.7	37122.3	1.205
1970	3.894	35604.9	35604.9	36947.8	1.230

	LC*	LS	M	MB	MF
1963	0.907	0.687	659.4	532.4	746.3
1964	1.020	0.702	930.5	922.7	1129.2
1965	1.005	0.712	1476.0	1281.7	1864.0
1966	0.959	0.739	2188.0	2047.0	2590.0
1967	1.029	0.804	2796.0	2481.4	3240.0
1968	1.043	0.825	3647.0	3615.9	4487.0
1969	1.084	0.869	5161.0	5124.7	6057.0
1970	1.133	0.927	7870.0	8722.4	10483.0

	NCF	NPROF	NTP	NYD	NYP
1963	1.161	1605.0	103.0	6658.7	6788.0
1964	1.195	2663.0	157.0	10251.2	10451.0
1965	1.214	3053.0	377.0	14118.0	14549.0
1966	1.226.	4031.0	599.0	19032.4	19799.0
1967	1.249	5680.0	818.0	24980.0	25754.0
1968	1.247	7657.0	1065.0	33543.4	34750.0
1969	1.285	12180.0	1463.0	47887.9	10266.0
1970	1.306	18918.0	2298.0	10031.8	72744.0

	P	PC	PCON	PM	PQ
1963	0.532	0.495	0.534	0.595	0.512
1964	0.776	0.732	0.761	0.771	0.745
1965	1.000	1.000	1.000	1.000	1.000
1966	1.229	1.296	1.243	1.196	1.303
1967	1.452	1.642	1.632	1.533	1.672
1968	1.838	2.196	1.121	1.982	2;188
1969	2.396	3.172	2.925	2.779	3.086
1970	3.182	4.282	4.011	3.774	4.274

TABLE 12.3 (continued)

	PS	PT	Q	QC	QCF
1963	0.536	0.528	16412.0	9323.0	9378.34
1964	0.763	0.746	17099.0	9870.0	9828.67
1965	1.000	1.000	17956.0	10241.0	10309.1
1966	1.312	1.298	19221.0	10935.0	11064.2
1967	1.712	1.612	19670.0	11242.0	10996.8
1968	2.177	2.099	20241.0	11475.0	11388.9
1969	2.975	2.967	10915.0	11832.0	11712.0
1970	4.221	4.046	21572.0	12054.0	12172.8

	QCFE	QS	R	REP	$(M/P.PO)^d$
1963	11981.5	7089.0	12839.2	911.634	1260.8
1964	12642.7	7288.0	12764.9	958.303	1241.2
1965	13310.1	7715.0	19653.2	1003.62	1470.2
1966	14119.0	8286.0	18744.4	1050.64	1788.8
1967	14644.7	8428.0	19799.0	1096.88	2042.0
1968	15534.1	8766.0	10960.7	1144.00	2044.7
1969	16674.2	9083.0	23940.4	1194.75	2084.4
1970	17828.5	9518.0	27345.8	1246.17	2299.9

	T	TMF	TNCF	TPF	TRF
1963	2560.8	431.1	209.7	202.5	1388.5
1964	2624.9	267.5	238.5	219.9	1529.6
1965	3209.1	347.2	354.5	280.7	1819.7
1966	3773.1	459.0	389.3	385.6	1986.3
1967	3916.8	433.1	462.1	176.5	2006.3
1968	4172.2	497.6	444.3	501.3	2226.5
1969	4404.5	522.3	458.4	581.5	2303.5
1970	4848.3	619.8	571.6	612.2	2431.9

	TSS	TW	U	UC	ULCC
1963	1218.6	2773.0	4.913E-02	5.872E-02	0.190
1964	1311.6	4148.0	5.120E-02	6.538E-02	0.270
1965	1585.0	6222.0	5.028E-02	6.159E-02	0.389
1966	1928.1	8713.0	4.922E-02	6.020E-02	0.509
1967	2028.9	11378.0	5.962E-02	7.679E-02	0.635
1968	2218.5	15917.0	5.685E-02	7.265E-02	0.870
1969	2516.3	22695.0	6.973E-02	9.070E-02	1.205
1970	2805.2	33889.0	6.632E-02	8.659E-02	1.766

TABLE 12.3 (continued)

	ULCS	*US*	*WC*	*WRC*	*WS*
1963	0.204	3.295E-02	1774.0	1574.2	1443.0
1964	0.303	2.701E-02	2665.0	2314.6	2191.0
1965	0.434	3.102E-02	3987.0	3395.2	3345.0
1966	0.578	3.105E-02	5567.0	4687.6	4788.0
1967	0.743	3.305E-02	7142.0	6006.2	6264.0
1968	0.995	3.304E-02	9983.0	8372.9	8724.0
1969	1.387	3.903E-02	14258.0	11835.1	12598.0
1970	1.976	3.800E-02	21285.8	17308.3	18809.2

	YD	*ZM*
1963	12464.8	−20.784
1964	13963.9	−42.404
1965	14118.0	5.829
1966	15308.8	−8.008
1967	15309.6	−115.697
1968	15817.7	−60.623
1969	16372.9	69.562
1970	17466.4	173.339

TABLE 12.4
Simulated values of endogenous variables (control values).

	A	W^e/C^e	*CA*	*CD*	*CK*
1963	2.862	19682.7	0.830	2229.01	8.721E-02
1964	2.884	16997.0	0.807	2517.16	0.140
1965	2.875	18088.2	0.813	2838.05	0.155
1966	2.856	21242.0	0.808	3242.63	0.207
1967	2.847	21624.7	0.778	3472.00	0.294
1968	2.852	21711.0	0.799	3870.18	0.376
1969	2.874	21744.1	0.744	4136.75	0.571
1970	2.843	21465.6	0.733	4668.68	0.887

	CND	*CP*	*CUC*	*De*	*ERSS*
1963	9265.91	11494.6	0.771	354.256	856.499
1964	9620.73	12137.9	0.760	444.76	915.980
1965	9993.34	12831.4	0.777	819.003	1110.72
1966	10384.7	13627.5	0.801	865.508	1263.00
1967	10790.8	14262.4	0.779	495.637	1372.34
1968	11119.1	14989.1	0.752	949.871	1585.41
1969	11605.5	15742.6	0.738	539.117	1783.87
1970	12075.0	16743.2	0.703	2607.25	1931.45

TABLE 12.4 (continued)

	F	FCCBT	GDI	GIM	H
1963	2525.19	−59.144	2733.79	2145.19	2199.11
1964	3019.37	−107.041	2604.51	2122.53	2454.74
1965	4769.97	96.203	2684.77	2172.75	2354.64
1966	3838.91	179.308	2958.86	2430.59	2684.98
1967	4231.46	150.737	3146.70	2649.26	2783.02
1968	4743.89	21.771	3337.60	2765.81	3197.98
1969	5082.80	−125.983	3451.13	2801.51	3360.21
1970	6656.13	596.854	3548.37	2908.86	3824.66

	HC	HI	HKM	I	IM
1963	193.773	868.500	583.557	0.548	1233.34
1964	235.407	971.475	550.430	0.518	1167.73
1965	231.419	1178.64	524.992	0.362	1177.08
1966	363.332	1359.70	565.775	0.407	1393.78
1967	387.512	1398.94	702.505	0.332	1563.40
1968	413.227	1428.62	757.140	0.334	1625.38
1969	452.009	1528.64	786.556	0.443	1604.38
1970	709.133	1706.13	927.827	0.616	1655.36

	IPK	KC	KCF	KC*	LC
1963	0.538	26046.8	26046.8	28801.1	1.130
1964	0.811	27280.1	27280.1	27973.0	1.153
1965	0.966	28447.9	28447.9	30606.9	1.173
1966	1.261	29624.9	29624.9	34490.9	1.183
1967	1.619	31018.7	31018.7	35941.4	1.193
1968	2.065	32582.1	32582.1	35977.7	1.200
1969	2.827	34207.5	34207.5	37926.9	1.212
1970	3.969	35811.9	35811.9	39043.8	1.227

	LC*	LS	M	MB	MF
1963	0.901	0.671	596.516	461.756	650.079
1964	1.013	0.683	785.608	759.215	952.834
1965	1.041	0.709	1251.31	1144.32	1625.40
1966	0.999	0.750	2004.93	1986.53	2531.52
1967	1.023	0.794	2734.08	2357.86	3150.79
1968	1.020	0.838	3717.48	3517.53	4591.59
1969	1.073	0.893	5185.40	4899.35	6228.04
1970	1.120	0.947	8194.45	8836.90	10888.1

TABLE 12.4 (continued)

	NCF	NPROF	NTP	NYD	NYP
1963	1.161	1595.25	99.192	6628.57	6757.14
1964	1.195	2520.16	148.135	9991.92	10139.8
1965	1.214	2830.27	343.860	13698.3	14009.5
1966	1.226	3952.98	580.084	19036.1	19640.8
1967	1.249	5792.50	853.228	25194.1	26017.6
1968	1.247	7596.63	1062.76	33597.1	34909.2
1969	1.285	12179.5	1441.98	48493.7	50977.0
1970	1.306	20701.7	2285.27	73970.7	77379.9

	P	PC	PCON	PM	PQ
1963	0.528	0.505	0.530	0.574	0.516
1964	0.737	0.702	0.739	0.771	0.732
1965	0.934	0.916	0.965	1.004	0.967
1966	1.221	1.291	1.277	1.199	1.310
1967	1.495	1.745	1.611	1.545	1.684
1968	1.830	2.150	2.091	2.006	2.176
1969	2.392	2.967	2.822	2.775	2.963
1970	3.460	4.553	4.115	3.745	4.376

	PS	PT	Q	QC	QCF
1963	0.530	0.527	16129.3	9206.05	9396.58
1964	0.773	0.733	16626.7	9639.82	9933.68
1965	1.038	0.969	18064.5	10418.9	10380.5
1966	1.334	1.303	19292.4	10967.3	10602.0
1967	1.606	1.633	19854.1	11177.7	10773.3
1968	2.210	2.093	20503.7	11593.2	11549.7
1969	2.956	2.911	21736.6	12141.8	11877.7
1970	4.159	4.180	22120.9	12260.2	11979.4

	QCFE	QS	R	REP	$(M/P.PO)^d$
1963	11934.7	6922.81	12826.0	911.638	1244.82
1964	12685.8	6986.79	12789.4	854.805	1097.45
1965	13407.2	7645.68	19191.9	995.675	1341.17
1966	13699.6	8325.67	19002.1	1036.87	1620.53
1967	14354.1	8675.13	21024.5	1085.66	1930.24
1968	15415.7	8910.04	21307.6	1140.37	2031.77
1969	16446.4	9596.35	23357.2	1197.26	2235.85
1970	17452.0	9859.43	27859.0	1253.42	2250.67

TABLE 12.4 (continued)

	T	TMF	TNCF	TPF	TRF
1963	2694.21	504.079	233.715	174.894	1452.36
1964	2739.35	360.392	261.317	194.680	1553.55
1965	3156.82	335.769	354.092	261.819	1798.15
1966	3715.71	395.153	375.853	386.393	2005.58
1967	3959.06	412.683	429.815	472.731	2104.69
1968	4158.69	489.624	468.117	482.987	2215.33
1969	4444.21	519.714	462.537	507.324	2416.27
1970	4784.68	606.073	518.858	564.888	2481.74

	TSS	TW	U	UC	ULCC
1963	1233.26	2743.52	5.573E-02	5.651E-02	0.194
1964	1322.13	4012.34	6.070E-02	6.439E-02	0.265
1965	1603.83	5977.59	5.228E-02	6.250E-02	0.354
1966	1823.49	8732.59	4.658E-02	6.414E-02	0.494
1967	1980.98	11506.4	6.300E-02	7.402E-02	0.660
1968	2287.39	16025.6	4.772E-02	6.697E-02	0.869
1969	2572.76	23299.6	5.597E-02	8.540E-02	1.205
1970	2785.03	36264.7	5.874E-02	8.890E-02	1.935

	ULCS	US	WC	WRC	WS
1963	0.204	5.443E-02	1784.89	1580.08	1411.01
1964	0.305	5.440E-02	2558.35	2219.62	2129.32
1965	0.436	3.488E-02	3683.52	3139.83	3331.70
1966	0.583	1.749E-02	5419.83	4582.84	4855.01
1967	0.712	4.593E-02	7376.51	6184.89	6180.56
1968	0.994	1.872E-02	10073.3	8397.23	8853.2
1969	1.349	1.287E-02	14626.5	12070.5	12941.0
1970	1.950	1.658E-02	23719.4	19336.1	19227.9

	YD	ZM
1963	12502.6	−116.138
1964	13527.1	−31.910
1965	14201.5	−1.685
1966	14911.1	21.874
1967	15638.8	−101.736
1968	16067.5	−0.538
1969	17188.6	−66.999
1970	17969.6	116.332

TABLE 12.5

Percentage errors for the backcast.

	A	W^e/C^e	CA	CD	CK
1963	5.964E-03	−1.741	0.804	−6.383	4.278
1964	0.508	−5.349	0.368	0.727	3.324
1965	0.662	−5.601	−0.333	8.613	−3.371
1966	−0.660	−1.704	−1.443	7.230	−3.054
1967	−0.584	1.593	1.080	0.784	0.527
1968	0.204	2.208	2.180	2.958	−1.696
1969	0.102	3.149	2.186	−0.511	−2.296
1970	−0.237	6.980	−0.939	−0.856	1.937

	CND	CP	CUC	De	$ERSS$
1963	−0.281	−1.528	−1.453	−16.747	2.624
1964	−1.959	−1.414	−2.255	−17.324	0.392
1965	0.436	2.136	0.333	3.292	6.510E-02
1966	−4.823	−2.207	2.159	9.816	−5.464
1967	−1.615	−1.045	3.702	−11.088	−1.744
1968	0.172	0.876	2.582	2.779	4.441
1969	4.799	3.352	5.105	−19.218	2.716
1970	5.256	3.474	2.891	15.045	−0.967

	F	$FCCBT$	GDI	GIM	H
1963	−3.590E-02	−614.298	−3.536	−4.446	0.187
1964	3.869E-02	653.806	−4.771	−5.791	7.334
1965	−4.749	37.236	−6.094	−7.424	−0.606
1966	−2.402	75.105	2.029	2.470	−10.65
1967	4.973	−29.496	6.994	8.443	−4.429
1968	2.619	−740.323	5.420	6.623	1.234
1969	−3.647	−12698.3	4.169	5.162	−4.891
1970	0.452	132.239	−0.355	−0.416	1.722E-02

	HC	HI	HKM	I	IM
1963	−33.662	−0.321	21.955	−2.080	−7.504
1964	−1.791	11.510	14.984	−11.931	−9.807
1965	−7.396	−1.911	5.441	−5.846	−12.380
1966	−13.161	−12.328	−11.501	25.955	5.478
1967	−8.173	−6.668	0.761	16.319	16.143
1968	−5.462	3.945	1.127	−11.960	12.095
1969	−21.294	4.508	−12.837	0.921	9.193
1970	−2.458	2.693	−2.794	27.565	−1.161

TABLE 12.5 (continued)

	IPK	KC	KCF	KC*	LC
1963	4.272	3.899E-04	3.899E-04	−2.420	0.236
1964	3.323	−0.365	−0.365	−5.956	0.106
1965	−3.370	−0.791	−0.791	−2.134	−9.680E-02
1966	−3.047	−1.310	−1.310	2.472	−0.420
1967	0.514	−1.024	−1.024	7.309E-02	0.300
1968	−1.701	−0.317	−0.317	−6.133E-02	0.613
1969	−2.281	0.210	0.210	2.168	0.582
1970	1.925	0.581	0.581	5.673	−0.253

	LC*	LS	M	MB	MF
1963	−0.677	−2.221	−9.536	−13.269	−12.893
1964	−0.640	−2.815	−15.571	−17.718	−15.619
1965	3.672	−0.398	−15.223	−10.719	−12.800
1966	4.237	1.400	−8.367	−2.954	−2.258
1967	−0.528	−1.332	−2.215	−4.979	−2.753
1968	−2.211	1.481	1.933	−2.720	2.331
1969	−0.975	2.722	0.473	−4.397	2.824
1970	−1.202	2.226	4.123	1.313	3.864

	NCF	NPROF	NTP	NYD	NYP
1963	0.0	−0.608	−3.697	−0.452	−0.455
1964	0.0	−5.364	−5.646	−2.529	−2.978
1965	0.0	−7.295	−8.790	−2.973	−3.708
1966	0.0	−1.935	−3.158	1.954E-02	−0.799
1967	0.0	1.981	4.307	0.857	1.023
1968	0.0	−0.788	−0.210	0.160	0.458
1969	0.0	−3.816E-03	−1.437	1.265	1.415
1970	0.0	9.429	−0.554	5.624	6.373

	P	PC	PCON	PM	PQ
1963	−0.688	2.134	−0.730	−3.548	0.702
1964	−4.992	−4.103	−2.937	0.000	−1.713
1965	−6.581	−8.448	−3.542	0.400	−3.257
1966	−0.647	−0.405	2.720	0.263	0.515
1967	2.932	6.295	−1.313	0.778	0.715
1968	−0.445	−2.127	−1.425	1.201	−0.559
1969	−0.159	−6.441	−3.517	−0.160	−3.985
1970	8.748	6.332	2.604	−0.771	2.397

TABLE 12.5 (continued)

	PS	PT	Q	QC	QCF
1963	−1.157	−0.216	−1.723	−1.254	0.195
1964	1.404	−1.725	−2.762	−2.332	1.068
1965	3.816	−3.097	0.604	1.737	0.692
1966	1.705	0.331	0.371	0.295	−4.178
1967	−6.153	1.290	0.936	−0.572	−2.032
1968	1.548	−0.280	1.298	1.030	1.412
1969	−0.660	−1.898	3.928	2.618	1.415
1970	−1.469	3.312	2.544	1.711	−1.589

	QCFE	QS	R	REP	$(M/P.PO)^d$
1963	−0.390	−2.344	−0.103	4.017E-04	−1.267
1964	0.341	−3.337	0.192	−0.365	−11.582
1965	0.730	−0.899	−2.347	−0.791	−8.776
1966	−2.970	0.479	1.375	−1.310	−9.407
1967	−1.984	2.932	6.190	−1.024	−5.473
1968	−0.768	1.643	1.655	−0.317	−0.633
1969	−1.366	5.652	−2.436	0.210	7.266
1970	−2.112	3.587	1.877	0.581	−2.141

	T	TMF	TNCF	TPF	TRF
1963	5.210	16.928	11.452	−13.633	4.599
1964	4.360	34.726	9.567	−11.469	1.566
1965	−1.629	−3.292	−0.115	−6.726	−1.184
1966	−1.521	−13.910	−3.454	0.206	0.971
1967	1.079	−4.714	−6.987	−0.791	4.904
1968	−0.324	−1.603	5.361	−3.653	−0.502
1969	0.902	−0.495	0.902	−12.756	4.895
1970	−1.312	−2.215	−9.227	−7.728	2.049

	TSS	TW	U	UC	ULCC
1963	1.203	−1.063	13.445	−3.762	1.892
1964	0.803	−3.270	18.551	−1.508	−1.710
1965	1.188	−3.928	3.975	1.470	−9.189
1966	−5.426	0.225	−5.381	6.548	−2.930
1967	−2.362	1.128	5.657	−3.609	3.878
1968	3.105	0.683	−16.059	−7.823	−0.124
1969	2.244	2.664	−19.739	−5.847	−3.292E-02
1970	−0.719	7.010	−11.429	2.675	9.559

TABLE 12.5 (continued)

	ULSC	US	WC	WRC	WS
1963	0.124	65.174	0.614	0.374	−2.217
1964	0.538	101.401	−4.002	−4.104	−2.815
1965	0.506	12.429	−7.612	−7.522	−0.397
1966	0.924	−43.688	−2.644	−2.235	1.400
1967	−4.157	38.966	3.284	2.975	−1.332
1968	−0.165	−43.346	0.905	0.291	1.481
1969	−2.756	−67.023	2.584	1.989	2.723
1970	−1.327	−56.365	11.433	11.716	2.226

	YD	ZM
1963	0.303	458.782
1964	−3.128	−24.746
1965	0.592	−128.910
1966	−2.598	−373.145
1967	2.150	−12.067
1968	1.579	−99.112
1969	4.982	−196.315
1970	2.881	−32.911

TABLE 12.6
Percentage differences for experiment No. 1.

	A	W^e/C^e	CA	CD	CK
1965	0.000	−3.077	0.783	0.213	−1.208
1966	2.976E-02	−7.876	2.243	0.454	−2.109
1967	0.269	−11.377	3.711	0.466	−2.577
1968	0.554	−13.727	4.649	0.268	−2.717
1969	0.733	−16.591	6.04	5.902E-02	−3.529
1970	0.935	−21.362	7.98	−0.271	−5.250

	CND	CP	CUC	De	ERSS
1965	−6.669E-02	−4.749E-03	0.461	−4.630	0.157
1966	−0.110	2.376E-02	0.999	−2.077	−0.192
1967	−0.213	−4.379E-02	1.127	3.495	−0.996
1968	−0.570	−0.352	1.109	3.435	−1.527
1969	−0.994	−0.720	1.327	11.323	−1.742
1970	−1.521	−1.171	1.968	−0.207	−2.010

TABLE 12.6 (continued)

	F	FCCBT	GDI	GIM	H
1965	0.000	−39.415	−0.610	−0.756	−0.357
1966	−3.601	−10.023	−1.967	−2.379	−0.804
1967	−2.635	11.490	−4.105	−4.902	−1.547
1968	−1.473	149.873	−5.901	−7.136	−2.204
1969	−1.211	−48.453	−7.308	−8.981	−2.898
1970	−3.742	−0.903	−8.535	−10.432	−3.328

	HC	HI	HKM	I	IM
1965	−2.600	−0.202	0.000	−13.562	−1.394
1966	−1.912	−0.289	−1.950	−8.938	−4.114
1967	−2.314	−0.618	−3.542	−4.970	−8.125
1968	−2.613	−1.062	−5.829	−2.387	−11.704
1969	−3.424	−1.469	−7.630	−8.575	−14.837
1970	−3.040	−1.657	−8.281	−11.582	−17.000

	IPK	KC	KCF	KC*	LC
1965	−1.208	0.000	0.000	−1.206	0.226
1966	−2.118	−5.537E-02	−5.537E-02	−3.910	0.646
1967	−2.562	−0.238	−0.238	−6.887	1.039
1968	−2.707	−0.616	−0.616	−9.315	1.327
1969	−3.543	−1.143	−1.143	−11.776	1.638
1970	−5.233	−1.757	−1.757	−15.093	2.140

	LC*	LS	M	MB	MF
1965	1.929	−0.208	−1.473	−3.314	−2.807
1966	4.320	−0.514	−2.442	−2.813	−2.272
1967	5.037	−0.897	−1.677	−1.176	−1.176
1968	5.095	−1.368	−0.329	−0.169	0.277
1969	5.797	−1.928	1.027	1.125	1.549
1970	7.947	−2.648	1.172	0.563	0.994

	NCF	NPROF	NTP	NYD	NYP
1965	0.0	−3.601	0.000	−2.142	−2.463
1966	0.0	−6.139	−6.288	−3.722	−4.507
1967	0.0	−7.495	−7.097	−4.883	−5.887
1968	0.0	−8.356	−6.986	−5.643	−6.740
1969	0.0	−11.212	−7.224	−7.725	−8.976
1970	0.0	−15.700	−11.499	−11.136	−12.961

TABLE 12.6 (continued)

	P	PC	PCON	PM	PQ
1965	−3.599	−5.445	−1.980	0.0	−2.805
1966	−6.112	−8.828	−3.559	0.0	−4.744
1967	−7.232	−10.350	−4.484	0.0	−5.728
1968	−7.760	−11.244	−4.544	0.0	−5.976
1969	−10.221	−14.533	−6.161	0.0	−7.862
1970	−14.153	−19.876	−8.882	0.0	−11.037

	PS	PT	Q	QC	QCF
1965	0.483	−2.310	−4.751E-02	0.461	0.570
1966	0.617	−3.735	−0.173	0.603	1.683
1967	0.711	−4.658	−0.465	0.479	3.323
1968	0.857	−4.893	−0.874	0.232	4.614
1969	0.935	−6.298	−1.233	0.128	5.807
1970	1.252	−8.774	−1.680	0.197	7.382

	QCFE	QS	R	REP	$(M/P.PO)^d$
1965	0.000	−0.740	0.000	0.000	1.189
1966	−0.393	−1.205	−2.463	−5.538E-02	2.298
1967	−0.640	−1.665	−0.942	−0.238	3.783
1968	−0.867	−2.303	0.240	−0.616	5.471
1969	−1.184	−2.971	0.530	−1.143	7.970
1970	−1.736	−3.998	−1.318	−1.757	12.521

	T	TMF	TNCF	TPF	TRF
1965	0.636	−0.466	3.736	3.736	−7.541E-02
1966	−0.308	−1.016	−3.703E-02	−0.585	−0.263
1967	−0.656	−1.941	−0.752	6.218E-02	−0.693
1968	−0.955	−2.678	−0.524	0.917	−1.279
1969	−0.784	−3.485	1.746	3.379	−1.753
1970	−1.224	−3.907	1.392	3.022	−2.366

	TSS	TW	U	UC	ULCC
1965	0.157	−3.470	−1.133	−3.391	−6.843
1966	−0.191	−6.246	−3.996	−9.415	−11.925
1967	−0.994	−8.088	−3.951	−13.002	−14.536
1968	−1.520	−9.064	−4.375	−18.491	−16.051
1969	−1.734	−11.618	−2.102	−17.536	−20.345
1970	−2.005	−15.768	−0.877	−21.941	−26.580

TABLE 12.6 (continued)

	ULCS	US	WC	WRC	WS
1965	0.536	5.755	−6.414	−6.624	−0.208
1966	0.689	28.905	−11.394	−11.960	−0.515
1967	0.798	18.628	−14.127	−15.009	−0.897
1968	0.969	71.722	−15.855	−16.958	−1.368
1969	1.059	147.845	−20.243	−21.525	−1.928
1970	1.425	157.074	−26.435	−27.982	−2.647

	YD	ZM
1965	−0.164	−586.337
1966	−0.188	120.486
1967	−0.385	−36.882
1968	−1.129	−9901.104
1969	−1.696	−137.637
1970	−2.441	122.513

12.2. Simulation experiment No. 1

The first experiment assumes that for the period 1965–1970 the real wage rate in the commodity sector is constant at a fixed unemployment rate (instead of growing at the historical rate of around 5%).

In table 12.6, we present the percentage differences between the results of the simulations for experiment No. 1, and the control values. Prices, as expected, are lower but output is also lower. The result can be due in part to a fault of the model arising from the lack of an endogenous income distribution process. In the model, the lower wages cut disposable income and therefore consumption and aggregate demand. But, in principle, profits can increase (if they are the residual), and this could result in a smaller reduction in disposable income than the value showed in the experiment. However, the important point to note is the fact that the cut in wages in the commodity sector creates an important increase in employment in that sector and a major cut in the unemployment rate of that sector, although the overall unemployment rate is only weakly affected because of the increase in the unemployment rate in services. If we accept the hypothesis that there is in the service sector an important disguised employment, this shift in employment toward the commodity sector can be desirable for the society.

12.3. Simulation experiment No. 2

One of the controversial policy decisions taken during the Frei government was the accumulation of foreign reserves to be used as a basis for the rationalization of the international trade system. In experiment No. 2, we study the behavior of the endogenous variables of the model assuming that, in the period 1965–1970, instead of accumulating foreign reserves, the Central Bank had maintained the foreign exchange reserves at the average level which existed in the three years before the Frei government. These values are shown in table 12.7. In the experiment, we assume that the government imports commodities which compete with domestic output and sells the products in the domestic market. As a conse-

TABLE 12.7
Foreign reserves (millions of US dollars).

	Available at end of the year	Possible* sale
1960	−33.9	
1961	−166.0	
1962	−234.5	
1963	−264.0	
1964	−238.7	
1965	−182.9	62.8
1966	−66.1	116.8
1967	−91.5	−25.4
1968	37.7	129.2
1969	220.0	182.3
1970	343.2	123.2

* Sale that keeps the average stock of period 1962–1964.
Source: ODEPLAN, Plan de la Economía Chilena 1960–1970, Santiago, Chile, 1971.

TABLE 12.8
Percentage differences for experiment No. 2.

	A	W^e/C^e	CA	CD	CK
1965	−3.317E-04	1.003	−0.723	−3.221	0.929
1966	0.299	0.483	−1.599	−5.663	6.420E-02
1967	0.385	−4.766	5.700E-03	−0.323	−3.823
1968	−0.348	−5.741	0.773	−2.279	−0.609
1969	0.645	−2.202	−1.137	−7.015	−9.498E-02
1970	0.786	−4.532	−1.450	−4.243	−2.919

	CND	CP	CUC	D	$ERSS$
1965	−0.399	−1.021	−1.611	6.094	−1.981
1966	−0.819	−1.968	−3.774	1.902	−1.798
1967	9.155E-02	−4.437E-03	−0.735	−25.627	4.042
1968	−0.246	−0.771	−0.818	39.980	−0.787
1969	−1.204	−2.738	−4.981	5.348	−2.602
1970	−1.288	−2.113	−4.680	−5.160	0.238

	F	$FCCBT$	GDI	GIM	H
1965	4.561E-02	51.879	−1.125	−1.397	8.633
1966	2.700	9.182	−3.320	−4.047	14.081
1967	−2.792	−84.263	−3.165	−3.807	−2.954
1968	−11.459	1744.35	−4.303	−5.192	13.078
1969	9.014	−22.886	−7.070	−8.665	17.562
1970	0.336	−22.539	−8.265	−10.083	10.427

	HC	HI	HKM	I	IM
1965	3.492E-02	−1.472	1.939E-02	10.144	−2.573
1966	−2.379	−3.000	−0.277	−9.341	−6.978
1967	−3.454	−0.603	−3.143	−44.504	−6.151
1968	−1.394	−2.877	−5.964	39.030	−8.351
1969	−3.233	−4.918	−4.573	4.534	−14.358
1970	−2.771	−3.982	−6.035	−19.604	−16.467

	IPK	KC	KCF	KC^*	LC
1965	0.932	8.651E-04	8.651E-04	−0.787	−0.209
1966	6.638E-02	−0.101	−0.101	−2.286	−0.460
1967	−3.794	−0.410	−0.410	−1.904	1.759E-03
1968	−0.610	−0.686	−0.686	−3.903	0.220
1969	−0.127	−1.050	−1.050	−6.160	−0.308
1970	−2.919	−1.646	−1.646	−5.859	−0.390

TABLE 12.8 (continued)

	LC*	LS	M	MB	MF
1965	−1.782	−0.720	−7.021	−13.381	−11.329
1966	−2.764	−2.178	−22.282	−30.150	−29.671
1967	2.958	−2.198	−27.089	−25.418	−25.298
1968	1.952	−3.090	−27.816	−30.004	−29.805
1969	−4.000	−4.672	−43.035	−53.626	−53.150
1970	−1.391	−5.678	−49.127	−47.500	−47.031

	NCF	NPROF	NTP	NYD	NYP
1965	0.0	2.767	7.448E-02	0.983	1.045
1966	0.0	−9.578E-02	3.913	−0.800	−0.859
1967	0.0	−11.449	−3.923	−5.837	−6.624
1968	0.0	−2.979	−17.549	−1.444	−2.293
1969	0.0	−1.987	8.168	−2.186	−2.286
1970	0.0	−9.939	−1.006	−6.448	−7.217

	P	PC	PCON	PM	PQ
1965	2.774	2.578	1.998	0.0	2.165
1966	1.195E-02	−2.103	0.739	0.0	0.149
1967	−11.002	−14.236	−6.882	0.0	−8.483
1968	−2.315	−3.579	−0.748	0.0	−1.347
1969	−1.037	−2.700	0.324	0.0	−0.283
1970	−8.435	−11.582	−4.878	0.0	−6.157

	PS	PT	Q	QC	QCF
1965	1.712	1.783	−2.018	−1.611	−0.528
1966	3.140	−0.148	−3.859	−2.608	−0.381
1967	−0.452	−7.202	−9.070E-02	1.026	0.851
1968	1.597	−0.836	−3.304	−2.217	−0.853
1969	3.042	−0.837	−5.820	−4.253	0.376
1970	1.338	−5.478	−4.728	−2.897	0.157

	QCFE	QS	R	REP	$(M/P.PO)^d$
1965	2.914E-05	−2.568	6.249E-03	8.582E-04	−2.570
1966	1.212	−5.503	0.979	−0.101	−12.756
1967	1.774	−1.492	−3.535	−0.410	−19.526
1968	−1.410	−4.721	−6.635	−0.686	−21.632
1969	0.765	−7.838	9.786	−1.050	−27.595
1970	1.871	−7.007	2.935E-02	−1.646	−43.513

TABLE 12.8 (continued)

	T	TMF	TNCF	TPF	TRF
1965	−1.134	11.261	−2.581	−2.61	−3.203
1966	−0.367	17.797	4.790	4.061	−5.866
1967	1.522	−3.706	10.136	7.577	−0.135
1968	−4.491	15.888	−16.897	−16.250	−4.831
1969	−0.260	21.119	5.585	10.207	−8.272
1970	−4.392E-02	12.239	8.343	8.075	−6.658

	TSS	TW	U	UC	ULCC
1965	−1.971	1.007	7.281	3.131	4.178
1966	−1.790	−1.576	23.060	6.712	1.557
1967	4.027	−7.897	13.036	−1.997E-02	−13.422
1968	−0.780	−3.024	22.767	−3.076	−0.782
1969	−2.592	−3.298	36.446	3.302	2.168
1970	0.234	−8.212	43.166	3.987	−7.588

	ULCS	US	WC	WRC	WS
1965	1.900	19.932	2.499	2.720	−0.721
1966	3.524	122.350	−1.092	−0.627	−2.178
1967	−0.677	45.664	−12.534	−12.549	−2.196
1968	1.708	162.012	−2.981	−3.193	−3.091
1969	3.392	358.334	−2.177	−1.867	−4.675
1970	1.425	336.762	−10.265	−9.912	−5.679

	YD	ZM
1965	−0.990	5522.34
1966	−1.523	−727.981
1967	1.187	−47.178
1968	−0.705	16890.2
1969	−2.566	455.479
1970	−1.652	−62.58

TABLE 12.9
Percentage differences for experiment No. 3

	A	W^e/C^e	CA	CD	CK
1965	−3.317E-04	7.472E-02	−3.881E-02	−0.415	5.037E-02
1966	1.346E-02	−0.280	0.140	−0.593	−0.327
1967	5.058E-03	−0.821	0.515	−0.443	−0.574
1968	6.688E-02	−1.016	0.830	0.164	−0.678
1969	0.165	−1.056	1.111	0.777	−0.785
1970	0.276	−1.268	1.372	1.547	−1.140

TABLE 12.9 (continued)

	CND	CP	CUC	De	ERSS
1965	−1.235E-02	−0.102	−7.708E-02	−2.694	−0.145
1966	0.138	−3.715E-02	2.400E-02	−7.936	0.526
1967	0.408	0.208	0.194	−19.769	1.087
1968	0.716	0.573	9.552E-02	−19.269	1.585
1969	1.056	0.978	−0.212	−60.259	2.086
1970	1.433	1.471	−0.380	−24.398	2.807

	F	FCCBT	FDV	GDI	GIM
1965	4.561E-02	−22.939	−62.451	5.278	6.526
1966	0.133	−38.307	−4.011	7.816	9.526
1967	−0.613	−65.004	−57.435	9.749	11.532
1968	0.504	−840.711	−3.547	10.866	13.112
1969	1.726	257.866	−30.161	11.648	14.391
1970	2.611	−106.578	3.497	12.190	14.835

	H	HC	HI	HKM	I
1965	6.158	29.011	6.624	−4.539E-02	0.500
1966	5.400	0.543	0.564	23.94	−3.767
1967	5.210	9.246	3.901	7.861	−2.702
1968	4.534	0.795	1.391	16.098	−1.186
1969	4.315	4.262	2.799	10.489	−1.037
1970	3.791	0.478	1.770	12.13	−2.132

	IM	IPK	KC	KCF	KC*
1965	12.045	4.777E-02	8.651E-04	8.651E-04	−2.573E-02
1966	16.251	−0.334	0.479	0.479	0.144
1967	18.737	−0.544	1.188	1.188	0.233
1968	20.889	−0.677	2.030	2.030	0.148
1969	22.939	−0.816	2.926	2.926	−1.730E-03
1970	23.179	−1.114	3.823	3.823	4.242E-03

	LC	LC*	LS	M	MB
1965	−1.114E-02	−9.477E-02	−2.846E-02	−0.983	−1.906
1966	4.064E-02	0.437	0.114	−3.297	−4.556
1967	0.144	1.011	0.403	−6.186	−7.994
1968	0.237	1.176	0.827	−9.028	−10.562
1969	0.301	1.112	1.299	−12.107	−14.214
1970	0.368	1.246	1.798	−14.277	−15.079

TABLE 12.9 (continued)

	MF	NCF	NPROF	NTP	NYD
1965	−1.610	0.0	0.199	7.448E-02	6.858E-02
1966	−4.452	0.0	−0.424	0.199	−0.281
1967	−7.576	0.0	−0.420	−1.472	−0.322
1968	−10.110	0.0	0.196	−0.938	−0.114
1969	−13.739	0.0	0.767	−0.335	9.292E-02
1970	−14.588	0.0	0.729	−0.190	−8.787E-03

	NYP	P	PC	PCON	PM
1965	7.330E-02	0.190	0.154	9.904E-02	0.0
1966	−0.312	−0.919	−1.070	−0.644	0.0
1967	−0.405	−1.504	−1.750	−1.075	0.0
1968	−0.167	−1.797	−2.044	−1.345	0.0
1969	5.936E-02	−2.185	−2.493	−1.618	0.0
1970	−3.514E-02	−2.912	−3.550	−2.076	0.0

	PQ	PS	PT	Q	QC
1965	0.111	7.340E-02	0.131	−9.084E-02	−7.705E-02
1966	−0.748	−0.314	−0.645	0.421	0.380
1967	−1.216	−0.591	−1.009	0.964	0.864
1968	−1.496	−0.814	−1.191	1.481	1.247
1969	−1.811	−0.824	−1.450	1.890	1.590
1970	−2.348	−0.816	−1.929	2.413	2.126

	QCF	QCFE	QS	R	REP
1965	−2.830E-02	2.914E-05	−0.113	6.249E-03	8.582E-04
1966	0.437	0.356	0.467	8.367E-03	0.479
1967	1.125	0.669	1.129	−0.501	1.188
1968	2.057	1.150	1.785	0.518	2.030
1969	3.104	1.806	2.235	1.357	2.926
1970	4.176	2.516	2.800	1.890	3.823

	$(M/P \cdot PO)^d$	T	TMF	TNCF	TPF
1965	−0.150	0.755	8.032	−8.363E-02	−0.113
1966	−0.722	1.312	6.825	1.195	1.109
1967	−2.078	1.453	6.535	0.211	4.689E-02
1968	−4.540	1.996	5.508	0.719	0.980
1969	−6.834	2.487	5.189	1.676	1.963
1970	−9.154	2.987	4.450	2.963	2.996

TABLE 12.9 (continued)

	TRF	TSS	TW	U	UC
1965	−0.144	−0.143	7.090E-02	0.322	0.168
1966	0.640	0.524	−0.440	−1.408	−0.586
1967	1.437	1.082	−0.635	−3.695	−1.806
1968	2.165	1.583	−0.414	−9.563	−3.301
1969	2.687	2.081	−0.242	−12.197	−3.224
1970	3.399	2.796	−0.462	−15.899	−3.773

	ULCC	ULCS	US	WC	WRC
1965	0.229	8.117E-02	0.788	0.152	0.163
1966	−1.300	−0.359	−6.405	−0.925	−0.963
1967	−2.284	−0.682	−8.378	−1.40	−1.584
1968	−2.668	−0.941	−43.330	−1.454	−1.688
1969	−3.119	−0.953	−99.642	−1.579	−1.863
1970	−4.246	−0.944	−106.665	−2.10	−2.568

	WS	YD	ZM
1965	−2.856E-02	−3.592E-02	819.385
1966	0.114	0.351	−128.736
1967	0.405	0.823	44.191
1968	0.826	1.249	10648.8
1969	1.296	1.675	103.863
1970	1.800	2.163	−59.261

quence, the money base is cut through the public buying the imports, and imports are increased by an amount equal to the foreign reserve surplus (with respect to the levels of 1962—1964). As expected, the consequence of this set of policies is a reduced level of output, especially in the last three years where the surplus was higher. Prices are lower as well, in the last four years, owing to the decrease in the demand for domestic output. A more interesting set of policies is to increase public investment in plant and equipment and to finance this expansion through credit from the Central Bank equal to the proceeds from the sale of foreign exchange to the public. This will be our experiment No. 3 which is described below.

12.4. Simulation experiment No. 3

In Chile, for the period 1962–1969 for which information exists, public investment was about 50% of the total investment in fixed capital (ODEPLAN), so that the public sector had a well establish-ed network to take care of investment projects, especially in some branches of the industrial sector. The experiment that we will do now assumes that the government is following a policy of increas-ing annual investment in plant and equipment during the period 1965–1970 by 145 millions of 1965 escudos (about 10% of the average investment for the period).

We assume further that this increase in investment is financed through the Central Bank selling foreign exchange to importers by an amount equal to the excess of reserves defined in experiment No. 2. For the importers to be willing to increase imports, it is necessary to make imports cheaper and/or to relax the restrictions on trade. The first alternative of making imports cheaper through lower devaluation was not used here, because it would have re-quired the treatment of exports as endogenous (at least non-copper exports) depending on the exchange rate. An unsuccessful attempt was made to endogenize exports on non-copper products. This failure can be due in part to the quota system for most of the agricultural products, and to the big promotion of exports by the government after 1965. The latter constitute major changes in the structure, difficult to capture with an 11-year time series. There-fore, in our experiment, we assume that the increase in imports is achieved by the Central Bank relaxing the quantitative control on trade (*FDV*). The consequences of this set of policies are: more output, especially in the last three years; reduced unemployment; lower prices.

APPENDIX A

In this appendix, the data used in the estimation of ch. 3 are presented.

For all the indexes used, the arithmetic base is the year 1965. The definitions and sources of the variables that appear in the tables are as follows.

CL = quarterly cost of living index. This index was computed as the average of the monthly retail price index. This last index was taken from the *Monthly Bulletin of the Central Bank* (MBCB).

PI = quarterly industrial price index. This index was computed as the average of the industrial price component of the monthly wholesale price index. This last index was taken from the MBCB.

P = quarterly wholesale price index. This index was computed as the average of the monthly wholesale price index.

PF = quarterly agricultural price index. This index was computed as the average of the agricultural component of the monthly wholesale price index.

PM = quarterly imported raw materials price index. This index was computed as the average of the imported raw materials component of the wholesale price index.

$QIPRO$ = quarterly industrial production index. This variable is defined as an average of the monthly index of industrial production computed by the Direction of Statistics and Census. The figures were taken from different issues of the MBCB.

$QMIPRO$ = quarterly maximum industrial production index. This variable is defined using linear interpolation through the peaks of the index of industrial production already defined.

CU = capacity utilization in the industrial sector. This variable is defined as the ratio between $QIPRO$ and $QMIPRO$, corrected by a factor to reproduce the figures taken from a survey of 42 industrial firms for the second half of 1961 by the Institute of Economics of the University of Chile (1963, p. 18).

UNIN = unemployment rate in the industrial sector. The variable is the unemployment rate computed in the sampling survey of the Institute of Economics of the University of Chile. The data were taken from different issues of the MBCB.

QIIEM = quarterly index of industrial employment. This index was built with the employment figures taken from the same source as *UNIN*.

WI = index of wages and salaries in the industrial sector, taken directly from the MBCB.

QMS = quarterly money supply. This variable is defined as the average of the end of the quarter figures for money supply. The definition of money supply is currency plus demand deposits in commercial banks.

TABLE A.1

Quarter	*CL*	*PI*	*P*
1959.1	0.235218	0.269726	0.272017
1959.2	0.262612	0.305302	0.301887
1959.3	0.286056	0.319443	0.320382
1959.4	0.293504	0.312742	0.315454
1960.1	0.294929	0.310791	0.313040
1960.2	0.294087	0.311901	0.314894
1960.3	0.305032	0.309561	0.321929
1960.4	0.308076	0.309789	0.323961
1961.1	0.313062	0.312834	0.315704
1961.2	0.318502	0.313531	0.318432
1961.3	0.327763	0.313182	0.323773
1961.4	0.335082	0.313896	0.325492
1962.1	0.343825	0.319804	0.326329
1962.2	0.350495	0.324266	0.327311
1962.3	0.364613	0.325506	0.336924
1962.4	0.415582	0.400131	0.398775
1963.1	0.464024	0.460691	0.475832
1963.2	0.508710	0.506549	0.522648
1963.3	0.551259	0.524955	0.553475
1963.4	0.602681	0.543644	0.583130
1964.1	0.683569	0.709822	0.725514
1964.2	0.756946	0.788037	0.795487
1964.3	0.808691	0.802922	0.836333
1964.4	0.855255	0.828176	0.857272
1965.1	0.998704	0.996749	0.988249
1965.2	0.998704	0.996749	0.988249
1965.3	1.029340	1.036980	1.041030
1965.4	1.076030	1.064310	1.061570
1966.1	1.143380	1.202360	1.157130
1966.2	1.204130	1.283540	1.205290
1966.3	1.277440	1.316370	1.267330
1966.4	1.289810	1.328330	1.280740
1967.1	1.335530	1.505280	1.380650
1967.2	1.422510	1.570380	1.447250
1967.3	1.502950	1.603910	1.502690
1967.4	1.545370	1.628670	1.528720
1968.1	1.672300	1.887930	1.751830
1968.2	1.790690	2.040250	1.860290
1968.3	1.913350	2.161360	2.003830
1968.4	1.976230	2.197330	2.038910

<table>
<tr><th colspan="3" align="center">TABLE A.2</th></tr>
<tr><th>Quarter</th><th>*PF*</th><th>*PM*</th></tr>
<tr><td>1959.1</td><td>0.194338</td><td>0.360557</td></tr>
<tr><td>1959.2</td><td>0.234526</td><td>0.386713</td></tr>
<tr><td>1959.3</td><td>0.282103</td><td>0.383603</td></tr>
<tr><td>1959.4</td><td>0.278495</td><td>0.379555</td></tr>
<tr><td>1960.1</td><td>0.274317</td><td>0.380122</td></tr>
<tr><td>1960.2</td><td>0.278031</td><td>0.383478</td></tr>
<tr><td>1960.3</td><td>0.307778</td><td>0.383924</td></tr>
<tr><td>1960.4</td><td>0.314290</td><td>0.385285</td></tr>
<tr><td>1961.1</td><td>0.280950</td><td>0.384949</td></tr>
<tr><td>1961.2</td><td>0.286680</td><td>0.384135</td></tr>
<tr><td>1961.3</td><td>0.303568</td><td>0.385023</td></tr>
<tr><td>1961.4</td><td>0.309806</td><td>0.383404</td></tr>
<tr><td>1962.1</td><td>0.306588</td><td>0.384284</td></tr>
<tr><td>1962.2</td><td>0.304212</td><td>0.383149</td></tr>
<tr><td>1962.3</td><td>0.335232</td><td>0.385332</td></tr>
<tr><td>1962.4</td><td>0.389006</td><td>0.425592</td></tr>
<tr><td>1963.1</td><td>0.398660</td><td>0.649812</td></tr>
<tr><td>1963.2</td><td>0.445229</td><td>0.711194</td></tr>
<tr><td>1963.3</td><td>0.515569</td><td>0.712180</td></tr>
<tr><td>1963.4</td><td>0.561470</td><td>0.724047</td></tr>
<tr><td>1964.1</td><td>0.637058</td><td>0.950273</td></tr>
<tr><td>1964.2</td><td>0.698389</td><td>0.995165</td></tr>
<tr><td>1964.3</td><td>0.777331</td><td>1.006220</td></tr>
<tr><td>1964.4</td><td>0.799777</td><td>1.008510</td></tr>
<tr><td>1965.1</td><td>0.886997</td><td>0.937831</td></tr>
<tr><td>1965.2</td><td>0.989294</td><td>0.985453</td></tr>
<tr><td>1965.3</td><td>1.054030</td><td>1.024220</td></tr>
<tr><td>1965.4</td><td>1.069670</td><td>1.052470</td></tr>
<tr><td>1966.1</td><td>1.151290</td><td>1.107320</td></tr>
<tr><td>1966.2</td><td>1.176940</td><td>1.141730</td></tr>
<tr><td>1966.3</td><td>1.340290</td><td>1.157420</td></tr>
<tr><td>1966.4</td><td>1.359640</td><td>1.164760</td></tr>
<tr><td>1967.1</td><td>1.338320</td><td>1.358010</td></tr>
<tr><td>1967.2</td><td>1.413860</td><td>1.420950</td></tr>
<tr><td>1967.3</td><td>1.524010</td><td>1.460490</td></tr>
<tr><td>1967.4</td><td>1.547770</td><td>1.501170</td></tr>
<tr><td>1968.1</td><td>1.617700</td><td>1.876980</td></tr>
<tr><td>1968.2</td><td>1.701430</td><td>1.964680</td></tr>
<tr><td>1968.3</td><td>1.967080</td><td>2.138110</td></tr>
<tr><td>1968.4</td><td>1.954360</td><td>2.181880</td></tr>
</table>

<table>
<tr><th colspan="3" align="center">TABLE A.3</th></tr>
<tr><th>Quarter</th><th>*QIPRO*</th><th>*QMIPRO*</th></tr>
<tr><td>1959.1</td><td>0.680105</td><td>0.766646</td></tr>
<tr><td>1959.2</td><td>0.744044</td><td>0.781307</td></tr>
<tr><td>1959.3</td><td>0.758501</td><td>0.788027</td></tr>
<tr><td>1959.4</td><td>0.800040</td><td>0.801466</td></tr>
<tr><td>1960.1</td><td>0.718183</td><td>0.811036</td></tr>
<tr><td>1960.2</td><td>0.704133</td><td>0.819996</td></tr>
<tr><td>1960.3</td><td>0.725106</td><td>0.829973</td></tr>
<tr><td>1960.4</td><td>0.764813</td><td>0.840358</td></tr>
<tr><td>1961.1</td><td>0.715332</td><td>0.850540</td></tr>
<tr><td>1961.2</td><td>0.778048</td><td>0.860924</td></tr>
<tr><td>1961.3</td><td>0.746487</td><td>0.870902</td></tr>
<tr><td>1961.4</td><td>0.876399</td><td>0.879658</td></tr>
<tr><td>1962.1</td><td>0.818570</td><td>0.907962</td></tr>
<tr><td>1962.2</td><td>0.833435</td><td>0.927713</td></tr>
<tr><td>1962.3</td><td>0.839543</td><td>0.937283</td></tr>
<tr><td>1962.4</td><td>0.921604</td><td>0.946854</td></tr>
<tr><td>1963.1</td><td>0.861127</td><td>0.956628</td></tr>
<tr><td>1963.2</td><td>0.904296</td><td>0.963755</td></tr>
<tr><td>1963.3</td><td>0.912033</td><td>0.970270</td></tr>
<tr><td>1963.4</td><td>0.961311</td><td>0.978415</td></tr>
<tr><td>1964.1</td><td>0.889635</td><td>0.990430</td></tr>
<tr><td>1964.2</td><td>0.931174</td><td>1.002240</td></tr>
<tr><td>1964.3</td><td>0.959885</td><td>1.022600</td></tr>
<tr><td>1964.4</td><td>1.030750</td><td>1.053350</td></tr>
<tr><td>1965.1</td><td>0.946446</td><td>1.083080</td></tr>
<tr><td>1965.2</td><td>0.983098</td><td>1.107920</td></tr>
<tr><td>1965.3</td><td>1.003660</td><td>1.129510</td></tr>
<tr><td>1965.4</td><td>1.066380</td><td>1.150890</td></tr>
<tr><td>1966.1</td><td>1.010990</td><td>1.172470</td></tr>
<tr><td>1966.2</td><td>1.068820</td><td>1.180410</td></tr>
<tr><td>1966.3</td><td>1.065360</td><td>1.181840</td></tr>
<tr><td>1966.4</td><td>1.133780</td><td>1.183260</td></tr>
<tr><td>1967.1</td><td>0.998167</td><td>1.184480</td></tr>
<tr><td>1967.2</td><td>1.068010</td><td>1.185710</td></tr>
<tr><td>1967.3</td><td>1.081860</td><td>1.187130</td></tr>
<tr><td>1967.4</td><td>1.110360</td><td>1.188560</td></tr>
<tr><td>1968.1</td><td>1.013440</td><td>1.189780</td></tr>
<tr><td>1968.2</td><td>1.060270</td><td>1.191200</td></tr>
<tr><td>1968.3</td><td>1.087760</td><td>1.192420</td></tr>
<tr><td>1968.4</td><td>1.086340</td><td>1.193650</td></tr>
</table>

TABLE A.4

Quarter	*CU*	*QMS*
1959.1	0.771269	318.000000
1959.2	0.827945	316.450000
1959.3	0.836835	325.150000
1959.4	0.867863	326.700000
1960.1	0.769873	337.400000
1960.2	0.746565	359.600000
1960.3	0.759559	397.500000
1960.4	0.791252	448.250000
1961.1	0.731202	482.550000
1961.2	0.785716	491.950000
1961.3	0.745208	488.650000
1961.4	0.866189	505.650000
1962.1	0.783813	545.900000
1962.2	0.781057	563.150000
1962.3	0.778747	573.400000
1962.4	0.846225	668.150000
1963.1	0.782616	772.950000
1963.2	0.815772	846.850000
1963.3	0.817226	889.300000
1963.4	0.854211	923.900000
1964.1	0.780931	1009.700000
1964.2	0.807762	1147.000000
1964.3	0.816088	1256.900001
1964.4	0.850757	1371.350001
1965.1	0.759732	1556.950001
1965.2	0.771458	1740.250000
1965.3	0.772542	1918.800000
1965.4	0.805570	2123.000001
1966.1	0.749668	2301.100001
1966.2	0.787217	2534.300002
1966.3	0.783723	2790.050002
1966.4	0.833051	2962.200002
1967.1	0.732653	3118.200002
1967.2	0.783110	3288.100001
1967.3	0.792312	3340.700002
1967.4	0.812209	3508.300002
1968.1	0.740552	3943.800002
1968.2	0.773846	4313.300006
1968.3	0.793097	4591.850004
1968.4	0.791250	5065.500003

TABLE A.5

Quarter	*WI*
1963.2	0.460563
1963.3	0.465854
1963.4	0.522736
1964.1	0.601223
1964.2	0.684782
1964.3	0.731963
1964.4	0.763269
1965.1	0.811111
1965.2	0.983079
1965.3	1.081850
1965.4	1.123960
1966.1	1.233090
1966.2	1.413000
1966.3	1.487740
1966.4	1.567330
1967.1	1.704020
1967.2	1.811830
1967.3	1.944330
1967.4	2.073530
1968.1	2.222120
1968.2	2.386370
1968.3	2.490000
1968.4	2.727000

Appendix A

TABLE A.6

Quarter	*QIIEM*	*UNIN*
1960.2	0.843181	7.000000
1960.3	0.799745	7.200000
1960.4	0.804429	6.500000
1961.1	0.825296	7.400000
1961.2	0.748217	7.900000
1961.3	0.804855	6.600000
1961.4	0.845310	5.700000
1962.1	0.822740	6.100000
1962.2	0.804429	6.400000
1962.3	0.850421	5.300000
1962.4	0.850846	5.100000
1963.1	0.836793	5.900000
1963.2	0.806132	5.400000
1963.3	0.818908	6.100000
1963.4	0.903652	4.400000
1964.1	0.871713	5.700000
1964.2	0.890025	4.700000
1964.3	0.920260	6.100000
1964.4	0.904929	5.000000
1965.1	0.966677	5.700000
1965.2	1.011390	3.900000
1965.3	1.013520	4.500000
1965.4	1.008410	4.200000
1966.1	0.953902	4.500000
1966.2	1.122540	5.200000
1966.3	1.027570	4.500000
1966.4	1.064620	4.100000
1967.1	0.961993	5.800000
1967.2	1.056960	5.300000
1967.3	1.076970	5.300000
1967.4	1.052700	6.700000
1968.1	0.996913	5.200000
1968.2	1.066330	5.300000
1968.3	1.115720	6.000000
1968.4	1.055250	4.800000

APPENDIX B

In this appendix, the method used to derive the different variables used in chs. 6–11 is presented. Only the method used for those variables which are a transformation of the variables available in the sources are described here.

The main sources used were:

(1) *Cuentas Nacionales de Chile 1940–1962*, Corporacion de Fomento de la Produccion, Santiago, Junio, 1963.

(2) *Cuentas Nacionales de Chile 1958–1963*, Corporacion de Fomento de la Produccion, Santiago, Junio, 1964.

(3) *Cuentas Nacionales de Chile 1960–1970*, Presidencia de la Republica, Oficina de Planificacion Nacional, Santiago, Febrero, 1972.

(4) *Boletin Mensual, Banco Central de Chile*, various issues. We will refer to this publication as MBCB (Monthly Bulletin of the Central Bank).

(5) *La Economia Chilena en el Período 1950–1963*, Universidad de Chile, Instituto de Economia, 1963.

(6) *Boletin Nacional de Estadistica*, formerly *Estadistica Chilena*, Direccion de Estadistica y Censos, various issues.

(7) *Plan de la Economia Nacional: Antecedentes Sobre el Desarrollo Chileno 1960–1970*, ODEPLAN, 1971. We will refer to this publication as *Antecedentes*.

In what follows, 1 and 2 will be referred to as the old accounts and 3 as the new ones.

Real gross domestic product of commodities

From the viewpoint of technological relations, we are interested in measuring a quantity related to physical output. Unfortunately, in the old accounts, the sectoral figures for gross domestic product, at current prices, are deflated by a general price index. This price index is the implicit deflator of the expenditure side of gross domestic product[1]. Therefore, the sectoral outputs at constant prices, in the old accounts, may be thought of roughly as the purchasing power of that sector's output.

To generate our series, an index was built from the old accounts of sectoral gross domestic product, at current prices, for the period 1950–1960 with 1960 = 100. Taking the current values for 1960 from the new accounts and multiplying them by this index, a series was obtained for the sectoral gross domestic product at current prices for the period 1950–1960.

Next, for the period 1950–1960, price indices that are closely related to the composition of the sectoral outputs were used as deflators for the figures at current prices. For the period 1960–1970, it was possible to use the real figures obtained directly from the new National Accounts which are themselves calculated using sectoral price indices.

Specifically, the gross domestic product of commodities was defined so as to include agriculture, fishing and forestry; mining; manufacturing; construction; electricity, gas, water, and transportation. These last two sectors were included in the above definition because, in the study of the investment function, it was not possible to separate investment in them from that for the other four sectors.

For the period 1950–1960, the sectoral figures were deflated by the corresponding price indices given below:
   (1) agriculture component wholesale price index,
   (2) mining component wholesale price index,
   (3) industrial component wholesale price index,
   (4) construction materials component wholesale price index,
   (5) national component wholesale price index.

---

[1] This implicit deflator is a weighted harmonic mean of the price deflators for consumption, government expenditures, investment, exports and imports, where the weights are the nominal values of these variables.

Real gross domestic product of services

This is defined as the difference between real gross domestic product and real gross domestic product of commodities.

Real gross investment in plant and equipment

For the period 1960–1970, our figures were obtained directly from the new accounts. For the period 1950–1960, an index was built with 1960 = 100 from the old account and then multiplied by the 1960 value from the new account.

Capital stock in plant and equipment in the sector producing commodities

Although there is a series of capital stock computed by ODEPLAN for the period 1958–1965, it was not utilized in this work because the series was derived on the basis of two different assumptions concerning depreciation. In deriving the depreciation series, a linear depreciation procedure was adopted and the capital stock was assumed to depend on gross investment over the last *m* years during which there was no deterioration until the final year, after which the stock disappeared. As was correctly pointed out in the ODEPLAN (1969) document where the figures are presented, the two depreciation procedures are clearly inconsistent. It is possible to derive this series starting with the stock of capital estimated for 1965 and assuming a capital–output ratio for that year of 2.8. The year 1965 was used as the initial point because, in that year, there was an important expansion in aggregate demand and, therefore, output was nearest to its long-run trend[2]. Utilizing the 1965 value of the capital stock as a benchmark, incorporating a series of gross investment and making the assumption that depre-

[2] For 1965, the ODEPLAN series implies a capital–output ratio of 2.4 which we decided to be too low.

ciation is a constant proportion (0.035) of the capital stock[3], it
was possible to build a capital series.

Employment in the sector producing commodities

For the years 1960–1969, again our figures were obtained from
the ODEPLAN publication, *Antecedentes*. For the year 1970,
the rate of growth of employment of the different sectors was
taken from a sampling survey study for metropolitan Santiago by
the University of Chile.

Employment in the sector producing services

Same sources as employment in the sector producing commodities.

Unemployment rate in the sector producing commodities

This rate was defined as a weighted average of the quarterly unemployment rate figures in the *Ocupación y desocupación* bulle-
tins.

Unemployment rate in the sector producing services

Same source as unemployment in the sector producing commodities.

---

[3] We can arrive at this result from still another hypothesis. The one
most commonly used is to assume that the flow of services from a given flow
of gross investment follows an expotential function with parameter δ (i.e., it
evaporates through time at a constant rate δ). Then it can be shown that total
depreciation is the same rate δ of the total capital stock (see Hahn and
Matthews, 1964; and Jorgenson, in Ferber, 1967).

Labor force in the sector producing commodities

This variable was obtained using eq. (56) from ch. 11, together with the other variables already defined in this equation.

Labor force in the sector producing services

This variable was obtained using eq. (57) from ch. 11.

Real private consumption

The same methodology was utilized as for real gross investment in plant and equipment.

Real private consumption in durables[4]

For the period 1960–1970, our data was taken from *Anteced-entes*. This figure refers mainly to production rather than consumption. For the period 1950–1960, an index of durable consumption was build with 1960 as the base. For this index, the weights from the ODEPLAN 1962 input–output study, the indices of production and imports for the period 1953–1960 given in the *Indice de producción industrial*, and the imports of durables found in various issues of MBCB were used. For the period 1950–1953, the indices of industrial production were taken from Muñoz's book (1968) and the imports of durables from different issues of MBCB. To use the production index as a proxy for production of consumption goods necessitated the assumption either that the sector considered did not produce capital goods or that the production of capital goods was a constant proportion of the production of consumption goods.

---

[4] The primary information used for this variable is available from the author.

Real private consumption in non-durables

This series was defined as real private consumption minus real private consumption in durables.

Real gross domestic investment in fixed capital

The same methodology was used as for real gross domestic product.

Real gross domestic investment in housing

This was defined as real gross domestic investment in fixed capital minus real gross domestic investment in plant and equipment.

Real government consumption expenditures

The same methodology was used as for real gross investment in plant and equipment.

Real exports

The same methodology was used as for real gross investment in plant and equipment.

Real imports

The same methodology was used as for real gross investment in plant and equipment.

Real gross personal disposable income

For the values at current prices, the same methodology was used as for real gross investment in plant and equipment. The real values were calculated by deflating the current figures with the implicit price deflator of consumption goods.

Real gross personal income

For the values at current prices, the same methodology was used as for real gross investment in plant and equipment. The real values were calculated by deflating the current figures with the cost of living index.

Real net transfers received by persons from the government and abroad

The same methodology was used as for real gross personal income.

Real direct taxes to persons

The same methodology was used as for real gross income.

Real social security contributions paid by persons

The same methodology was used as for real gross personal income.

Profit rate

This variable was defined as the ratio between real profits (deflated by the cost of living index) and the stock of capital.

Different imports components

The figures in current dollars were taken from unpublished material from ODEPLAN for the period 1950–1960 and from ODE-PLAN, *Antecedentes* for the years 1960–1970. This classification of imports is compatible with the national accounts classification. To obtain imports in current escudos, the rate of exchange used in the national accounts is needed and, for the period 1950–1970, the latter figures were taken directly from ODEPLAN (1972).

To derive the different components of imports in real terms, it was necessary to have the corresponding price indices. For imports of consumption goods, the consumption component of the index of unit value of imports multiplied by an index of the national account foreign exchange rate was utilized, both with 1965 = 100. For imports of raw materials, this component of the wholesale price index was used (see MBCB issues).

For imported capital goods, it was possible to employ the capital goods index of unit value of imports multiplied by an index of the national accounts foreign exchange rate. The real imports of services were calculated as a residual from the total imports figures already discussed.

Prices of commodities and services

These variables were computed as implicit price deflators. For the period 1960–1970, the current values were obtained directly from the new accounts. For the period 1950–1960, an index was built from the old accounts with 1960 = 100. This index was multiplied by the 1960 value for the new accounts. The calculation of the real figures was previously discussed.

Total labor cost in the sector producing commodities and services

Once again, these figures were obtained directly from an ODE-PLAN publication (*Distribucion...*).

Unit labor cost in the sector producing commodities and services

These variables were defined as the ratio between total labor cost and output in the commodity and the service sectors. The calculation of both variables has been discussed above.

The wage rate in the commodity and service sector

These variables were defined as the ratio between total labor cost and employment in the respective sectors. The calculation of both variables has been discussed above.

Real direct taxes on persons in the fiscal accounts

For the period 1950–1959, the figures at current prices were obtained from *La economía Chilena en el período 1950–63*. For the period 1960–1963, the ODEPLAN *Antecedentes* was used and, for 1970, various issues of MBCB were utilized. To derive the real figures, the cost of living index was used as a price deflator.

Real taxes on non-copper business in the fiscal accounts

For the figures at current prices, the same sources as for taxes on persons were used. For the real figures, the cost of living index was used as a price deflator.

Real taxes on imports in the fiscal accounts

For the nominal figure, the same sources were used as for taxes on persons; for the real figures, an implicit deflator was employed as the price deflator.

Real taxes on copper in the fiscal accounts

For the current figures, the same source was used as for the last two items; for real figures, an implicit deflator of exports was employed as the price deflator.

Other taxes in the fiscal accounts

For the current figures, the same sources were used as for the previous tax items. For real figures, the implicit price deflator of expenditure in gross domestic product was used as the price deflator.

Real government expenditures in the fiscal account

For the current figures, the same sources as for the tax items were used. For real figures, the implicit deflator of taxes was used as the price deflator.

Nominal deficit in the fiscal account

The same source was used as in the tax items.

Nominal supply of money

The annual money supply was defined as the average of the end of the month figures of: bills and currency held by the public, plus demand deposits in commercial banks, minus demand deposits held by the treasury and public institutions. For the period 1952–1969, it was necessary to draw upon information from the thesis of Ffrench-Davis (1971). For the year 1970, it was possible to obtain the basic information from different issues of MBCB.

Real money supply

The cost of living was used as the price deflator.

Money base

This is defined as: lending from Central Bank to the government, plus lending from Central Bank to the banking system and the public, plus net result of foreign exchange operation, plus public documents computed as legal reserves. The information for this variable was obtained from unpublished material by the Central Bank.

APPENDIX C

The purpose of this appendix is to show that Kmenta's (1967, pp. 180–189) approximation of the CES function cannot distinguish between two commonly used production functions: the CES and the VES.

In this note we first see that the variable elasticity of substitution (VES) production function initially used by Hildebrand and Liu (1957) and developed by Bruno (Nerlove, 1967, pp. 55–122), has the same form as Kmenta's approximation of the CES when we develop a linear approximation around $\rho = 0$. Furthermore, we investigate how well the approximation of the VES function performs for the same parameter values employed by Kmenta, and how, in addition, it is possible to perform a sensitivity analysis by investigating our approximation for alternative values of the parameters.

We can conclude that Kmenta's approximation (for the values of the parameters he employs) is a better approximation of a VES than a CES. Therefore, once the Kmenta approximation has been accepted, we must be cautious when interpreting its coefficients. Furthermore, given the availability of nonlinear estimation procedures, it would be best to utilize these procedures to estimate a CES or a VES rather than Kmenta's approximation.

Kmenta's approximation of the CES

Starting with a function of the form

$$V = \gamma \left[\delta K^{-\rho} + (1-\delta)L^{-\rho} \right]^{-\nu/\rho}$$

and

$$0 \leqslant \delta \leqslant 1, \quad \rho > -1, \quad \gamma > 0,$$

where V = output, L = input of labor services, K = input of capital services. Kmenta approximated it with a Taylor series expansion of the first- and second-order terms around ρ equal to zero and obtained

$$\ln V = \ln \gamma + \nu\delta \ln K + \nu(1-\delta) \ln L - \tfrac{1}{2}\nu\rho\delta(1-\delta)(\ln K - \ln L)^2. \quad (C.1)$$

Taylor expansion of the VES

Nerlove (1967), in his excellent survey of production functions, presents a VES function with constant returns to scale that he attributed to Bruno. The same type of function has been presented recently also by Lu and Fletcher (1968). Here we will follow the Nerlove nomenclature.

The Bruno production function allowing for non-constant returns to scale can be written as

$$V = \gamma[\delta K^{-\rho} + (1-\delta)K^{-m\rho}L^{\rho(m-1)}]^{-\nu/\rho} \text{ with } 0 < \delta < 1, \gamma > 0 . \quad (C.2)$$

For any positive ν, a non-negative marginal product of labor requires that $m \leqslant 1$, and a non-negative marginal product of capital requires that $\delta + m(1-\delta)k^{-m\rho+\rho} \geqslant 0$, where $k = K/L^1$. This function is homogeneous of degree ν and has a variable elasticity of substitution of $\sigma = 1/(1+\rho-m\rho\nu/\alpha_K)$ where α_K is the elasticity of output with respect to capital. Strict quasi-concavity of the production function requires that $\rho\delta(1-m) + \delta + m(1-\delta)k^{\rho(1-m)} > 0$

---

[1] It can be shown that within a range of K and L this function has diminishing marginal returns to each factor. This range obviously depends on ν, δ, ρ, and m.

(this condition and the non-negative marginal product condition implies that $\sigma \geqslant 0$).

For $m = 0$ we have, as a special case, the CES function and for $m = 1$, we have a non-constant returns to scale Leontief function with capital as the limiting factor.

Taking a Taylor series expansion of (C.2) around $\rho = 0$ and considering only the first- and second-order terms we obtain

$$\ln V = \ln \gamma + \nu[\delta + m(1-\delta)] \ln K - \nu(m-1)(1-\delta) \ln L$$

$$-\frac{\nu\rho}{2} (m-1)^2 \delta(1-\delta) [\ln K - \ln L]^2. \tag{C.3}$$

But (C.3) is the same form as (C.1) and so (C.1) is not identified. A similar problem was hinted at by McCarthy (1967, pp. 190–192) when he showed that, for the constant returns to scale case, a general production function (previously presented by Allen (1938, pp. 281–289)) of the form

$$V = \beta[AK^\alpha + BK^\delta L^{\alpha-\delta} + CL^\alpha]^{1/\alpha},$$

where $A + B + C > 0$, yielded a form similar to Kmenta's approximation when expanded in a Taylor series about $\alpha = 0$ and $\delta = 0$ and when the terms of order 3 and above were ignored. The Allen function presents two problems: (a) as far as I know it has never been used empirically; and (b) as noted by Kmenta (1967, p. 193), we do not know how good the approximation of Allen's function is for 'reasonable' values of the parameters.

In general, the error in approximating the VES function by (C.3) is given by.

$$\ln V_{appr} - \ln V_{exact} = -\nu(m-1)(1-\delta) \ln (L/K)$$

$$-\frac{\nu\rho}{2} (m-1)^2 \delta(1-\delta) [\ln L/K]^2 + \frac{\nu}{\rho} \ln [\delta + (1-\delta)(L/K)^{\rho(m-1)}]. \tag{C.4}$$

Measuring the 'goodness' of the approximation

To study how well (C.3) approximates (C.2), we perform numerical experiments for different values of the parameters involved. For our first case, we employ the same parameter values as Kmenta ($\nu = 0.9$ and $\delta = 4/9$) so that our results will be comparable. However, there is an additional parameter, m, for which we must have values. In order to obtain some idea of tha range of values that m might assume, it is possible to use the Hildebrand and Liu estimates (presented by Nerlove (1967)). Their estimates are presented in the table below. We have to be cautious in the use of these estimates because they were derived for the constant returns to scale case. In any event, we are interested only in those cases within the neighborhood of constant returns.

From table C.1, it can be seen that in 13 of 17 cases m is a number less than one in absolute value and, in 10 of the 13, m was between zero and one. Thus, in our experiments we let m take on the values of -1.00, -0.60, -0.20, 0, 0.20, 0.60, 1.00. (For $m = 1$, the higher order terms vanish.)

For the case where $m = 0$, (C.2) reduces to (C.1) so that our

TABLE C.1
Value of the parameter m in different industries.

Industry	m
Food and kindred products	0.752
Textile mill products	6.400
Apparel and related products	−1.366
Lumber and wood products	0.200
Furniture and fixtures	0.597
Pulp, paper, and products	0.539
Chemicals and products	1.763
Petroleum and coal products	0.344
Rubber products	−0.065
Leather and leather goods	−0.455
Stone, clay, and glass products	0.640
Primary metal products	0.451
Fabricated metal products	0.297
Machinery except electrical	−0.327
Electrical machinery	0.397
Transportation equipment	−26.750
Instruments and related products	0.544

Source: Nerlove (1967, p. 78).

results should be equal to those of Kmenta as indeed they are. For the case where $m = 1$, (C.2) reduces to a Leontief production function and is therefore equal to (C.3).

The ratio of V_{appr} to V_{exact} can be calculated for the same range of values of ρ and L/K as Kmenta, and these results appear in the tables that follow.

From the tables, it is clear that for the most common case of $0 < m < 1$ (ten out of seventeen in the Hildebrand and Liu estimates) the approximation in (C.3) is a better approximation of (C.2) than of (C.1) (case $m = 0$).

If we consider alternative values of ν and δ, these conclusions do not change as is shown by the second and third set of tables.

Control values are: $m = -1.00$; $\delta = 0.44$; $\nu = 0.90$.

RHO	Labor–capital ratios					
	0.10	0.50	1.00	2.00	5.00	10.00
−1.00	2.1651	1.0055	1.0000	1.0242	1.4396	2.8184
−0.50	1.1312	0.9994	1.0000	1.0046	1.0821	1.2913
−0.10	0.9980	0.9999	1.0000	1.0001	1.0018	1.0059
0.10	0.9941	0.9999	1.0000	1.0001	1.0009	1.0020
0.20	0.9740	0.9994	1.0000	1.0003	1.0015	0.9996
0.50	0.7744	0.9954	1.0000	1.0006	0.9761	0.8840
1.00	0.3548	0.9763	1.0000	0.9945	0.7963	0.4619
10.00	0.0000	0.1952	1.0000	0.2198	0.0000	0.0000

Control values are: $m = -0.60$; $\delta = 0.44$; $\nu = 0.90$.

RHO	Labor–capital ratios					
	0.10	0.50	1.00	2.00	5.00	10.00
−1.00	1.4449	1.0013	1.0000	1.0113	1.2003	1.7255
−0.50	1.0474	0.9995	1.0000	1.0022	1.0380	1.1315
−0.10	0.9988	1.0000	1.0000	1.0001	1.0009	1.0028
0.10	0.9972	0.9999	1.0000	1.0000	1.0005	1.0012
0.20	0.9859	0.9997	1.0000	1.0002	1.0012	1.0015
0.50	0.8838	0.9978	1.0000	1.0005	0.9929	0.9547
1.00	0.5795	0.9888	1.0000	0.9987	0.9073	0.6921
10.00	0.0000	0.3769	1.0000	0.4127	0.0021	0.0000

Control values are: $m = -0.20; \delta = 0.44; \nu = 0.90$.

RHO	Labor–capital ratios					
	0.10	0.50	1.00	2.00	5.00	10.00
−1.00	1.1369	0.9998	1.0000	1.0043	1.0748	1.2558
−0.50	1.0108	0.9997	1.0000	1.0008	1.0142	1.0485
−0.10	0.9994	1.0000	1.0000	1.0000	1.0004	1.0011
0.10	0.9989	1.0000	1.0000	1.0000	1.0002	1.0006
0.20	0.9946	0.9999	1.0000	1.0001	1.0007	1.0013
0.50	0.9538	0.9992	1.0000	1.0003	0.9995	0.9893
1.00	0.7963	0.9957	1.0000	1.0002	0.9717	0.8796
10.00	0.0006	0.6133	1.0000	0.6533	0.0387	0.0008

Control values are: $m = 0.00; \delta = 0.44; \nu = 0.90$.

RHO	Labor–capital ratios					
	0.10	0.50	1.00	2.00	5.00	10.00
−1.00	1.0636	0.9997	1.0000	1.0023	1.0403	1.1363
−0.50	1.0034	0.9998	1.0000	1.0005	1.0077	1.0259
−0.10	0.9996	1.0000	1.0000	1.0000	1.0002	1.0006
0.10	0.9994	1.0000	1.0000	1.0000	1.0001	1.0004
0.20	0.9970	0.9999	1.0000	1.0000	1.0004	1.0010
0.50	0.9747	0.9995	1.0000	1.0002	1.0004	0.9967
1.00	0.8800	0.9977	1.0000	1.0003	0.9880	0.9402
10.00	0.0066	0.7339	1.0000	0.7709	0.1169	0.0081

Control values are: $m = 0.20; \delta = 0.44; \nu = 0.90$.

RHO	Labor–capital ratios					
	0.10	0.50	1.00	2.00	5.00	10.00
−1.00	1.0234	0.9997	1.0000	1.0011	1.0188	1.0637
−0.50	1.0002	0.9999	1.0000	1.0002	1.0036	1.0121
−0.10	0.9998	1.0000	1.0000	1.0000	1.0001	1.0003
0.10	0.9997	1.0000	1.0000	1.0000	1.0001	1.0002
0.20	0.9986	1.0000	1.0000	1.0000	1.0003	1.0006
0.50	0.9880	0.9998	1.0000	1.0001	1.0006	0.9998
1.00	0.9401	0.9989	1.0000	1.0003	0.9965	0.9771
10.00	0.0457	0.8416	1.0000	0.8720	0.2805	0.0538

Control values are: $m = 0.60$; $\delta = 0.44$; $v = 0.90$.

RHO	Labor–capital ratios					
	0.10	0.50	1.00	2.00	5.00	10.00
−1.00	1.0001	0.9999	1.0000	1.0001	1.0018	1.0060
−0.50	0.9996	1.0000	1.0000	1.0000	1.0004	1.0012
−0.10	1.0000	1.0000	1.0000	1.0000	1.0000	1.0000
0.10	1.0000	1.0000	1.0000	1.0000	1.0000	1.0000
0.20	0.9998	1.0000	1.0000	1.0000	1.0000	1.0001
0.50	0.9988	1.0000	1.0000	1.0000	1.0002	1.0004
1.00	0.9940	0.9999	1.0000	1.0001	1.0003	0.9999
10.00	0.5342	0.9772	1.0000	0.9871	0.8094	0.5741

Control values are: $m = -1.00$; $\delta = 0.56$; $v = 0.90$.

RHO	Labor–capital ratios					
	0.10	0.50	1.00	2.00	5.00	10.00
−1.00	2.8184	1.0242	1.0000	1.0055	1.2557	2.1651
−0.50	1.2913	1.0046	1.0000	0.9994	1.0245	1.1312
−0.10	1.0059	1.0001	1.0000	0.9999	0.9991	0.9981
0.10	1.0020	1.0001	1.0000	0.9999	0.9982	0.9941
0.20	0.9996	1.0003	1.0000	0.9994	0.9910	0.9704
0.50	0.8840	1.0006	1.0000	0.9954	0.9241	0.7744
1.00	0.4619	0.9945	1.0000	0.9763	0.6946	0.3548
10.00	0.0000	0.2198	1.0000	0.1952	0.0000	0.0000

Control values are: $m = -0.60$; $\delta = 0.56$; $v = 0.90$.

RHO	Labor–capital ratios					
	0.10	0.50	1.00	2.00	5.00	10.00
−1.00	1.7255	1.0113	1.0000	1.0013	1.1021	1.4449
−0.50	1.1315	1.0022	1.0000	0.9995	1.0071	1.0474
−0.10	1.0029	1.0001	1.0000	1.0000	0.9995	0.9988
0.10	1.0012	1.0000	1.0000	0.9999	0.9991	0.9972
0.20	1.0015	1.0002	1.0000	0.9997	0.9957	0.9859
0.50	0.9547	1.0005	1.0000	0.9978	0.9634	0.8838
1.00	0.6921	0.9987	1.0000	0.9888	0.8332	0.5795
10.00	0.0000	0.4127	1.0000	0.3769	0.0017	0.0000

Control values are: $m = -0.20; \delta = 0.56; v = 0.90$.

RHO	Labor–capital ratios					
	0.10	0.50	1.00	2.00	5.00	10.00
−1.00	1.2558	1.0043	1.0000	0.9998	1.0292	1.1369
−0.50	1.0485	1.0008	1.0000	0.9997	1.0005	1.0108
−0.10	1.0011	1.0000	1.0000	1.0000	0.9998	0.9994
0.10	1.0006	1.0000	1.0000	1.0000	0.9996	0.9989
0.20	1.0013	1.0001	1.0000	0.9999	0.9983	0.9946
0.50	0.9893	1.0003	1.0000	0.9992	0.9860	0.9538
1.00	0.8796	1.0002	1.0000	0.9957	0.9304	0.7963
10.00	0.0008	0.6533	1.0000	0.6133	0.0326	0.0006

Control values are: $m = 0.00; \delta = 0.56; v = 0.90$.

RHO	Labor–capital ratios					
	0.10	0.50	1.00	2.00	5.00	10.00
−1.00	1.1363	1.0023	1.0000	0.9997	1.0122	1.0636
−0.50	1.0259	1.0005	1.0000	0.9998	0.9996	1.0034
−0.10	1.0006	1.0000	1.0000	1.0000	0.9999	0.9996
0.10	1.0004	1.0000	1.0000	1.0000	0.9998	0.9994
0.20	1.0010	1.0000	1.0000	0.9999	0.9991	0.9970
0.50	0.9967	1.0002	1.0000	0.9995	0.9924	0.9747
1.00	0.9402	1.0003	1.0000	0.9977	0.9613	0.8800
10.00	0.0081	0.7709	1.0000	0.7339	0.1015	0.0066

Control values are: $m = 0.20; \delta = 0.56; v = 0.90$.

RHO	Labor–capital ratios					
	0.10	0.50	1.00	2.00	5.00	10.00
−1.00	1.0637	1.0011	1.0000	0.9997	1.0036	1.0234
−0.50	1.0121	1.0002	1.0000	0.9999	0.9994	1.0002
−0.10	1.0003	1.0000	1.0000	1.0000	0.9999	0.9998
0.10	1.0002	1.0000	1.0000	1.0000	0.9999	0.9997
0.20	1.0006	1.0000	1.0000	1.0000	0.9996	0.9986
0.50	0.9998	1.0001	1.0000	0.9998	0.9964	0.9880
1.00	0.9771	1.0003	1.0000	0.9989	0.9815	0.9401
10.00	0.0538	0.8720	1.0000	0.8416	0.2516	0.0457

Control values are: $m = 0.60; \delta = 0.56; v = 0.90.$

RHO	Labor–capital ratios					
	0.10	0.50	1.00	2.00	5.00	10.00
−1.00	1.0060	1.0001	1.0000	0.9999	0.9997	1.0001
−0.50	1.0012	1.0000	1.0000	1.0000	0.9998	0.9996
−0.10	1.0000	1.0000	1.0000	1.0000	1.0000	1.0000
0.10	1.0000	1.0000	1.0000	1.0000	1.0000	1.0000
0.20	1.0001	1.0000	1.0000	1.0000	1.0000	0.9998
0.50	1.0004	1.0000	1.0000	1.0000	0.9996	0.9988
1.00	0.9999	1.0001	1.0000	0.9999	0.9982	0.9940
10.00	0.5741	0.9871	1.0000	0.9772	0.7743	0.5342

Control values are: $m = -1.00; \delta = 0.56; v = 1.10.$

RHO	Labor–capital ratios					
	0.10	0.50	1.00	2.00	5.00	10.00
−1.00	3.5481	1.0297	1.0000	1.0067	1.3209	2.5706
−0.50	1.3667	1.0057	1.0000	0.9992	1.0300	1.1626
−0.10	1.0073	1.0002	1.0000	0.9999	0.9989	0.9976
0.10	1.0024	1.0001	1.0000	0.9998	0.9978	0.9928
0.20	0.9995	1.0004	1.0000	0.9993	0.9891	0.9639
0.50	0.8601	1.0008	1.0000	0.9944	0.9080	0.7317
1.00	0.3890	0.9933	1.0000	0.9712	0.6406	0.2812
10.00	0.0000	0.1569	1.0000	0.1358	0.0000	0.0000

Control values are: $m = -0.60; \delta = 0.56; v = 1.10.$

RHO	Labor–capital ratios					
	0.10	0.50	1.00	2.00	5.00	10.00
−1.00	1.9479	1.0139	1.0000	1.0015	1.1262	1.5680
−0.50	1.1630	1.0027	1.0000	0.9993	1.0087	1.0582
−0.10	1.0035	1.0001	1.0000	0.9999	0.9994	0.9985
0.10	1.0015	1.0001	1.0000	0.9999	0.9989	0.9965
0.20	1.0018	1.0002	1.0000	0.9997	0.9948	0.9828
0.50	0.9450	1.0007	1.0000	0.9973	0.9554	0.8599
1.00	0.6377	0.9985	1.0000	0.9863	0.8000	0.5134
10.00	0.0000	0.3390	1.0000	0.3034	0.0004	0.0000

Control values are: $m = -0.20$; $\delta = 0.56$; $\nu = 1.10$.

RHO	Labor−capital ratios					
	0.10	0.50	1.00	2.00	5.00	10.00
−1.00	1.3210	1.0052	1.0000	0.9998	1.0358	1.1697
−0.50	1.0595	1.0010	1.0000	0.9996	1.0007	1.0132
−0.10	1.0014	1.0000	1.0000	1.0000	0.9997	0.9993
0.10	1.0007	1.0000	1.0000	1.0000	0.9996	0.9986
0.20	1.0016	1.0001	1.0000	0.9999	0.9980	0.9934
0.50	0.9869	1.0004	1.0000	0.9990	0.9829	0.9438
1.00	0.8549	1.0002	1.0000	0.9948	0.9156	0.7570
10.00	0.0002	0.5943	1.0000	0.5502	0.0152	0.0001

Control values are: $m = 0.00$; $\delta = 0.56$; $\nu = 1.10$.

RHO	Labor−capital ratios					
	0.10	0.50	1.00	2.00	5.00	10.00
−1.00	1.1691	1.0028	1.0000	0.9996	1.0149	1.0782
−0.50	1.0318	1.0006	1.0000	0.9996	0.9995	1.0041
−0.10	1.0008	1.0000	1.0000	1.0000	0.9998	0.9996
0.10	1.0004	1.0000	1.0000	1.0000	0.9998	0.9992
0.20	1.0012	1.0001	1.0000	0.9999	0.9989	0.9964
0.50	0.9959	1.0003	1.0000	0.9994	0.9907	0.9692
1.00	0.9274	1.0004	1.0000	0.9972	0.9529	0.8554
10.00	0.0028	0.7276	1.0000	0.6851	0.0611	0.0022

Control values are: $m = 0.20$; $\delta = 0.56$; $\nu = 1.10$.

RHO	Labor−capital ratios					
	0.10	0.50	1.00	2.00	5.00	10.00
−1.00	1.0784	1.0013	1.0000	0.9997	1.0043	1.0287
−0.50	1.0148	1.0003	1.0000	0.9999	0.9992	1.0002
−0.10	1.0004	1.0000	1.0000	1.0000	0.9999	0.9998
0.10	1.0002	1.0000	1.0000	1.0000	0.9999	0.9996
0.20	1.0007	1.0000	1.0000	1.0000	0.9995	0.9983
0.50	0.9998	1.0001	1.0000	0.9997	0.9956	0.9854
1.00	0.9721	1.0003	1.0000	0.9987	0.9774	0.9273
10.00	0.0281	0.8459	1.0000	0.8099	0.1852	0.0230

Control values are: m =0.60; δ = 0.56; v = 1.10.

RHO	Labor−capital ratios					
	0.10	0.50	1.00	2.00	5.00	10.00
−1.00	1.0074	1.0001	1.0000	0.9999	0.9996	1.0001
−0.50	1.0014	1.0000	1.0000	1.0000	0.9998	0.9995
−0.10	1.0000	1.0000	1.0000	1.0000	1.0000	1.0000
0.10	1.0000	1.0000	1.0000	1.0000	1.0000	1.0000
0.20	1.0001	1.0000	1.0000	1.0000	0.9999	0.9998
0.50	1.0005	1.0000	1.0000	1.0000	0.9996	0.9986
1.00	0.9999	1.0001	1.0000	0.9999	0.9978	0.9927
10.00	0.5075	0.9842	1.0000	0.9723	0.7315	0.4647

REFERENCES

Ahrensdorf, J., 1959, 'Central Bank policies and inflation. A case study of four less developed economies, 1949–57', *International Monetary Fund Staff Papers,* Vol. 7, October.

Ahumada, J., 1958, 'Una tesis sobre el estancamiento de la economía Chilena', *Economía,* No. 60–61, Santiago.

Allen, R.G.D., 1938, *Mathematical analysis for economists,* London, Macmillan.

Allen, R.G.D., 1967, *Macroeconomic theory: a mathematical treatment* New York, St Martin's Press.

Arrow, K.J. et al., 1961, 'Capital–labor substitution and economic efficiency', *Review of Economics and Statistics,* Vol. 43, August.

Behrman, J.R., 1970, *Price determination in an inflationary economy: the dynamics of Chilean inflation revisited,* Discussion Paper No. 151, Department of Economics, University of Pennsylvania, revised (mimeo).

Bernstein, E.M., 1958, 'Wage–price links in a prolonged inflation', *International Monetary Fund Staff Papers,* Vol. 6, November.

Bernstein, E.M. and Patel, I.G., 1952, 'Inflation in relation to economic development', *International Monetary Fund Staff Papers,* Vol. 6, November.

Bodkin, R.G., 1966, *The wage, price, productivity nexus,* Philadelphia, University of Pennsylvania Press.

Brown, M., 1966, *On the theory and measurement of technological change,* Cambridge, Cambridge University Press.

Brown, M. (ed.), 1967, *The theory and empirical analysis of production,* National Bureau of Economic Research.

Cagan, P., 1956, 'The monetary dynamics of hyperinflation', *Studies in the quantity theory of money,* Friedman, M. (ed.), Chicago, University of Chicago Press.

Cauas, J., 1970, 'Stabilization policy – the Chilean case', *Journal of Political Economy,* Vol. 78, No. 4, Supplement to July–August.

Chenery, H.B. and Bruno, M., 1962, 'Development alternatives in an open economy: the case of Israel', *Economic Journal,* March.

Chile, Oficina de Planificacion Nacional (ODEPLAN), undated, *Cuadro de Transacciones Intersectoriales para la Economia Chilena, 1962.*

Chile, ODEPLAN, undated, *Distribucion de ingreso y cuentas de produccion 1960–1968*, Tomo III.

Chile, ODEPLAN, 1969, *Estimación del stock de capital por sectores en la economía Chilena,* Docto No. C/69-001, 28 January.

Chile, ODEPLAN, 1972, *Tabla de conversion de moneda extranjera a escudos*, Depto de Cuentas Sociales, 24 August.

Chile, Banco Central, *Boletin Mensual,* various issues.

Chile, Corporacion de Fomento de la Produccion, 1963, Cuentas Nacionales 1940–1962, Santiago, June.

Chile, Corporacion de Fomento de la Produccion, 1964, Cuentas Nacionales 1958–1963, Santiago, June.

Chile, Oficina de Planification Nacional (ODEPLAN), 1972, Cuentas Nacionales 1960–1970, Santiago, February.

Chile, Oficina de Planificacion Nacional (ODEPLAN), 1971, *Plan de la Economía Nacional: Antecedentes sobre el Desarrollo Chileno, 1960–1970*, Santiago.

Chile, Direccion de Estadísticas y Censos, *Boletin Nacional de Estadistica,* various issues.

Corbo, V., 1968, 'Models of two gaps as a policy instrument for programming', mimeo, M.I.T.

Cortes, H. and Tapia, D., 1970, 'La demanda de dinero. Un informe preliminar', *Estudios Monetarios II*, Banco Central de Chile.

De La Cuadra, S., undated, *El Control de Precios en Chile*, Centro de Estudios Socio-Economicos (CESEC).

Deaver, J., 1961, *The Chilean inflation and demand for money*, unpublished PhD thesis, Department of Economics, University of Chicago.

Duesenberry, J.S. et al., (eds.), 1969, *Brookings econometric model of the United States; some further results,* Chicago, Rand McNally and Company.

Eckaus, R.S., 1955, 'The factor proportion problem in underdeveloped areas', *American Economic Review,* Vol. 45, September.

Eckstein, O. and Fromm, G., 1968, 'The price equation', *American Economic Review,* Vol. 58, December.

Fair, R.C., 1970, 'The estimation of simultaneous equation models with lagged endogenous variables and first order serially correlated errors', *Econometrica,* Vol. 38, No. 3, May.

Fair, R.C. and Jaffee, D.M., 1970, *Methods of estimation for markets in disequilibrium,* Paper presented at the Second World Congress of the Econometric Society, England, September 1970.

Ferber, R. (ed.), 1967, *Determinants of investment behavior,* National Bureau of Economic Research.

Ffrench-Davis, R., 1971, *Economic policies and stabilization programs, Chile, 1952–69,* unpublished PhD thesis, Department of Economics, University of Chicago, December.

Fisher, F.M., 1965, 'Embodied technical change and the existence of an aggregate capital stock', *Review of Economic Studies,* Vol. 32, No. 4.

Fisher, F.M., 1968, 'Embodied technology and the existence of labor and output aggregates', *Review of Economic Studies,* Vol. 35.

Fisher, F.M., 1969, 'The existence of aggregate production functions', *Econometrica,* Vol. 37, October.

Fisher, F.M., 1970, 'Test of equality between sets of coefficients in two linear regressions: an expository note', *Econometrica,* Vol. 38, March.

Friedman, B., 1968, *The demand for money: testing a neo-Fisherian approach,* unpublished PhD thesis, M.I.T.

Friedman, M., 1968, 'The role of monetary policy', *The American Economic Review,* Vol. 58, No. 1, March.

Friedman, M., 1969, *The optimum quantity of money and other essays,* Chicago, Aldine Publishing Company.

García, E., 1964, *Inflation in Chile: a quantitative analysis,* unpublished PhD thesis, Department of Economics, M.I.T.

Garretón, O. and Cisternas, J., 1970, *Algunas caracteristicas del proceso de toma de decisiones en la Gran Empresa: la dinámica de concentración,* Servicio Cooperación Técnica, Marzo.

Grubel, H., 1970, *The international monetary system,* Harmondsworth, Penguin.

Hahn, F.M. and Matthews, R.C.D., 1964, 'The theory of economic growth: a survey', *Economic Journal,* Vol. 74, No. 296.

Hall, R.E., 1967, *Polynomial distributed lags,* Working Paper No. 7, Department of Economics, M.I.T., 28 July.

Hall, R.E. and Jorgenson, D.W., 1967, 'Tax policy and investment behavior', *American Economic Review,* Vol. 57, June.

Hansen, B., 1970, 'Excess demand, unemployment, vacancies, and wages', *Quarterly Journal of Economics,* Vol. 84, No. 1.

Harberger, A.C., 1963, 'The dynamics of inflation in Chile', *Measurement in Economics,* Christ, C. (ed.), Stanford University Press.

Harberger, A.C., 1964, 'Some notes in inflation', *Inflation and Growth in Latin America,* Baer, W. and Kerstenetzky, I. (eds.), Yale University Press.

Harberger, A.C., 1966a, *The inflation problem in Latin America,* unpublished paper, February.

Harberger, A.C., 1966b, *The case of three numeraires,* paper presented at The Annual Meeting of the Economics Society, December.

Harberger, A.C., 1970, 'Economic policy problems in Latin America: a review', *Journal of Political Economy,* Vol. 78, No. 4.

Hildebrand, G.H. and Liu, T.C., 1957, *Manufacturing Production Functions in the U.S.,* Cornell Studies in Industrial and Labor Relations, No. 15, Ithaca, New York.

Hynes, A., 1967, 'The demand for money and monetary adjustments in Chile', *Review of Economic Studies,* Vol. 34, No. 99.

Johnson, H., 1967, *Essays in monetary theory,* Cambridge, Mass., Harvard University Press.

Jorgenson, D.W. and Stephenson, J.A., 1967a, 'Investment behaviour in U.S. manufacturing, 1947–1960', *Econometrica*, Vol. 35, April.

Jorgenson, D.W. and Stephenson, J.A., 1967b, 'The time structure of investment behaviour in U.S. manufacturing', *Review of Economic and Statistics*, Vol. 49, February.

Klein-Saks, Misión, 1958, *El programa de estabilización de la economia Chilena y el trabajo de la misión Klein-Saks*, Santiago, Editorial del Pacifico.

Kmenta, J., 1967a, 'On estimation of the CES production function', *International Economic Review*, Vol. 8, No. 2.

Kmenta, J., 1967b, 'The approximation of CES type functions: a reply', *International Economic Review*, Vol. 8, No. 2.

Kuh, E., 1965, 'Cyclical and secular labor productivity in the United States manufacturing industry', *Review of Economics and Statistics*, Vol. 47, February.

Lagos, R., 1966, *La industria en Chile: antecedentes estructurales*, Universidad de Chile, Instituto de Economia.

Lipsey, R.G., 1960, 'The relation between unemployment and the rate of change of money wage rates in the United Kingdom, 1862–1957: a further analysis', *Economica*, Vol. 27, February.

Lipsey, R.G. and Parkin, J.M., 1970, 'Income policy: a reappraisal', *Economica*, May.

Lu, Y. and Fletcher, L.B., 1968, 'A generalization of C.E.S. production function, *Review of Economics and Statistics*, Vol. 50, No. 4.

Lüders, R.J., 1968, *A monetary history of Chile, 1925–1958*, unpublished PhD thesis, Department of Economics, University of Chicago.

Mamalakis, M. and Reynolds, C.W., 1965, *Essays on the Chilean economy*, Illinois, Richard Irwin Inc.

McCarthy, M.D., 1967, 'Approximation of the CES production function: a comment', *International Economic Review*, Vol. 8, No. 2.

Mieselman, D. (ed.), 1970, *Varieties of monetary experience*, Chicago, University of Chicago Press.

Muñoz, O., 1968, *Crecimiento industrial de Chile, 1914–1965*, Universidad de Chile, Instituto de Economia y Planificacion.

Muth, J., 1960, 'Optimal properties of exponentially weighted forecasts' *Journal of the American Statistical Association*, Vol. 55.

Perry, G.L., 1966, *Unemployment, money wage rates, and inflation*, Cambridge, Mass., The M.I.T. Press.

Phelps, E.S., 1968, 'Money wage dynamics and labor market equilibrium', *Journal of Political Economy*, Vol. 76, No. 4, Part II, July/August.

Pinto, A., 1960, *Ni estabilidad ni desarrollo. La politica del Fondo Monetario Internacional*, Santiago.

Pinto, A., 1964, *Chile, una economía difícil*, Editorial del Fondo de Cultura Económica.

Ramos, J., 1970, *Politica de renumeraciones en inflaciones persistentes,* Instituto de Economía y Planificación, Universidad de Chile.

Samuelson, P.A., 1968, 'What classical and neoclassical monetary theory really was', *Canadian Economic Journal,* Vol. 1, No. 1, February. (Also in *Readings in monetary theory,* Clower, R. (ed.), Harmondsworth, Penguin, 1970.)

Seers, D., 1962, 'A theory of inflation and growth based on Latin American experience', *Oxford Economic Papers.* June.

Solow, R.M., 1969, *Price expectations and the behaviour of the price level,* Manchester University Press.

Starleof, D., 1970, 'The specification of money demand—supply models which involve the use of distributed lags', *Journal of Finance,* Vol. 25, September.

Sunkel, O., 1953, 'Metodologia para analizar la estructura de los ahorros', *Trimestre Economico,* No. 80, October—December.

Sunkel, O., 1958, 'La inflación Chilena, un enfoque heterodoxo', *El Trimestre Economico,* Vol. 25, No. 14, October—December. (English version in *International Economic Papers,* No. 10, 1960.)

Theil, H., 1961, *Economic forecasts and policy,* second edition, Amsterdam, North-Holland.

Theil, H., 1971, *Principles of Econometrics,* New York, John Wiley and Sons

Universidad de Chile, 1963a, *Utilizacion de la capacidad instalada en 42 empresas industriales,* Instituto de Economia, Santiago, Chile.

Universidad de Chile, 1963b, *La economia Chilena en el periodo 1950—1963,* Instituto de Economio, Santiago, Chile.

Universidad de Chile, *Ocupacion y desocupacion, Gran Santiago,* Instituto de Economia, Santiago, Chile, various issues.

Wolfe, J., 1968, *Value, capital and growth: Papers in honour of Sir John Hicks,* Edinburgh, University of Edinburgh Press.

INDEX

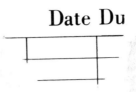

Date Du